ALSO BY LIANA FINCK

PASSING FOR HUMAN: A GRAPHIC MEMOIR

A BINTEL BRIEF: LOVE AND LONGING IN OLD NEW YORK

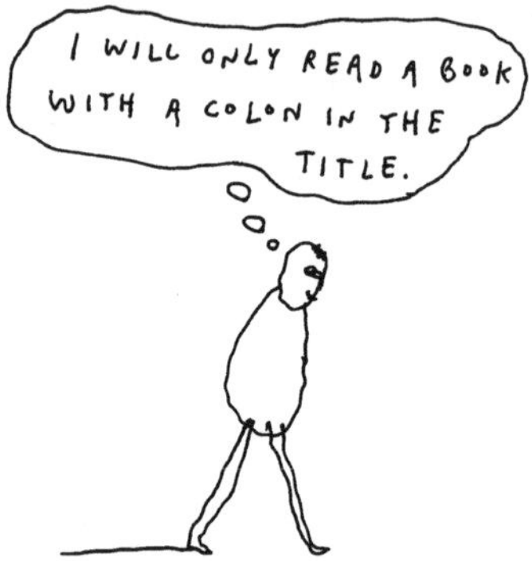
I WILL ONLY READ A BOOK WITH A COLON IN THE TITLE.

EXCUSE ME

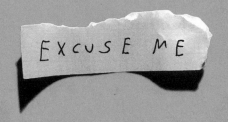

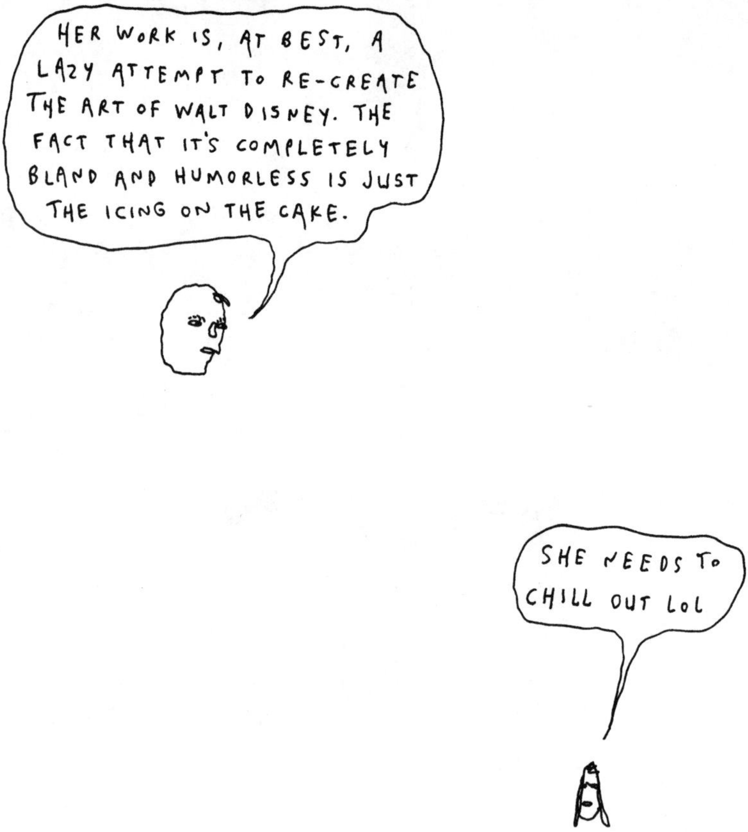
HER WORK IS, AT BEST, A LAZY ATTEMPT TO RE-CREATE THE ART OF WALT DISNEY. THE FACT THAT IT'S COMPLETELY BLAND AND HUMORLESS IS JUST THE ICING ON THE CAKE.
SHE NEEDS TO CHILL OUT LOL

EXCUSE ME

CARTOONS, COMPLAINTS, AND NOTES TO SELF

LIANA FINCK

RANDOM
HOUSE
NEW YORK

A RANDOM HOUSE TRADE PAPERBACK ORIGINAL

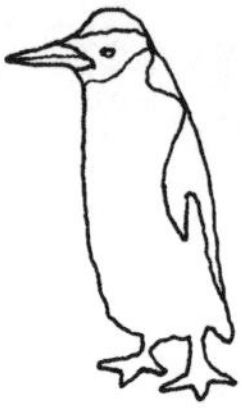
PROUD BUSINESS OWNER

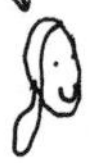
DO NOT SUE

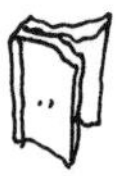
THE GENUINE ARTICLE

PUBLISHED IN THE UNITED STATES BY RANDOM HOUSE, AN IMPRINT AND DIVISION OF PENGUIN RANDOM HOUSE LLC, NEW YORK.

RANDOM HOUSE AND THE **HOUSE** COLOPHON ARE REGISTERED TRADEMARKS OF PENGUIN RANDOM HOUSE LLC.

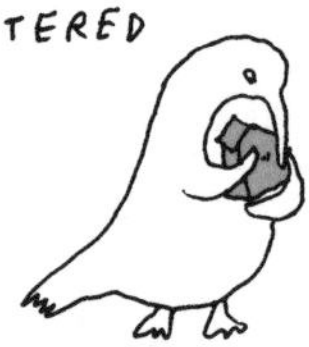
MINE

MEMORIZE THIS →

ISBN 978-1-9848-0151-7
EBOOK ISBN 978-1-9848-0150-0

PRINTED IN THE UNITED STATES OF AMERICA ON ACID-FREE PAPER

RANDOMHOUSEBOOKS.COM

9 8 7 6 5 4 3 2 1

← YES, THERE THEY ALL ARE

IT CERTAINLY HASN'T THE DRAMA OF: I SAW THE OLD, WHITE-
BEARDED FRIGATE MASTER ON THE DOCK AND SIGNED UP FOR
THE JOURNEY. BUT AFTER ALL "I" AM A WOMAN.

— ELIZABETH HARDWICK, SLEEPLESS NIGHTS

IN MODERN CITIES, COFFEE HOUSES, OR "CAFÉS," AS THEY ARE
SOMETIMES CALLED, CAN BE FOUND IN ABUNDANCE. THEY CAN
SERVE AS A PLEASANT "GETAWAY" FROM DAILY ROUTINE,
AND PEOPLE GO THERE NOT JUST TO GET THEIR COFFEE, BUT
ALSO TO MEET UP WITH FRIENDS, RELAX, OR ENGAGE IN
CONVERSATIONS WITH STRANGERS.

— HENK STAATS AND PIET GROOT, "SEAT CHOICE IN A CROWDED
CAFÉ: EFFECTS OF EYE CONTACT, DISTANCE, AND ANCHORING"

"WE'LL EAT YOU UP — WE LOVE YOU SO!"

— MAURICE SENDAK, WHERE THE WILD THINGS ARE

MOST OF THE DRAWINGS IN THIS BOOK WERE PUBLISHED ON INSTAGRAM, @LIANAFINCK. SOME WERE PUBLISHED ELSEWHERE, INCLUDING @NEWYORKERCARTOONS ON INSTAGRAM, *HARPER'S*, *THE AWL*, *THE STRANGER*, *TOPIC*, *THE TOAST*, *CATAPULT*, AND *STONECUTTER JOURNAL*. MY GRATITUDE TO ALL OF THESE VENUES.

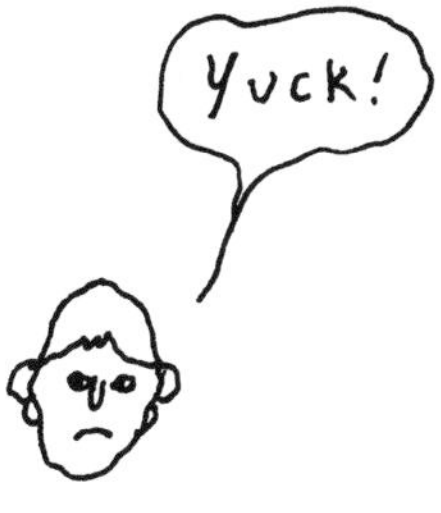
YUCK!

LOVE AND DATING

HOW TO FIND ROMANCE

PUT YOURSELF IN HUNDREDS
OF DANGEROUS AND HUMILIATING
SITUATIONS. DON'T LET YOURSELF
BE DESTROYED OR BROKEN.
NEVER GIVE UP. FORGET, FORGET,
FORGET. FORGIVE, FORGIVE,
FORGIVE. PRETEND NOT TO NOTICE
THE UNFAIRNESS. OTHERWISE,
WHAT ARE WE LIVING FOR?

BUT WHAT IF
HE HAS A
FOOT FETISH?

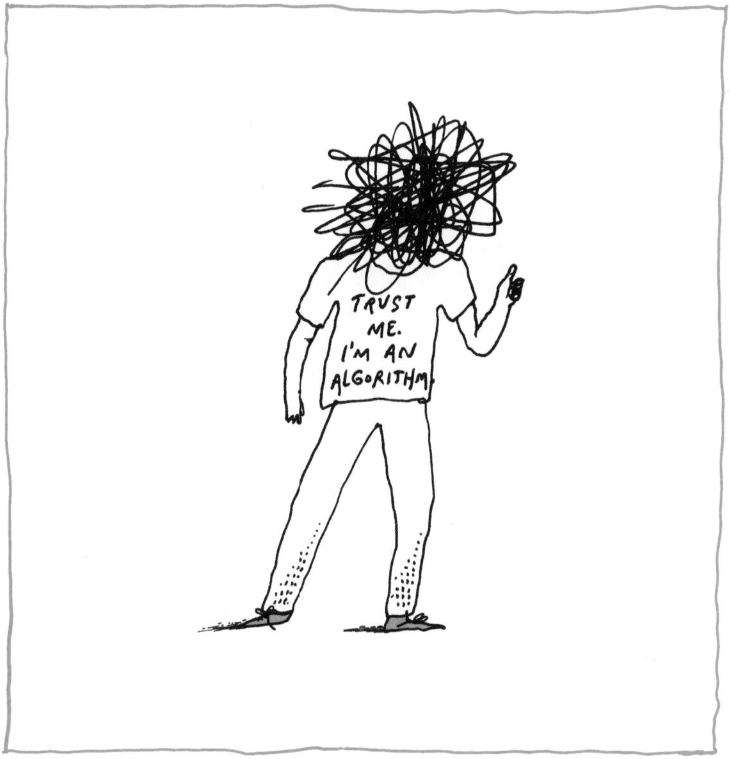
TRUST ME. I'M AN ALGORITHM.

○ AMOUNT YOU ARE LOVED

CAN DO VOLUNTEER WORK

CAN SPEND TIME WITH PEOPLE JUST TO MAKE THEM HAPPY

CAN LAUGH AT BAD JOKES

CAN BE GRACIOUS

NOT PARANOID

CAN SMILE AT CHILDREN

CAN RELATE TO THE NEWS

CAN ENJOY FRIENDS

DON'T HATE OWN BODY

CAN RELATE TO FAIRY TALES

CAN GET OUT OF BED

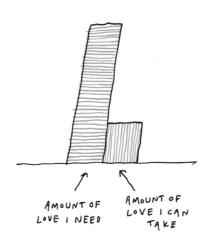

AMOUNT OF LOVE I NEED

AMOUNT OF LOVE I CAN TAKE

4

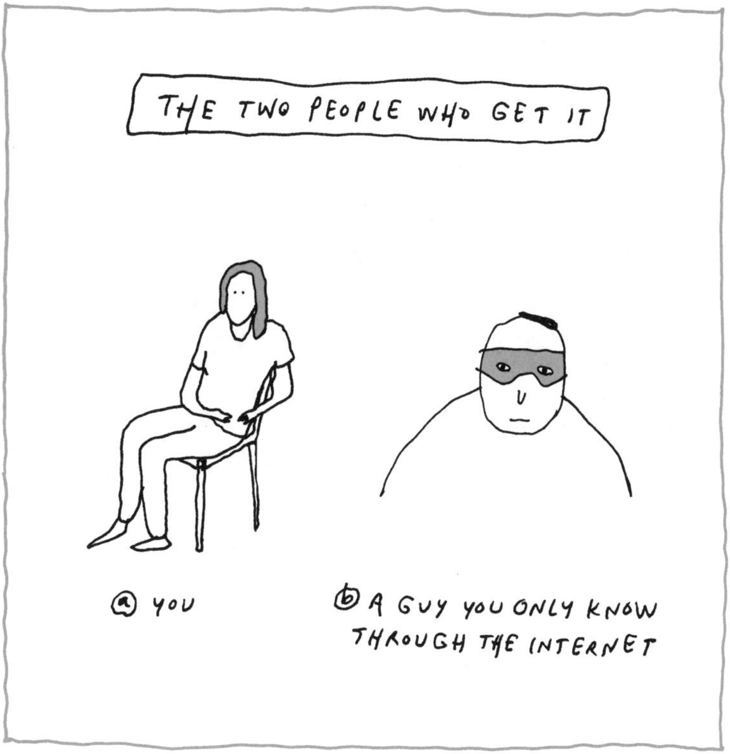
THE TWO PEOPLE WHO GET IT
ⓐ YOU
ⓑ A GUY YOU ONLY KNOW THROUGH THE INTERNET

I WANT A BOY WHO IS WILD WITHIN
REASON. I WANT A BOY WHO'S ABOUT
MY AGE. I WANT A BOY WHO IS REALLY
REALLY KIND WHO LIKES ANIMALS AS
MUCH AS I DO AND THINKS I'M BRILLIANT
BUT DOESN'T WORSHIP ME. I WANT A
BOY WHO WILL LEARN TO THINK I'M
VERY BEAUTIFUL (NOT SOMEONE WHO
ALREADY FETISHIZES MEDIUM-SIZED
SLAVIC-LOOKING WOMEN IN THEIR THIRTIES).
I WANT A BOY WHO UNDERSTANDS
PRIVACY BUT IS WARMER THAN ME.
I WANT A BOY WHO IS NOT BORING (I'VE
BEEN BURNED TOO MANY TIMES BY
BORING MEN). I WANT A BOY WHO LIKES
THINGS BUT NOT WHAT I LIKE. I WANT
A BOY WHO DOES 50% OF HOUSEHOLD
LABOR AND WOULD GENUINELY COPARENT
IF COPARENTING WERE TO COME UP.
I WANT A BOY WHO IS NOT ASEXUAL
AND DOESN'T THINK MY BODY IS GROSS.*

*AFTER THE SONG
"SHORT SKIRT/LONG JACKET"
BY **CAKE**

6

〈 SOMEWHERE 〉

WAITING PATIENTLY
FOR MY MEEK PRINCE

BEING "SINGLE BUT OPEN"

NOW I JUST
WAIT.

LOVE: PLEASE CHECK ONE

UN-
☐ CONDITIONAL
☐ REQUITED

A GENTLEMAN THROWING HIS JACKET
OVER A HOLE FOR A LADY

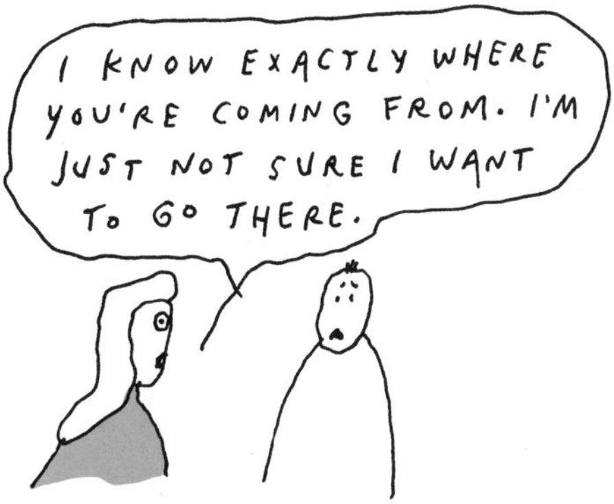
I KNOW EXACTLY WHERE YOU'RE COMING FROM. I'M JUST NOT SURE I WANT TO GO THERE.

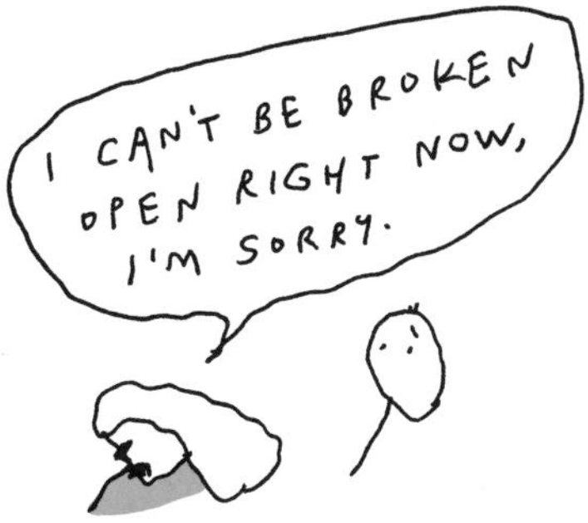
I CAN'T BE BROKEN OPEN RIGHT NOW, I'M SORRY.

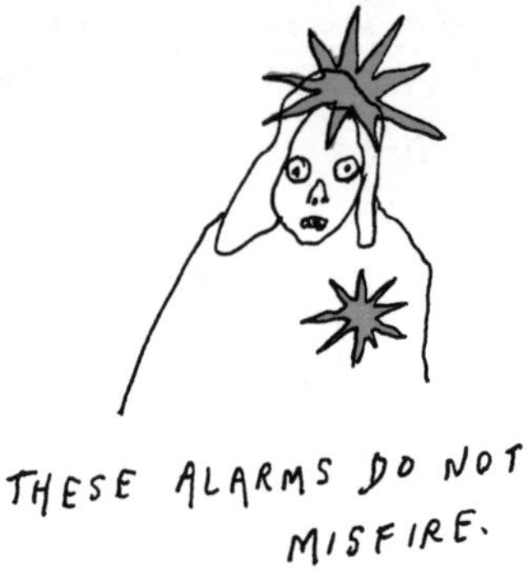
THESE ALARMS DO NOT MISFIRE.

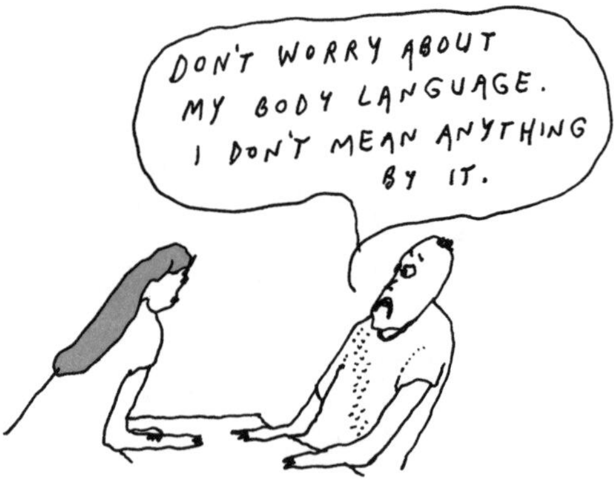
DON'T WORRY ABOUT MY BODY LANGUAGE. I DON'T MEAN ANYTHING BY IT.

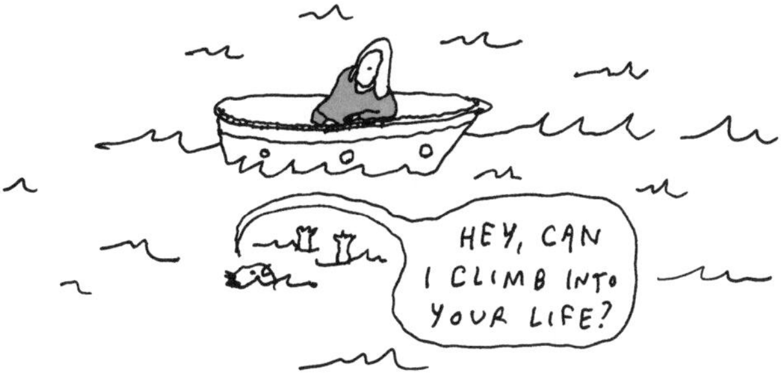
HEY, CAN I CLIMB INTO YOUR LIFE?

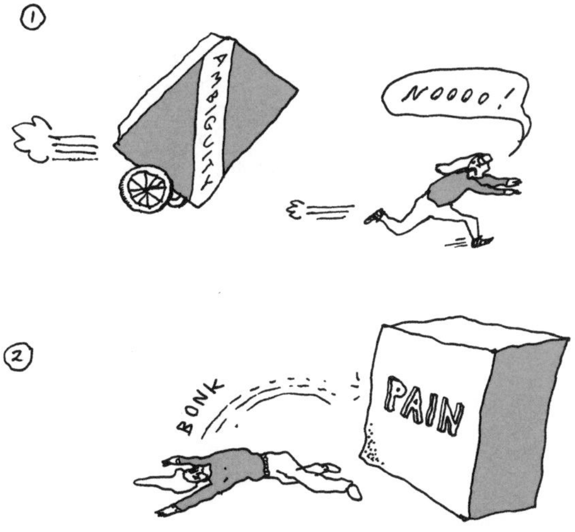
①
AMBIGUITY
NOOOO!
②
BONK
PAIN

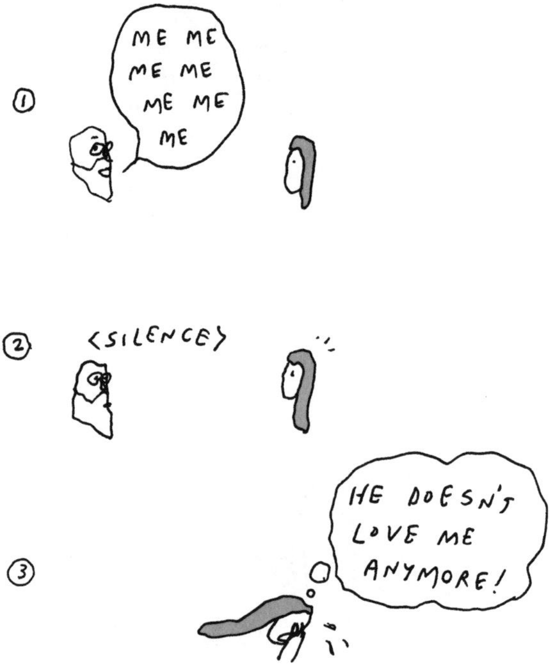
1
ME ME ME ME ME ME ME
2
<SILENCE>
3
HE DOESN'T LOVE ME ANYMORE!

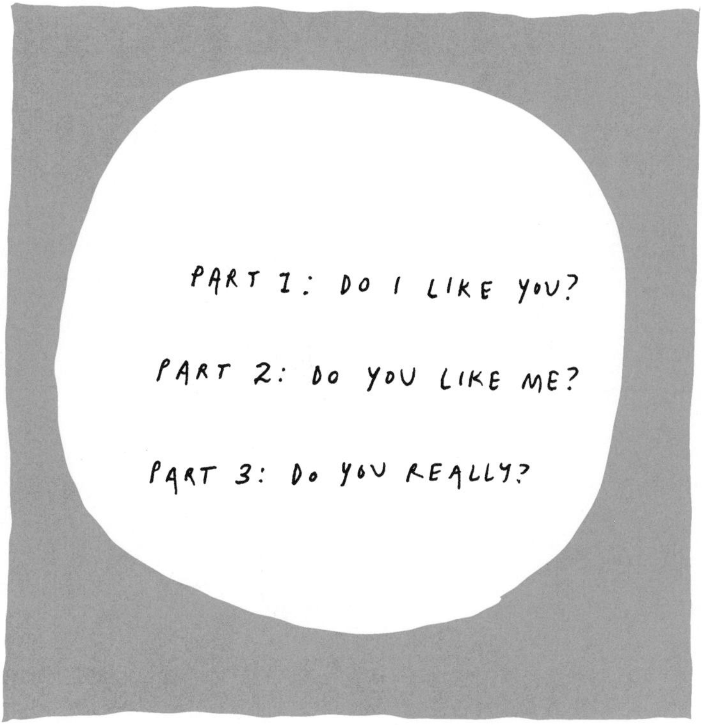
PART 1: DO I LIKE YOU?
PART 2: DO YOU LIKE ME?
PART 3: DO YOU REALLY?

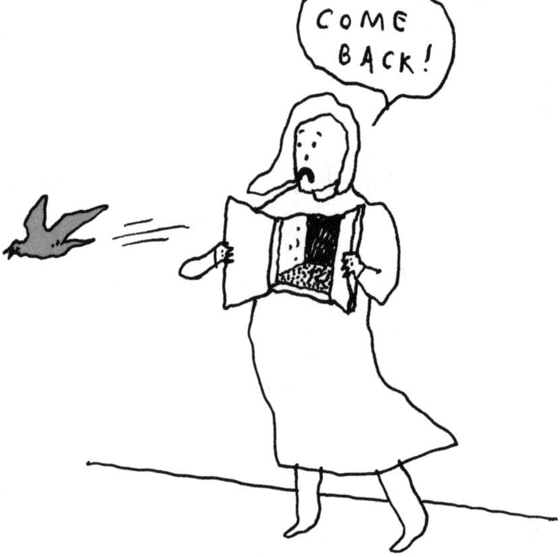
COME BACK!

THE ULTIMATUM

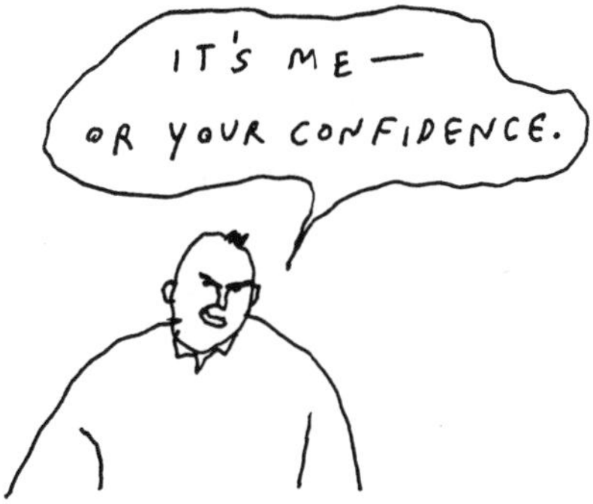
IT'S ME—
OR YOUR CONFIDENCE.

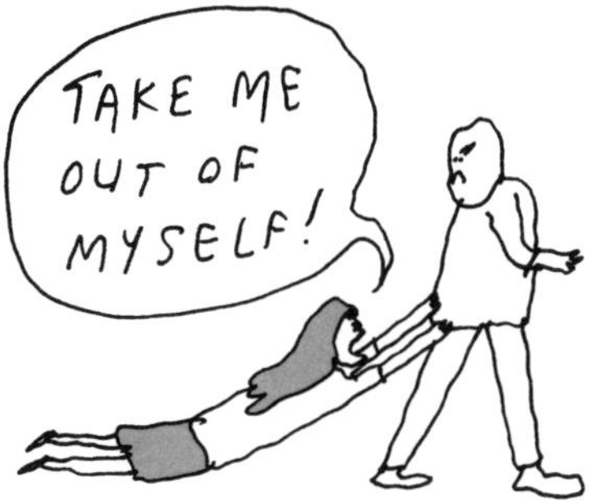
TAKE ME OUT OF MYSELF!

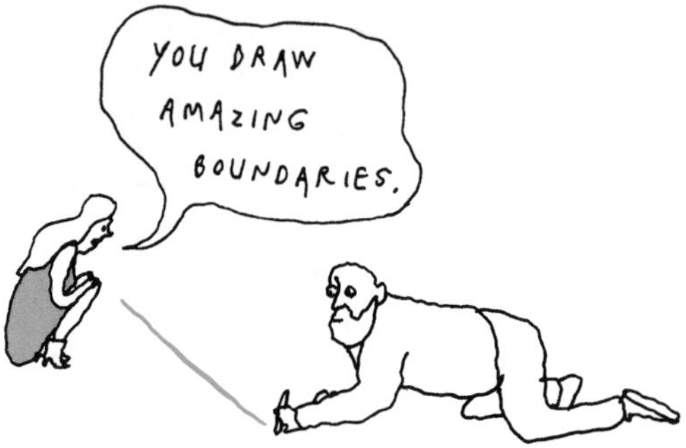
YOU DRAW AMAZING BOUNDARIES.

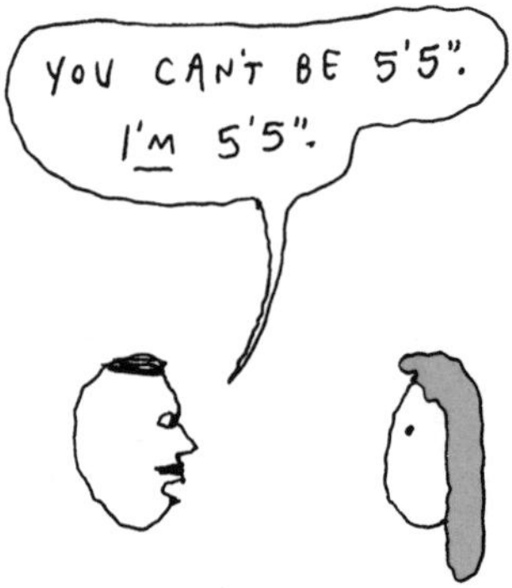
YOU CAN'T BE 5'5". I'M 5'5".

IMPOSSIBLY
HANDSOME

POSSIBLY
HANDSOME

IT IS SO EXHAUSTING
PRETENDING I'M NOT
SMARTER THAN YOU.

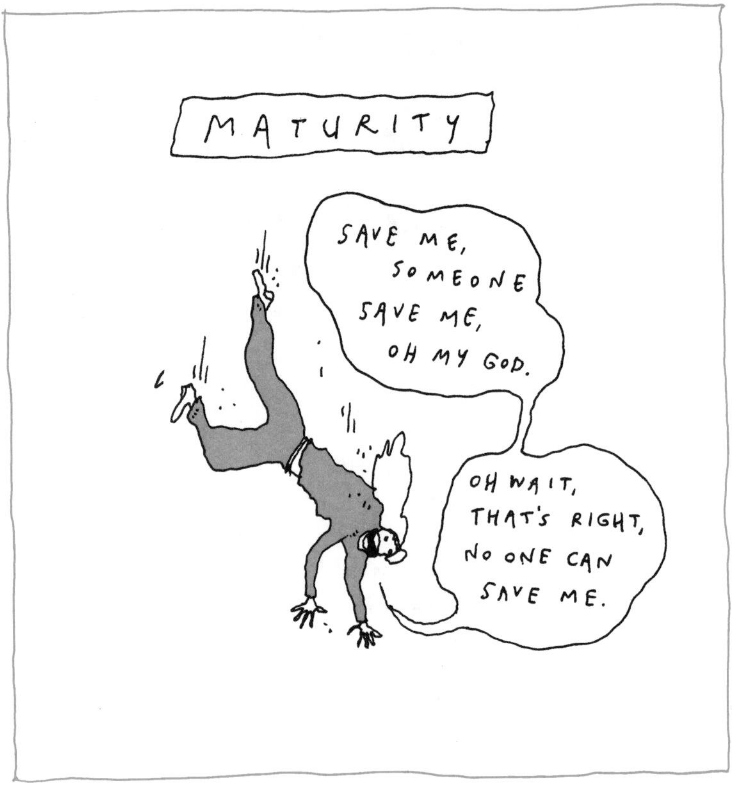
MATURITY
SAVE ME, SOMEONE SAVE ME, OH MY GOD.
OH WAIT, THAT'S RIGHT, NO ONE CAN SAVE ME.

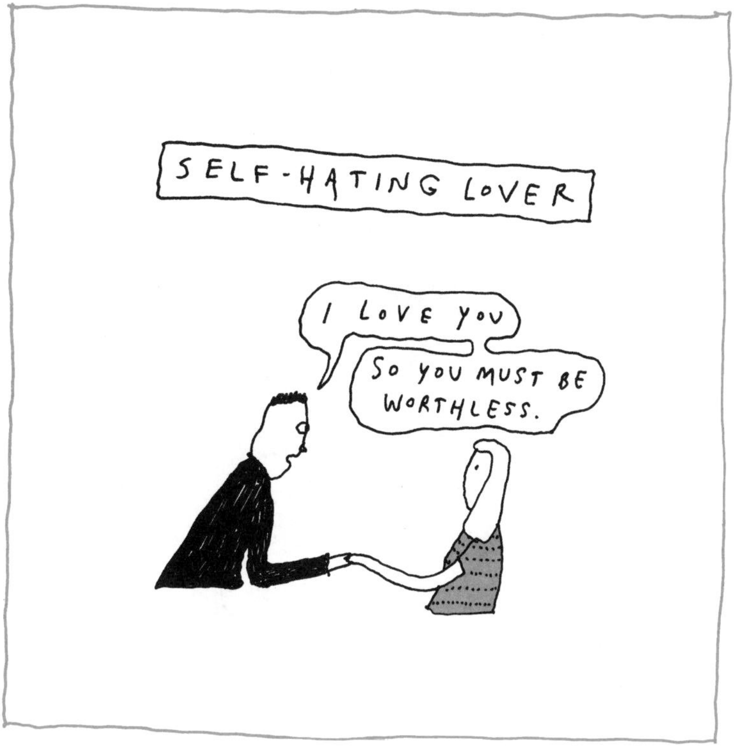
SELF-HATING LOVER
I LOVE YOU
SO YOU MUST BE WORTHLESS.

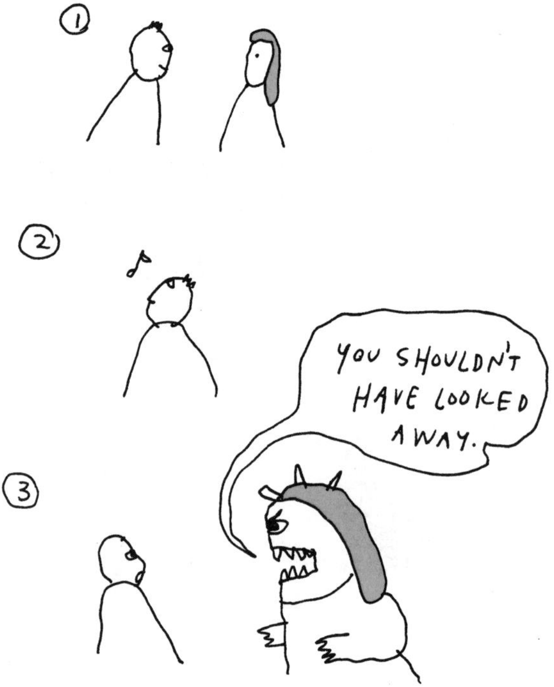
①
②
③
YOU SHOULDN'T HAVE LOOKED AWAY.

(1)  ← NORMAL GUY

(2) BLINK

(3)  HORRIBLE, SOULMATE-SHAPED VOID

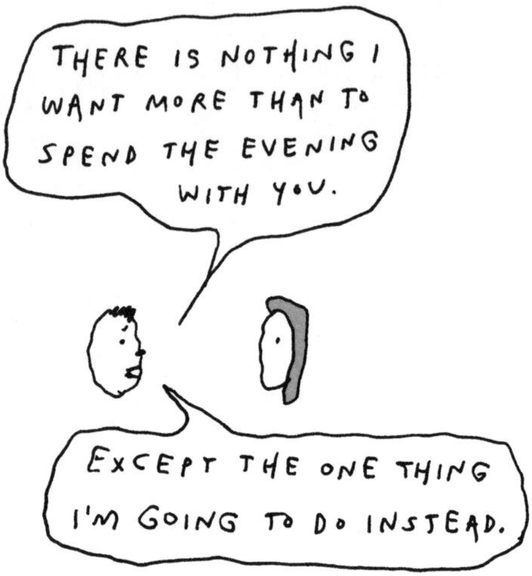
THERE IS NOTHING I WANT MORE THAN TO SPEND THE EVENING WITH YOU.
EXCEPT THE ONE THING I'M GOING TO DO INSTEAD.

THE DISTRACTION OF GETTING TEXTS $<$ THE DISTRACTION OF NOT GETTING TEXTS

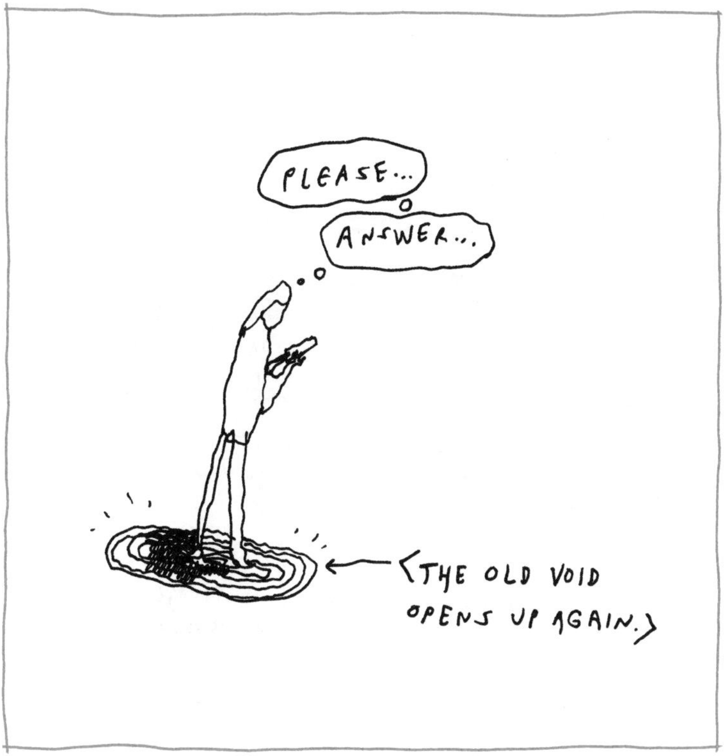
PLEASE...
ANSWER...
(THE OLD VOID OPENS UP AGAIN.)

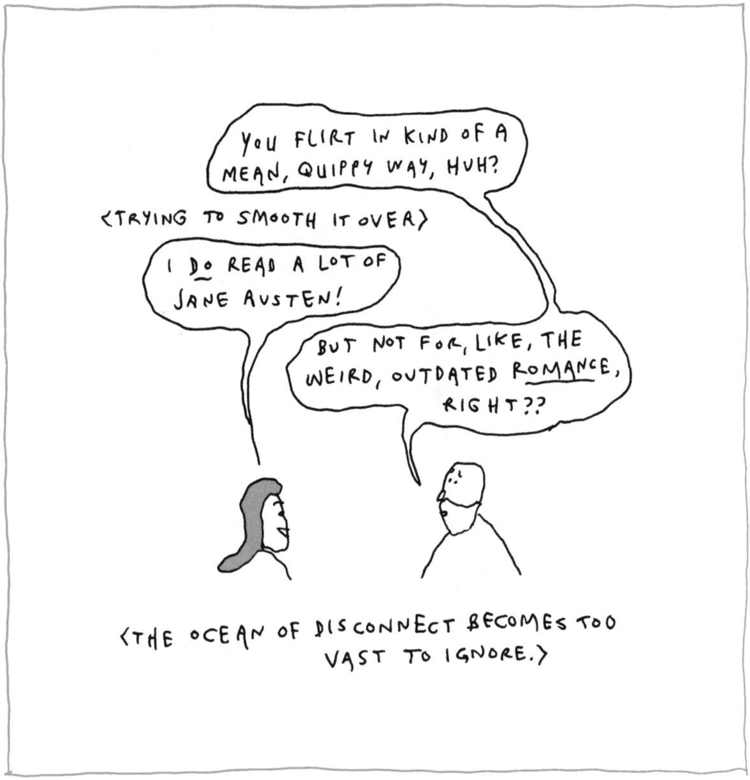
YOU FLIRT IN KIND OF A MEAN, QUIPPY WAY, HUH?
<TRYING TO SMOOTH IT OVER>
I DO READ A LOT OF JANE AUSTEN!
BUT NOT FOR, LIKE, THE WEIRD, OUTDATED ROMANCE, RIGHT??
<THE OCEAN OF DISCONNECT BECOMES TOO VAST TO IGNORE.>

THAT GUY WAS
HORRIBLE TO ME.
I BETTER NOT SEE
HIM AGAIN.

HEY, WHEN ARE WE
HANGING OUT AGAIN?

KEY
☐ = AMNESIA

THE FIVE LANGUAGES OF WHAT YOU
CAN CONVINCE YOURSELF IS LOVE

1. TEXTING YOU
2. SENDING A LINK
3. TELLING YOU HE LIKES DOGS
4. BELONGING TO THE SAME RELIGION AS YOU
5. HAVING SAD EYES

IF YOU DON'T WANT TO SEE ME AGAIN, PLEASE SAY SO.
NO, NO, I INSIST ON GHOSTING YOU.

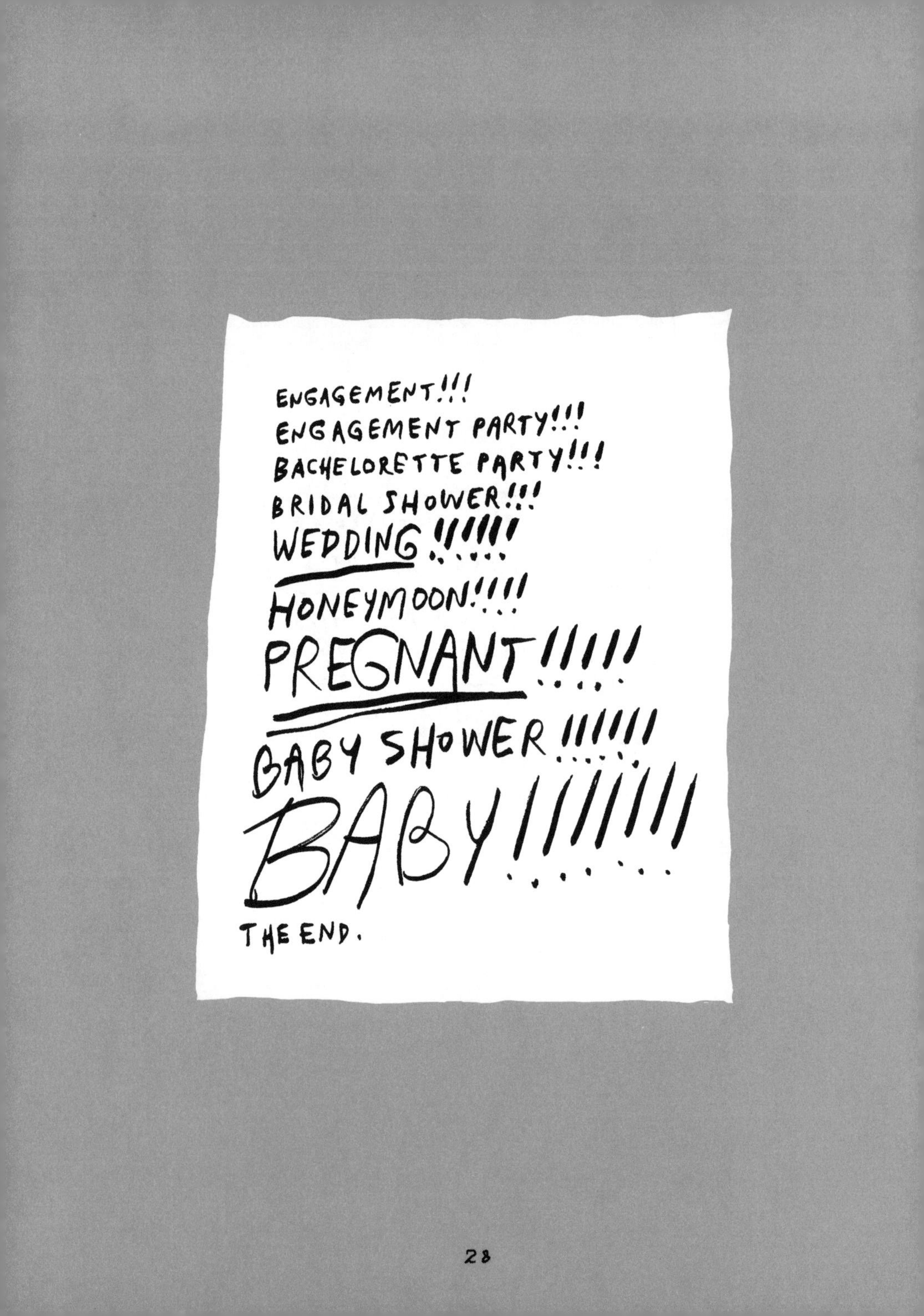
ENGAGEMENT!!!
ENGAGEMENT PARTY!!!
BACHELORETTE PARTY!!!
BRIDAL SHOWER!!!
WEDDING!!!!!!
HONEYMOON!!!!
PREGNANT!!!!!
BABY SHOWER!!!!!!
BABY!!!!!!!!
THE END.

A FEW RELATIONSHIP MODELS

A TANGO

CAT & MOUSE

COMEDY ROUTINE

KNIGHT IN SHINING
ARMOR / DAMSEL
IN DISTRESS

BIG FISH/
LITTLE FISH

GEMINI, THE
TWINS

PUNCH & JUDY

MOTHER & CHILD

A GIRL TRYING TO
DECIPHER A PRECIOUS
LETTER IN A FOREIGN
LANGUAGE

DANGERS of SEX

- HIV
- PREGNANCY
- CHLAMYDIA
- HERPES
- SYPHILIS
- POWERLESSNESS
- ABANDONMENT

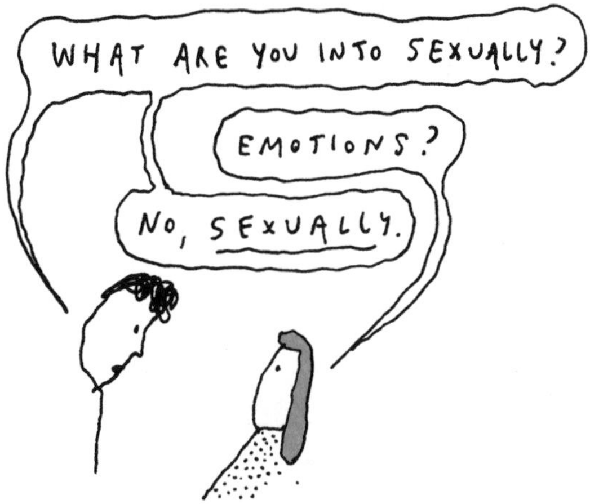
WHAT ARE YOU INTO SEXUALLY?
EMOTIONS?
NO, SEXUALLY.

THE SEX CRITIC

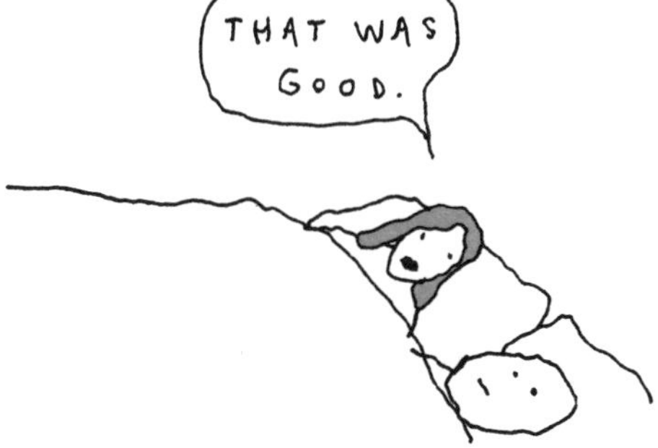
THAT WAS GOOD.

WHAT IN GOD'S NAME ARE YOU TWO DOING?

MERMAN SPERM

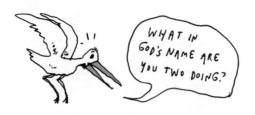

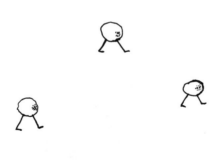

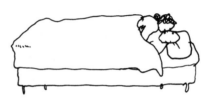

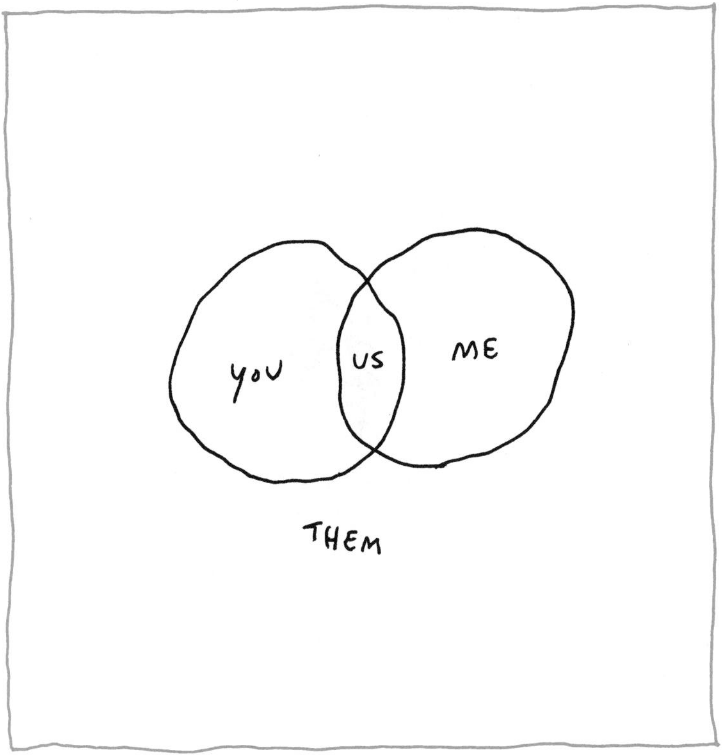
YOU
US
ME
THEM

PORTRAITS OF HIS EX

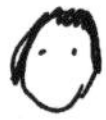

FIRST, A PERSON

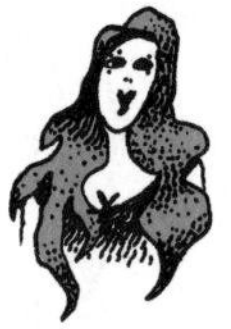

THEN, A BEAUTIFUL SIREN WITH WHOM YOU CAN NEVER COMPETE

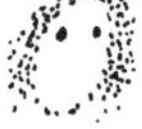

THEN, SOMEONE WHO USED TO DATE SOMEONE YOU USED TO DATE

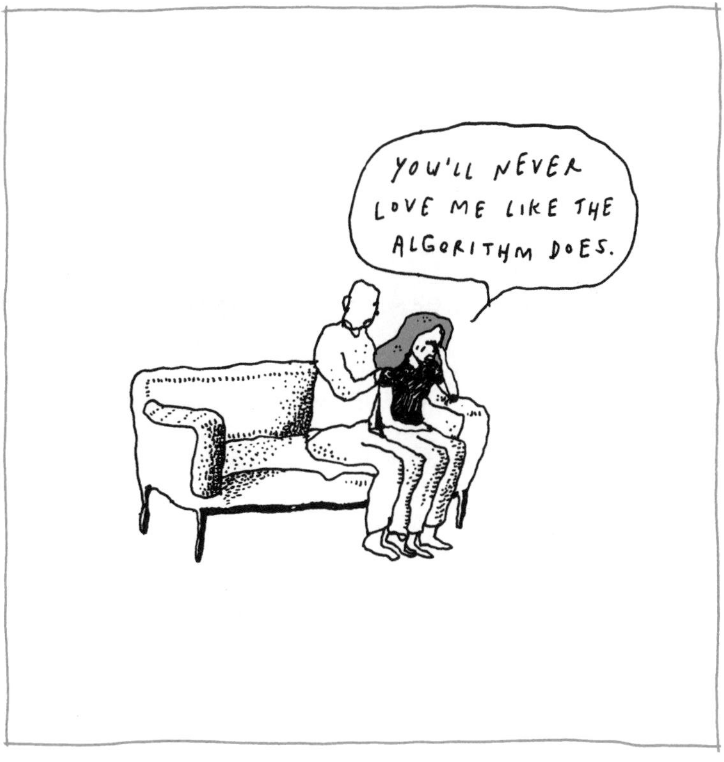
YOU'LL NEVER LOVE ME LIKE THE ALGORITHM DOES.

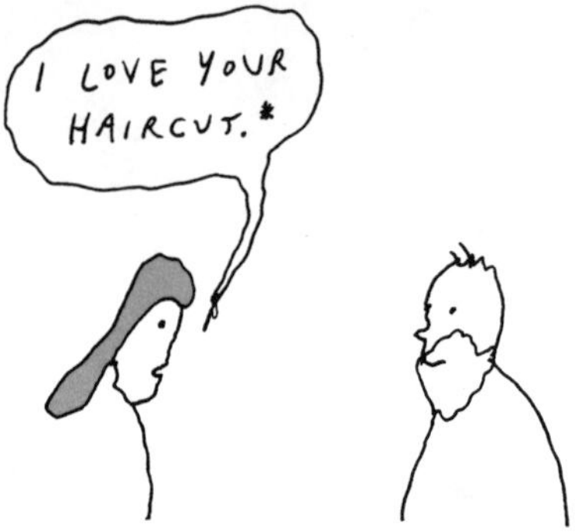
I LOVE YOUR HAIRCUT.*

*I WILL LEARN TO LOVE YOUR HAIRCUT.

LIARS

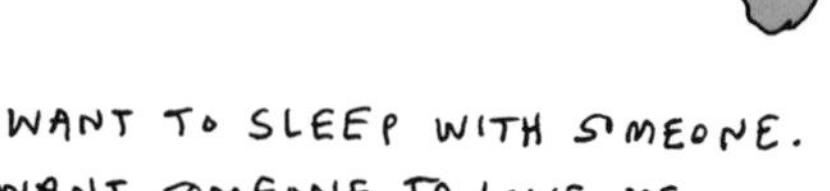
I LOVE YOU.*
I LOVE YOU, TOO.**

*I WANT TO SLEEP WITH SOMEONE.
**I WANT SOMEONE TO LOVE ME.

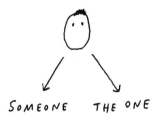

SOMEONE   THE ONE

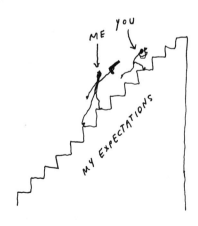

ME YOU

MY EXPECTATIONS

A SKEPTIC'S GUIDE TO TINDER

IF HE LOOKS	HE MIGHT BE
KIND	VERY, VERY BORING
SMART	PRETENTIOUS
SENSITIVE	UNHINGED
SWEETLY NERDY	A PICKUP ARTIST
INTERESTING	IMMATURE
HOT	SUBURBAN

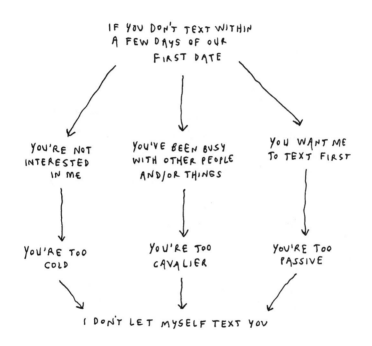

IF YOU DON'T TEXT WITHIN
A FEW DAYS OF OUR
FIRST DATE

YOU'RE NOT
INTERESTED
IN ME

YOU'VE BEEN BUSY
WITH OTHER PEOPLE
AND/OR THINGS

YOU WANT ME
TO TEXT FIRST

YOU'RE TOO
COLD

YOU'RE TOO
CAVALIER

YOU'RE TOO
PASSIVE

I DON'T LET MYSELF TEXT YOU

FEARS OF DATING

- HE IS BAD IN WAYS YOU DON'T YET KNOW. ONCE YOU KNOW, IT WILL BE TOO LATE.

- ONCE YOU LET YOUR GUARD DOWN, HE WILL ABANDON YOU IN AN ABRUPT AND BRUTAL WAY.

- HE WILL KILL YOU.

- THERE WILL BE SOMETHING THAT MAY OR MAY NOT BE A RED FLAG. WITHOUT GIVING YOURSELF PERMISSION TO WORRY, YOU WILL WORRY. THUS DIVIDED FROM YOUR TRUE MIND, YOU WILL LOSE YOURSELF.

- INSTEAD OF WORKING, YOU WILL SECRETLY WORRY. YOU WON'T EVEN KNOW IT.

- YOUR WORLD WILL SHRINK.

- YOU'LL BECOME A NAG.

- YOU WON'T BE ABLE TO SHARE YOUR FEELINGS ANYMORE, SINCE YOUR FEELINGS BELONG TO HIM.

- YOU WILL SHARE YOUR FEELINGS DESPITE THE GUILT. THE GUILT WILL KILL YOU.

- HE WILL BE WONDERFUL. YOUR FEARS WILL DISSIPATE. (YOU WILL HAVE LOST YOUR FEARS.)

FLIRTATION CHART

	HE LIKES YOU	HE MIGHT LIKE YOU	HE DOESN'T LIKE YOU
YOU LIKE HIM	NO GAMES NECESSARY	PLAY IT COOL	DISDAIN HIM; STUDY HIM
YOU MIGHT LIKE HIM	VERY DIFFICULT	PEACOCK IT UP	LOOK INSIDE YOURSELF; ABANDONMENT ISSUES?
YOU DON'T LIKE HIM	DON'T SEE HIM MUCH	BE CAREFUL	YAHTZEE

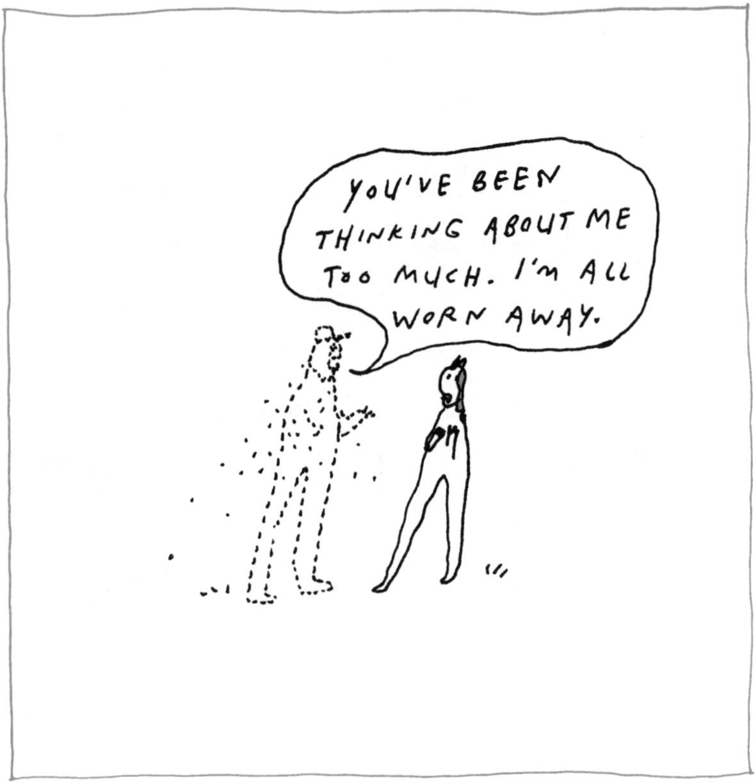
YOU'VE BEEN THINKING ABOUT ME TOO MUCH. I'M ALL WORN AWAY.

THREE ONE-YEAR RELATIONSHIPS

LOVE
LIKE
NEUTRAL
DISLIKE
HATE
1 YEAR
KEY
= JOSH
= IKE
= STANLEY

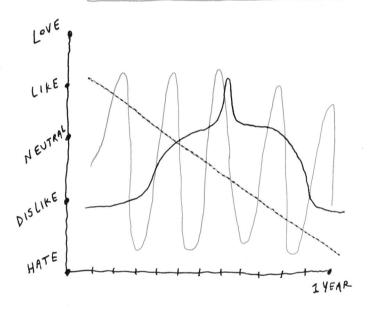

CAN'T SEE

ME
ME
ME
+
ME
ME
ME
=
US
US
US

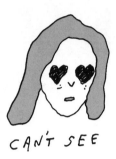

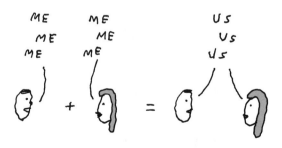

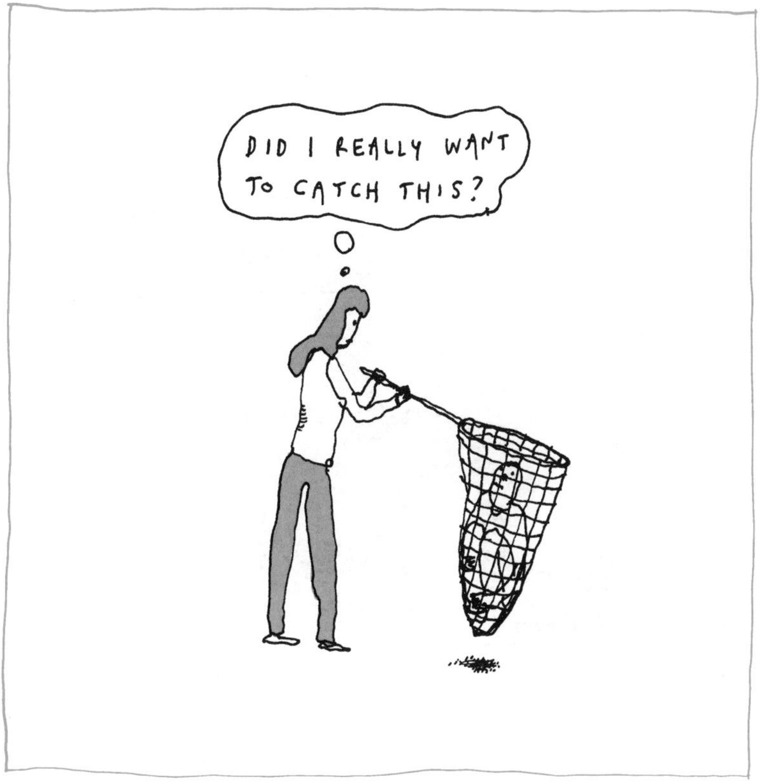
DID I REALLY WANT TO CATCH THIS?

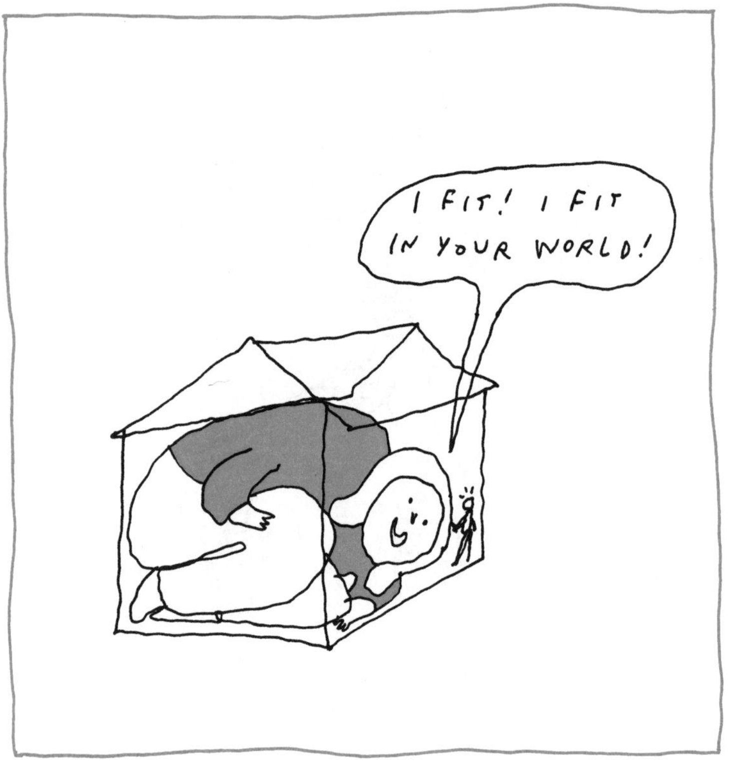
I FIT! I FIT IN YOUR WORLD!

THE MORE GENEROUS YOU ARE,
  THE MORE GENEROUS I AM.
THE MORE GENEROUS I AM,
  THE LESS GENEROUS YOU ARE.
THE LESS GENEROUS YOU ARE,
  THE LESS GENEROUS I AM.
THE LESS GENEROUS I AM,
  THE MORE GENEROUS YOU ARE.

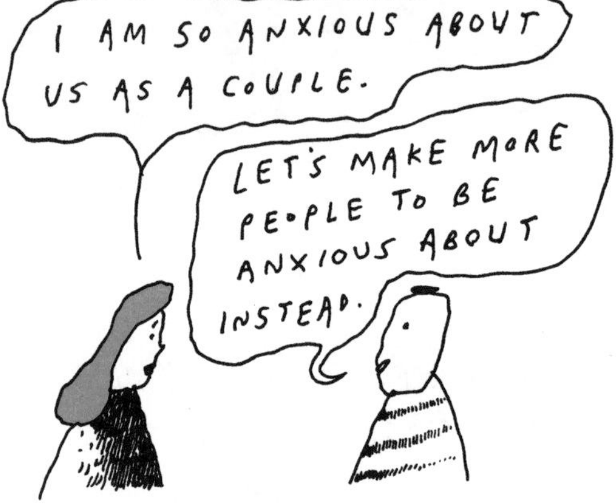
I AM SO ANXIOUS ABOUT US AS A COUPLE.
LET'S MAKE MORE PEOPLE TO BE ANXIOUS ABOUT INSTEAD.

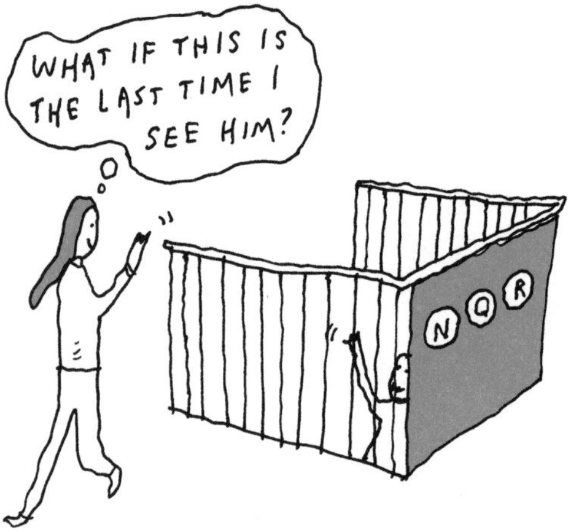
WHAT IF THIS IS THE LAST TIME I SEE HIM?
N Q R

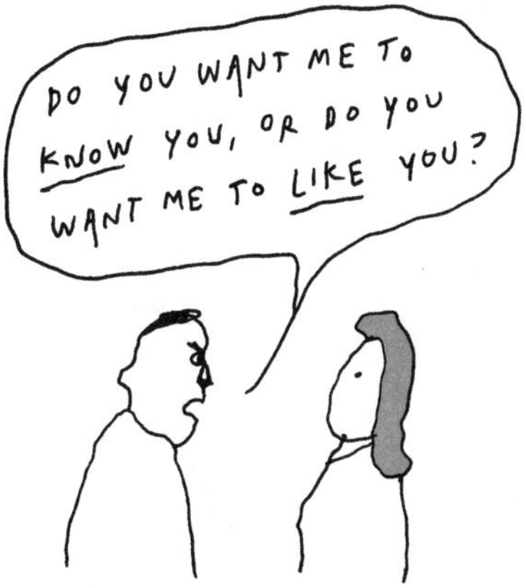
DO YOU WANT ME TO KNOW YOU, OR DO YOU WANT ME TO LIKE YOU?

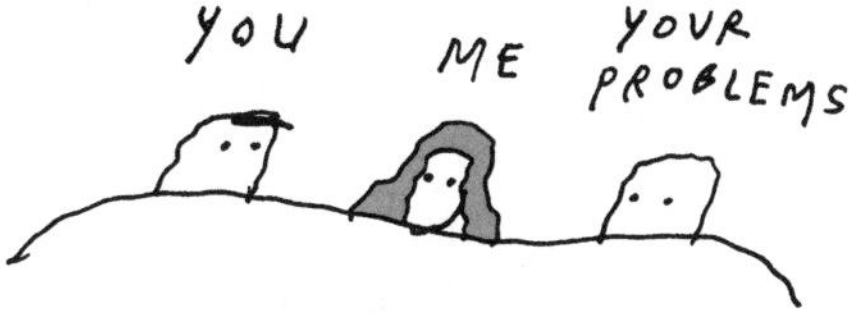
YOU
ME
YOUR PROBLEMS

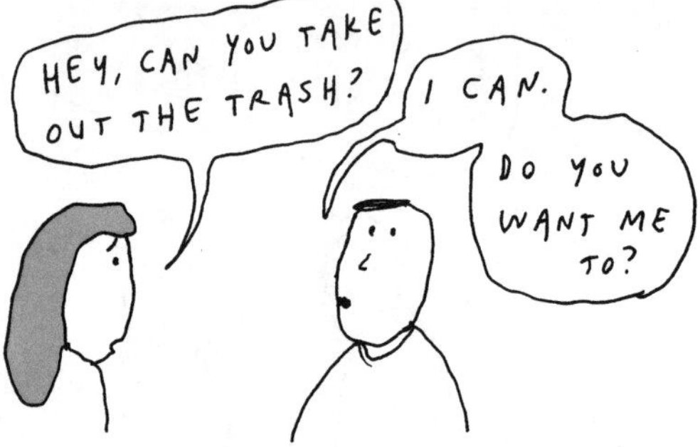
HEY, CAN YOU TAKE OUT THE TRASH?
I CAN.
DO YOU WANT ME TO?

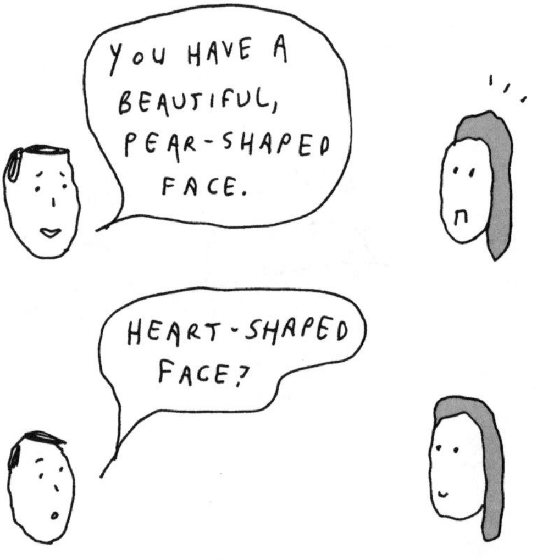
YOU HAVE A BEAUTIFUL, PEAR-SHAPED FACE.
HEART-SHAPED FACE?

THE ROMANTIC
THE PRAGMATIST

THIS IS UNBEARABLE.
MY DARLING, FINALLY YOU GET IT.

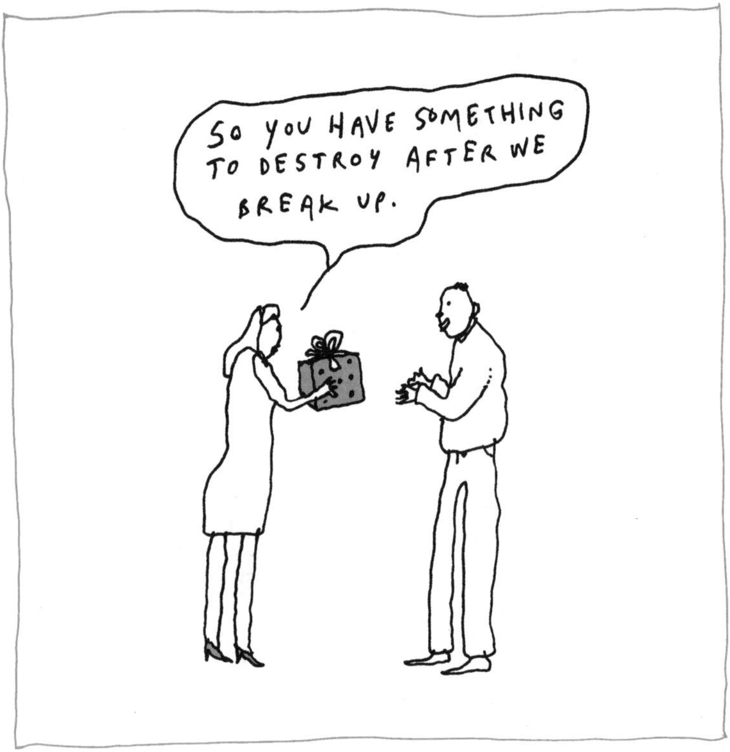
SO YOU HAVE SOMETHING TO DESTROY AFTER WE BREAK UP.

	RISK	REWARD
BELIEVING IN THE TRADITIONAL IDEA OF ROMANCE	LIVING A LIE	JOY, CONNECTION TO THE PAST
HAVING LOST THE TRADITIONAL IDEA OF ROMANCE	LIVING A FAILED UTOPIAN EXPERIMENT	THE POSSIBILITY OF REALLY CONNECTING TO ANOTHER PERSON ON YOUR TERMS

I'M NOT DRAWING YOU. I'M DRAWING MY FEARS.

↑
MY FEARS

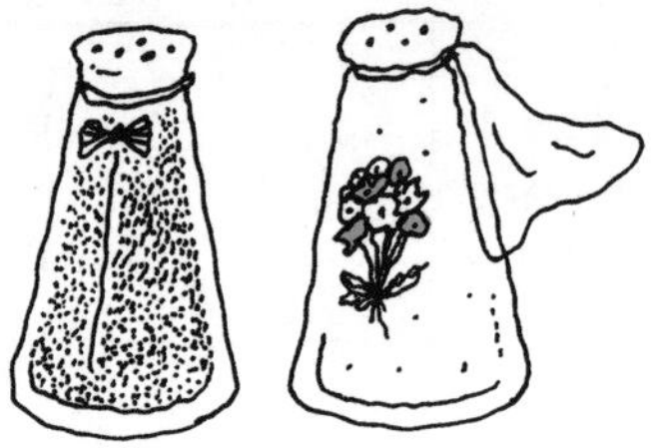

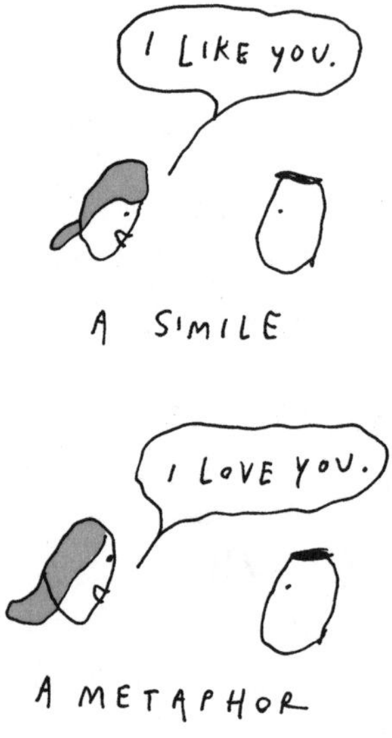
I LIKE YOU.
A SIMILE
I LOVE YOU.
A METAPHOR

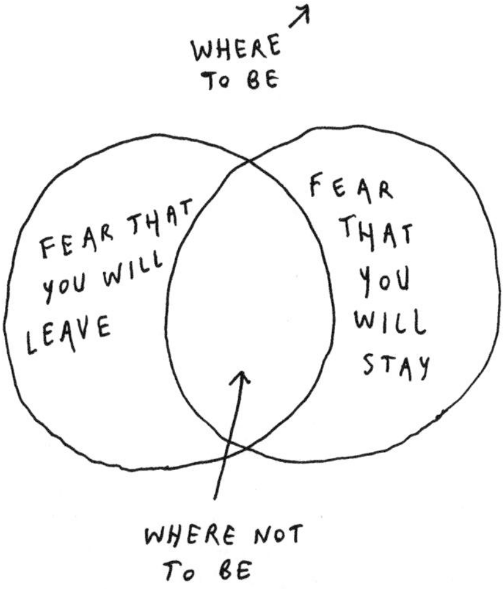
WHERE TO BE
FEAR THAT YOU WILL LEAVE
FEAR THAT YOU WILL STAY
WHERE NOT TO BE

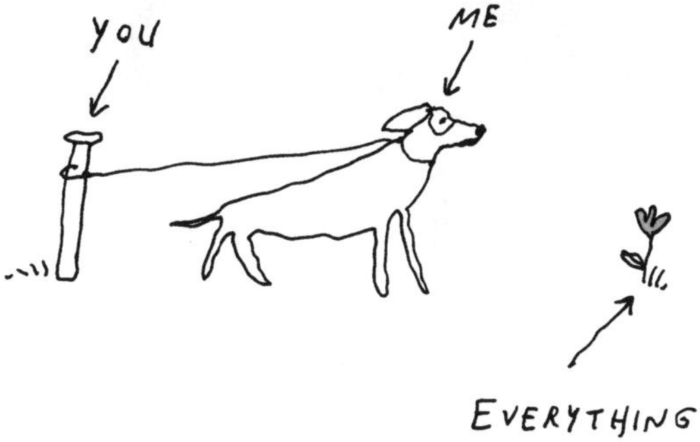
YOU
ME
EVERYTHING

THE CHORUS
HE TREATS YOU LIKE SHIT!
"I DIDN'T UNDERSTAND HIM TILL NOW."
HE TREATS YOU LIKE SHIT!
"HE'S JUST SHY."
HE TREATS YOU LIKE SHIT!
"I DON'T KNOW ENOUGH ABOUT HIM YET TO JUDGE."

THE SERIES OF
EVER-SMALLER
BOXES YOU WILL
BE EXPECTED TO
FIT YOURSELF INTO

AGAIN?

PIT OF DESPAIR

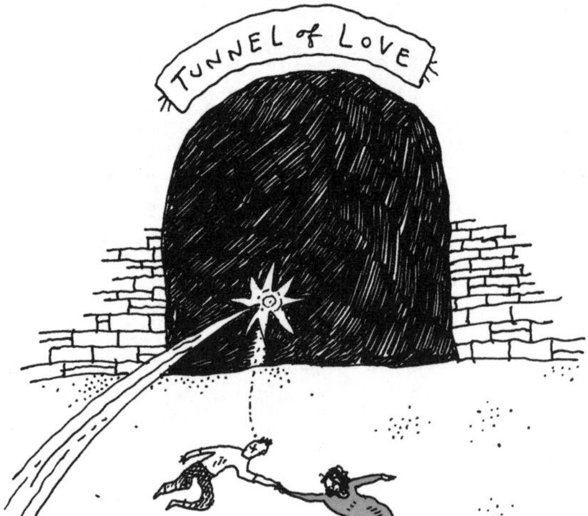
TUNNEL of LOVE

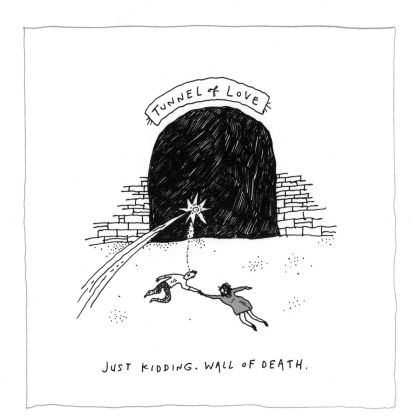

JUST KIDDING. WALL OF DEATH.

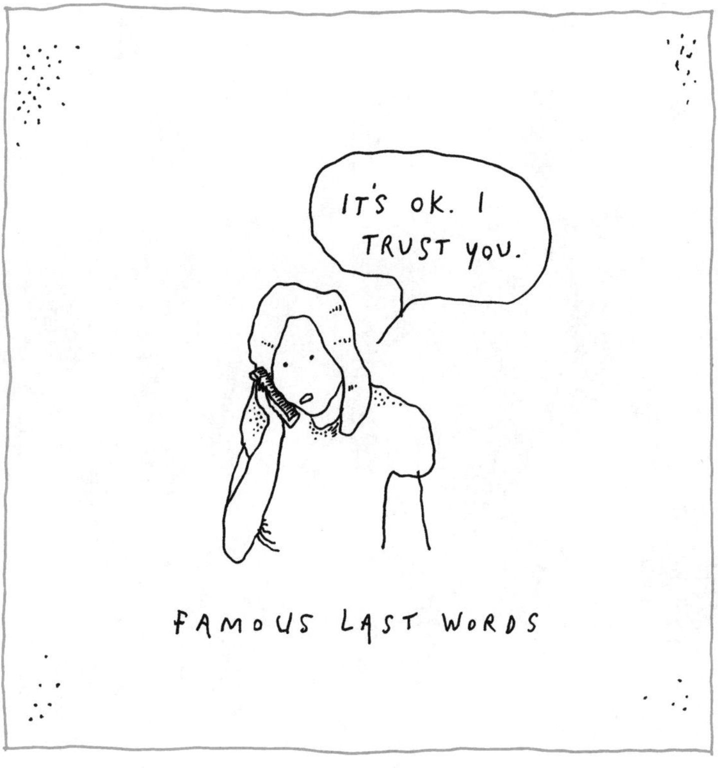
IT'S OK. I TRUST YOU.
FAMOUS LAST WORDS

I DID MY BEST
TO KEEP YOU.

_____

I DON'T THINK I COULD
TAKE YOU BACK. BUT
I ACHE FOR ALL THE
PARTS OF YOU THAT DIDN'T
BETRAY ME.

MY HEART IS
BREAKING AND
I LOVE IT.

WE DON'T NEED TO USE A CONDOM BECAUSE THIS IS THE REAL THING BECAUSE

YOU WERE JUST SOME
RANDOM PERSON. I THINK
I ALMOST LET YOU ABDUCT
ME FOR THE REST OF
MY LIFE.

I LIKED YOU BECAUSE
YOU WEREN'T AN IDIOT.

YOU LIKED ME BECAUSE
I WASN'T WEIRD.

WE WERE BOTH SO DISAPPOINTED.

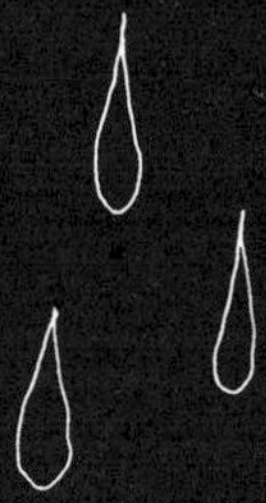

I WANT TO INFLICT
THESE TEARS ON YOU.

I WISH I'D
WONDERED WHAT
YOU WERE THINKING
INSTEAD OF WONDERING
WHAT YOU WERE
THINKING ABOUT ME.

HOW TO CLEAR
YOUR HEAD

BETTER TO HAVE LOVED AND LOST AND LOVED AND LOST AND LOVED AND LOST AND LOVED AND LOST AND LOVED AND LOST AND LOVED AND LOST AND LOVED AND LOST AND LOVED AND LOST AND LOVED AND LOST THAN NEVER TO HAVE LOVED AT ALL.

PERKS I HAVE LOST

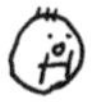 → CANADIAN CITIZENSHIP

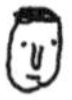 → CHILDREN WOULD GET TO HAVE TWO INTERESTING CULTURES

 → PAID FOR DRINKS (!!!)

 → FUNCTIONING PENIS

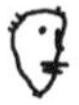 → ROOMMATE HAD A CAT

"IT'S ME, YOUR EX. CAN WE PLEASE MEET? BLAH BLAH BLAH HEALTHY FOR BOTH OF US."
OK
"NO, WE ONLY DATED FOR A WEEK AND A HALF, AND I'VE ALREADY BROKEN UP WITH YOU THREE TIMES!"
DON'T ANSWER
"COOL LET'S GET BACK TOGETHER."
YES
NO
"YOU ARE A MONSTER AND YOU WILL SUFFER FOR IT."

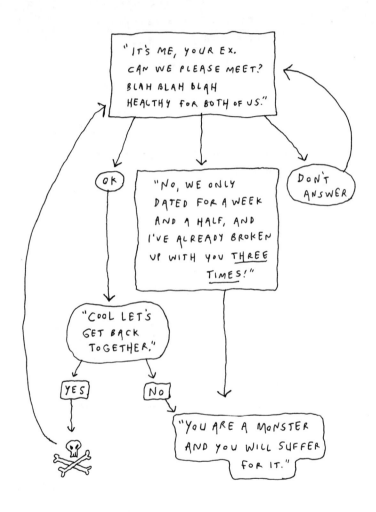

NEVER TRUST
AN HONEST MAN.

HAPPY
SAD
FALL IN LOVE
MAKE THINGS
BREAK UP
ETC.
MAKE THINGS

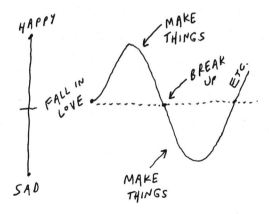

ALL THE MEN I'VE BEEN WITH.
ALL THE WOMEN I'VE BEEN.

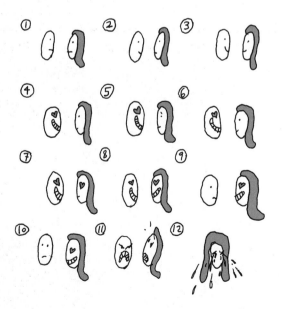

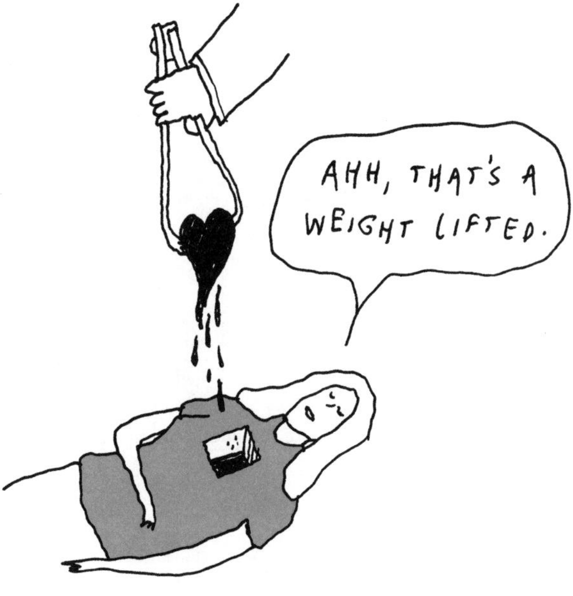
AHH, THAT'S A WEIGHT LIFTED.

GENDER POLITICS AND
POLITICS IN GENERAL

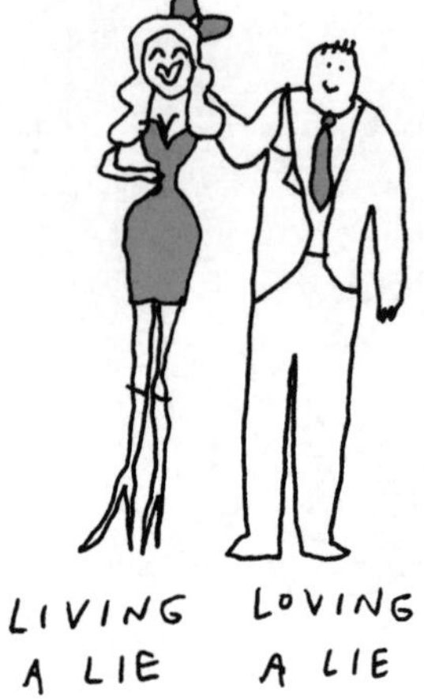
LIVING
A LIE
LOVING
A LIE

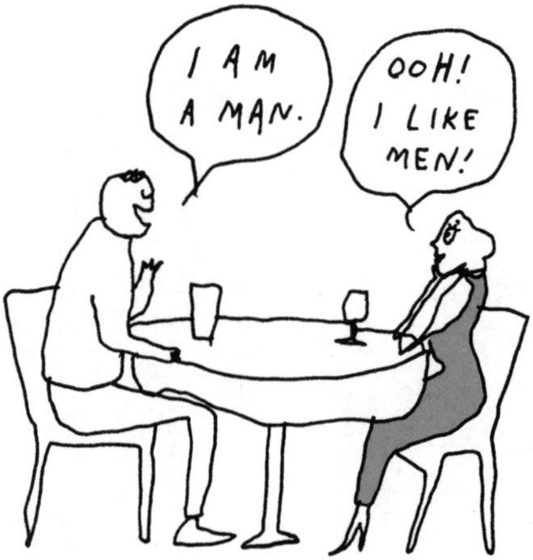
I AM
A MAN.
OOH!
I LIKE
MEN!

SELF-PORTRAIT AT 26 (PRE-FEMINIST)

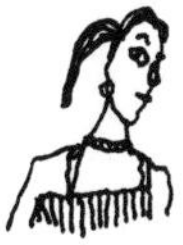

ABLE TO BE A ROMANTIC BECAUSE "WOMEN <u>DO</u> HAVE EQUAL RIGHTS"

SELF-PORTRAIT NOW (FEMINIST)

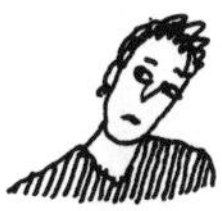

GUARDED AND VERY UNROMANTIC, NOT BECAUSE I'M EMANCIPATED AND STRONG, BUT BECAUSE I'M AWARE OF MY OWN OVERWHELMING VULNERABILITY AND LACK OF AUTONOMY

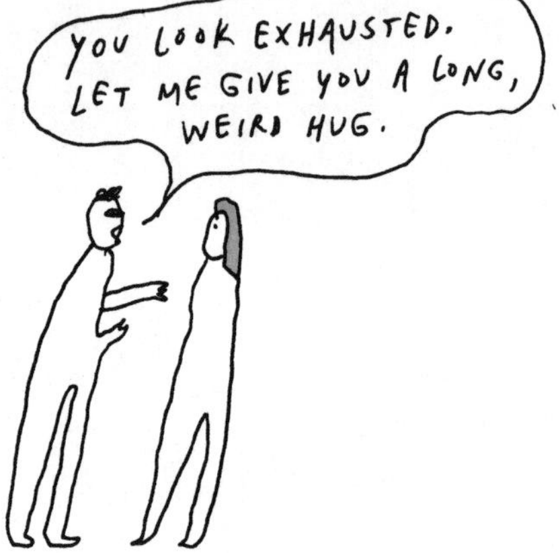
YOU LOOK EXHAUSTED. LET ME GIVE YOU A LONG, WEIRD HUG.

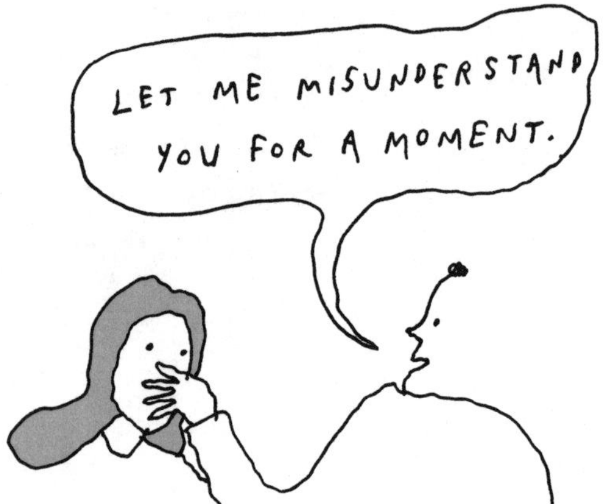
LET ME MISUNDERSTAND YOU FOR A MOMENT.

THE DIRECT STARE VS. THE
SIDELONG, ANXIOUS GLANCE

- NOTICE MASKED AGGRESSION

- REACT

- INCITE OVERT AGGRESSION

GRAB
GRAB
GRAB

NEW MANTRA

"I DO NOT GRANT YOU
MY ATTENTION."

LOW SELF-ESTEEM RED RIDING HOOD

I'M GOING TO VISIT A WOLF!

ENTITLEMENT
FOR MEN
Internalize
FOR WOMEN

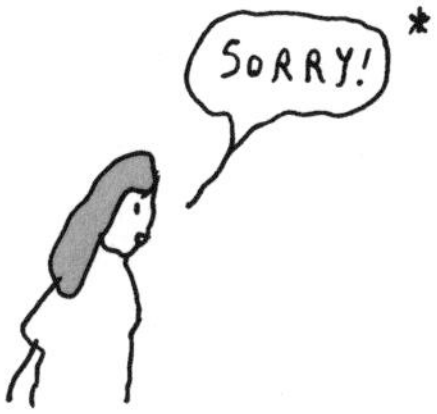
SORRY!*

* DON'T HURT ME, YOU ALL-POWERFUL BEING!!!

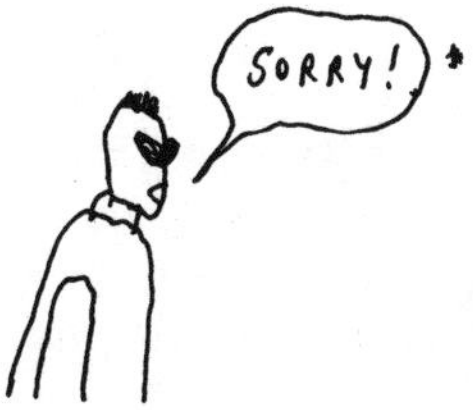
SORRY!*

*I NEED YOU TO TELL ME IT'S OK, THEREBY ACKNOWLEDGING THAT WHAT HAPPENED TO YOU WAS NOT MY FAULT, BECAUSE THIS IS ABOUT ME.

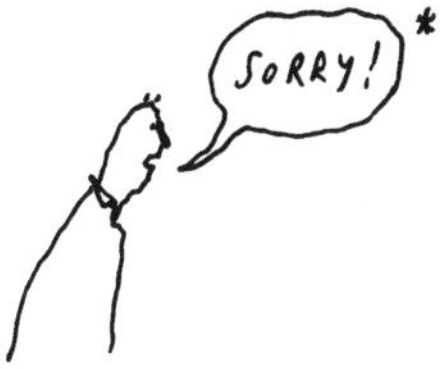
SORRY!*

*I AM BRITISH AND I WANT YOU TO BE HAPPY.

THE SHIT
I'VE TAKEN

THE MISTAKES
I'VE MADE

THINGS I "LIKED" FOR MEN

STAR TREK
VICTORIA'S SECRET
HERMAN HESSE
AARON SORKIN
TV IN GENERAL
FRISBEE GOLF
PINK FLOYD
STEELY DAN
JAY-Z
ULTIMATE FRISBEE
THE CARDINALS
THE BROWNS
THE YANKEES
THE METS
THE JETS
THE HEAT
LIBERTARIANISM
MEAT
BEN LERNER
NBC
HARI KRISHNA MUSIC
JUDAISM
CHRISTIANITY
MONEY
FRUGALITY
"FUN"
FRIED FOOD
VIDEO GAMES
COMPUTER GAMES
KARAOKE
BOCCE
HERRING
WHISKEY
VODKA
BEER
STAYING UP LATE
WAKING UP EARLY
POLYAMORY
SCUBA DIVING
HEGEL
GATORADE

83

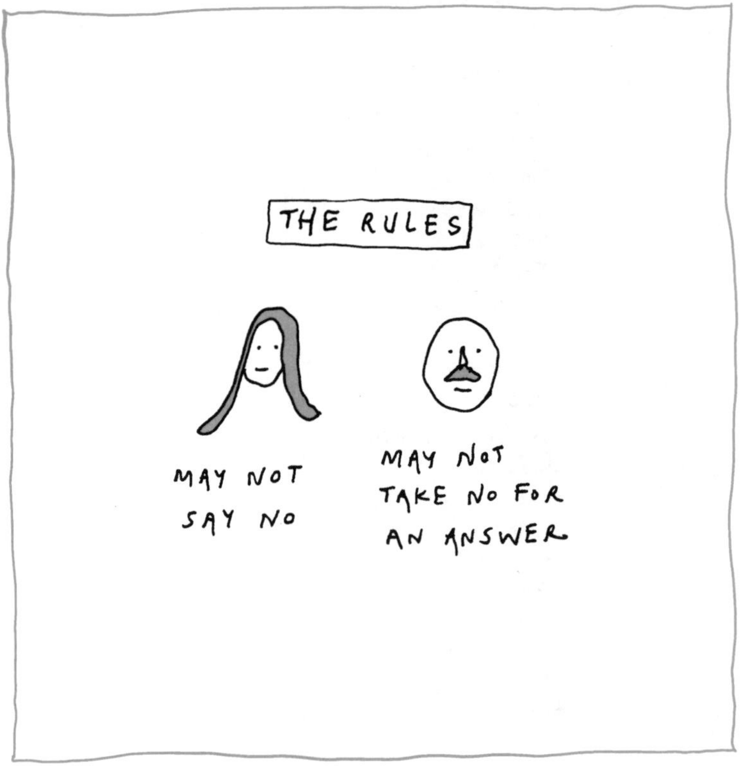
THE RULES
MAY NOT SAY NO
MAY NOT TAKE NO FOR AN ANSWER

IF YOU CAN'T
SAY NO YOU
CAN'T SAY YES.

TRANSLATOR

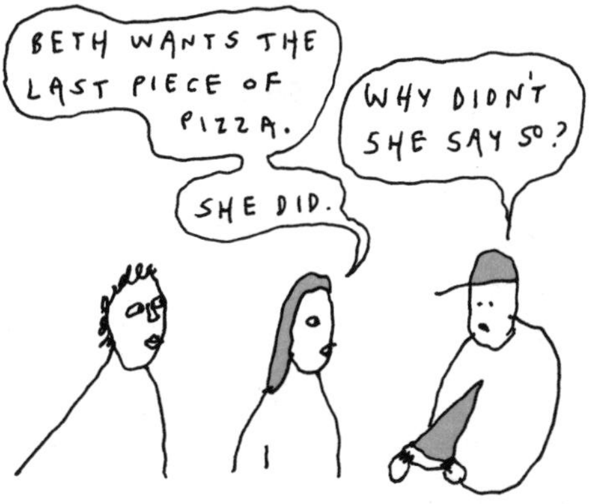
BETH WANTS THE LAST PIECE OF PIZZA.
SHE DID.
WHY DIDN'T SHE SAY SO?

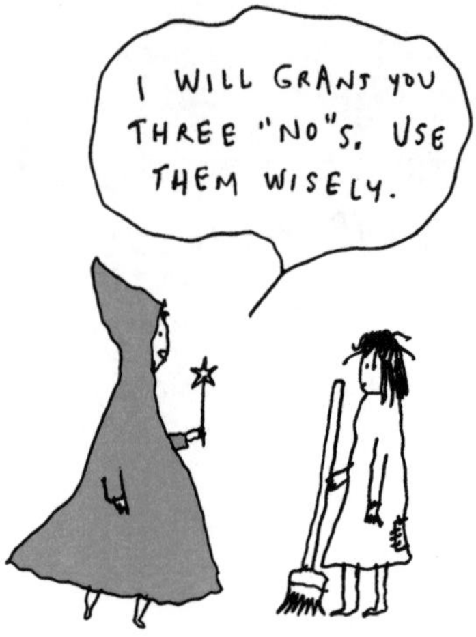
I WILL GRANT YOU THREE "NO"S. USE THEM WISELY.

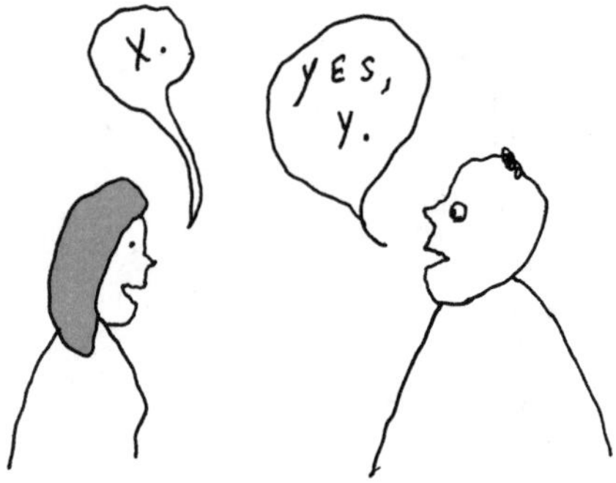
X.
YES, Y.

ASSERTIVE
YET INEPT

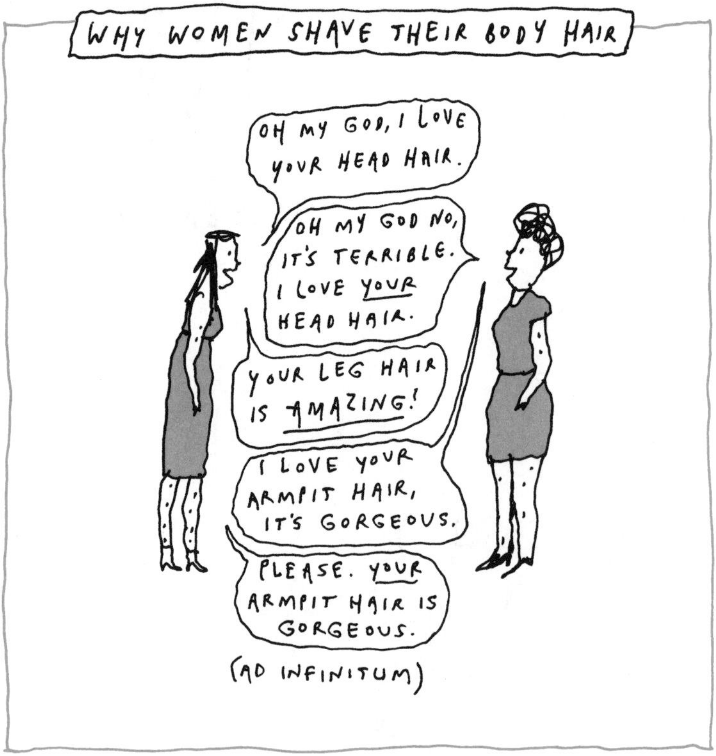
WHY WOMEN SHAVE THEIR BODY HAIR
OH MY GOD, I LOVE YOUR HEAD HAIR.
OH MY GOD NO, IT'S TERRIBLE. I LOVE YOUR HEAD HAIR.
YOUR LEG HAIR IS AMAZING!
I LOVE YOUR ARMPIT HAIR, IT'S GORGEOUS.
PLEASE. YOUR ARMPIT HAIR IS GORGEOUS.
(AD INFINITUM)

OCCAM'S RAZOR   OCCAM'S UNWANTED
                             HAIR

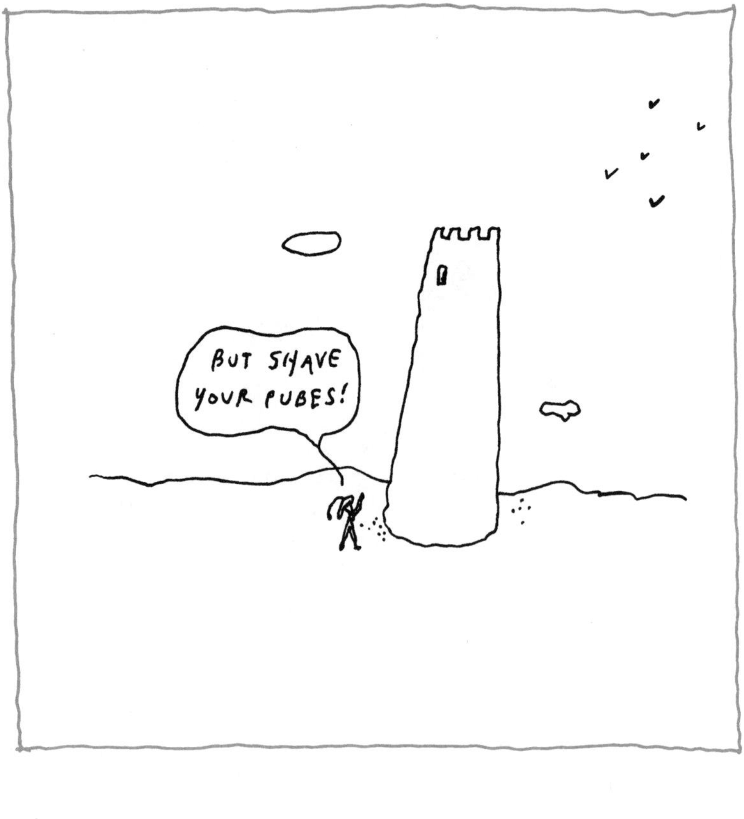
BUT SHAVE YOUR PUBES!

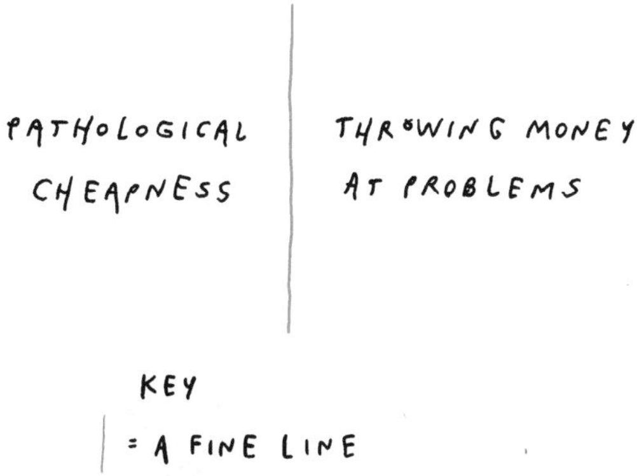
PATHOLOGICAL CHEAPNESS
THROWING MONEY AT PROBLEMS
KEY
= A FINE LINE

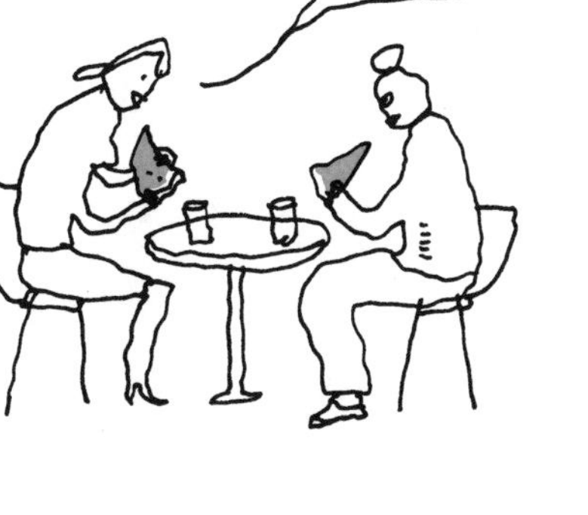
EVERYTHING I EAT GOES STRAIGHT TO MY BELLY AND OUT MY ANUS.

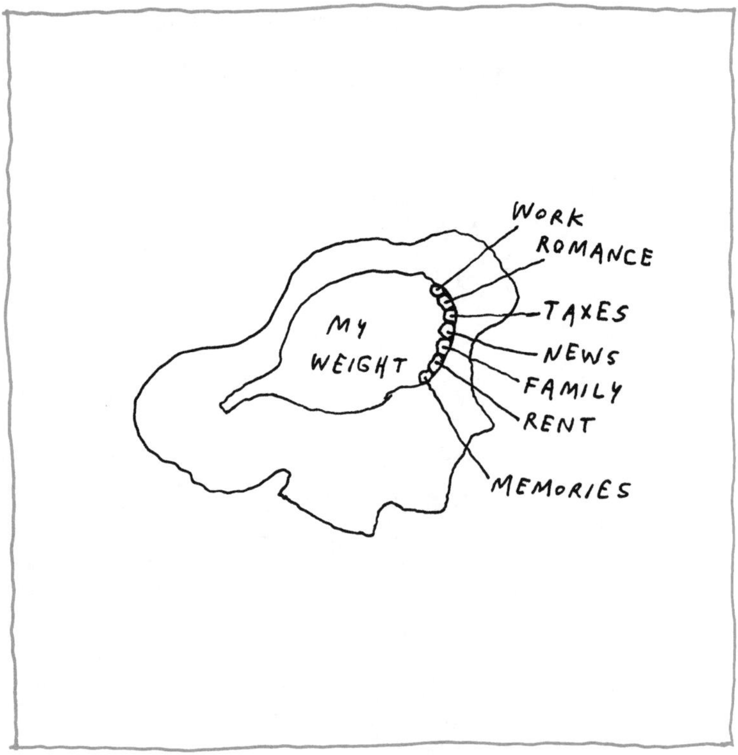
MY WEIGHT
WORK
ROMANCE
TAXES
NEWS
FAMILY
RENT
MEMORIES

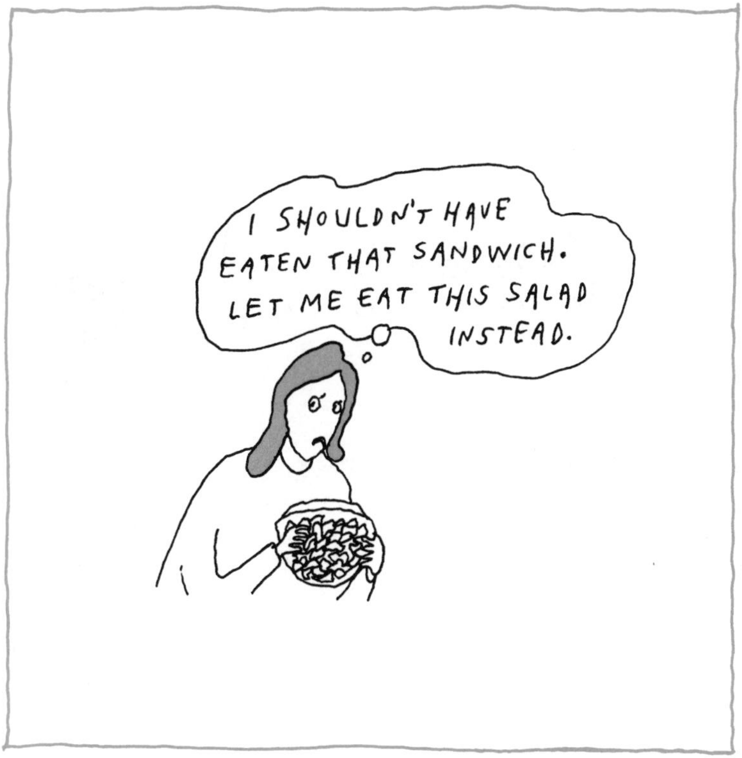
I SHOULDN'T HAVE EATEN THAT SANDWICH. LET ME EAT THIS SALAD INSTEAD.

THE SALAD

1. SPEAR SALAD WITH FORK?
(NO.)

2. SCOOP SALAD.

3. SALAD POURS OUT OF MOUTH,
OFF FORK. MORE POURS
OUT THAN COMES IN, IF
POSSIBLE.

4. SO HUNGRY. FIND
MORE SALAD.

A NOVEL IDEA

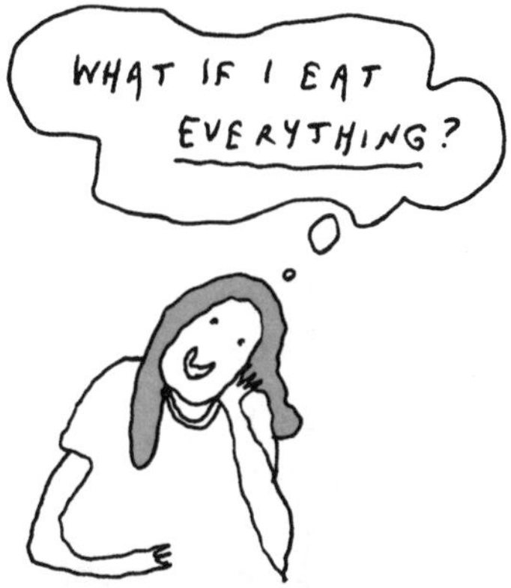
WHAT IF I EAT EVERYTHING?

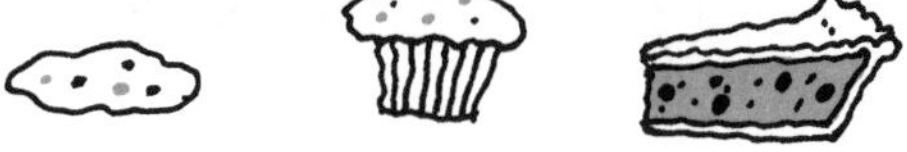

COLLECT THEM ALL!

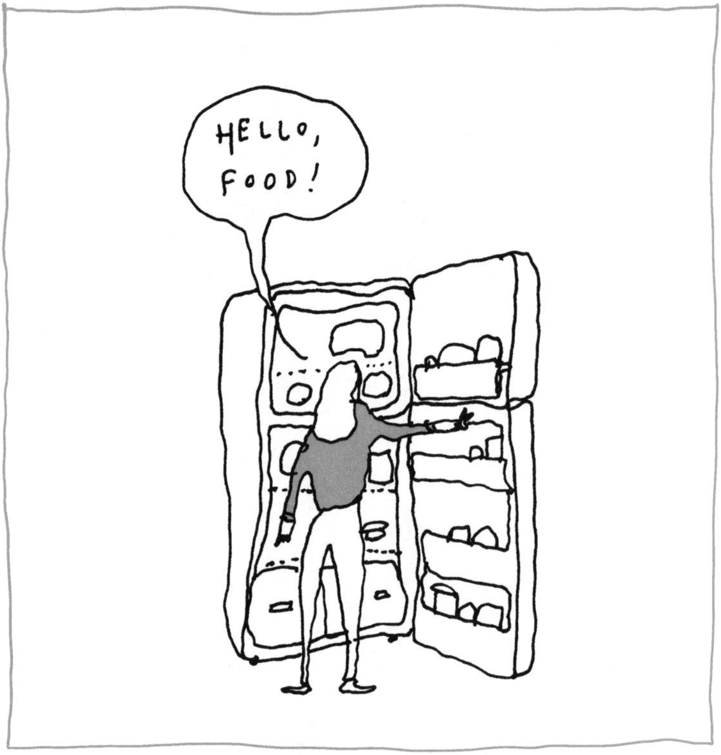
HELLO, FOOD!

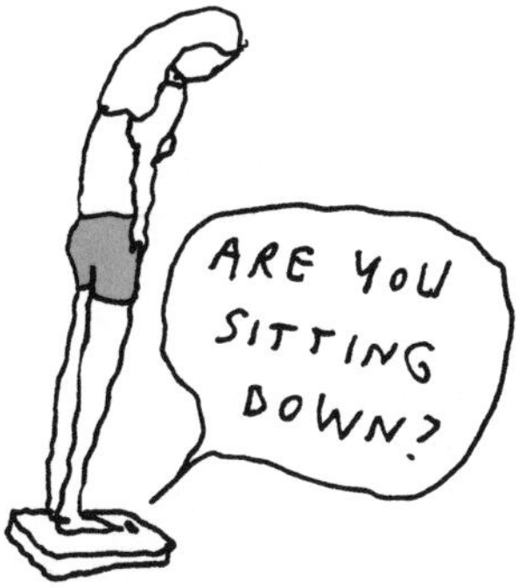
ARE YOU SITTING DOWN?

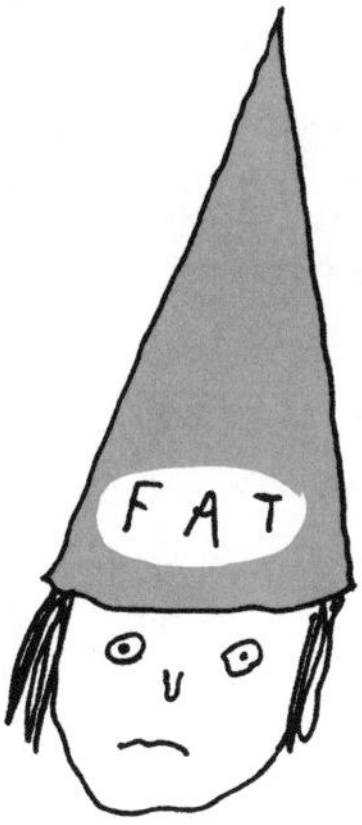
FAT

BATHING SUIT

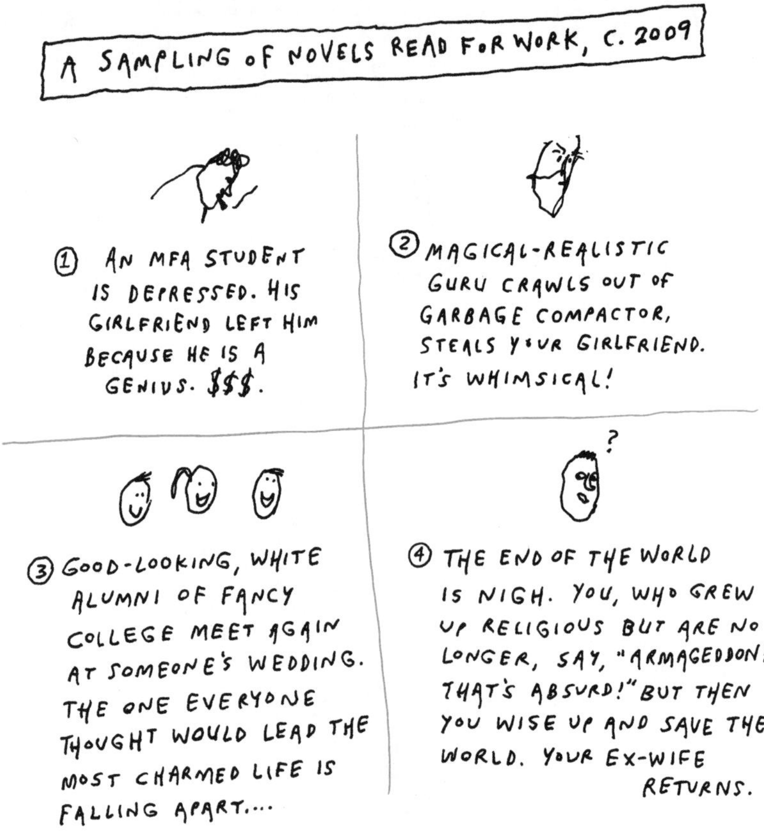
A SAMPLING OF NOVELS READ FOR WORK, C. 2009
① AN MFA STUDENT IS DEPRESSED. HIS GIRLFRIEND LEFT HIM BECAUSE HE IS A GENIUS. $$$.
② MAGICAL-REALISTIC GURU CRAWLS OUT OF GARBAGE COMPACTOR, STEALS YOUR GIRLFRIEND. IT'S WHIMSICAL!
③ GOOD-LOOKING, WHITE ALUMNI OF FANCY COLLEGE MEET AGAIN AT SOMEONE'S WEDDING. THE ONE EVERYONE THOUGHT WOULD LEAD THE MOST CHARMED LIFE IS FALLING APART....
?
④ THE END OF THE WORLD IS NIGH. YOU, WHO GREW UP RELIGIOUS BUT ARE NO LONGER, SAY, "ARMAGEDDON?! THAT'S ABSURD!" BUT THEN YOU WISE UP AND SAVE THE WORLD. YOUR EX-WIFE RETURNS.

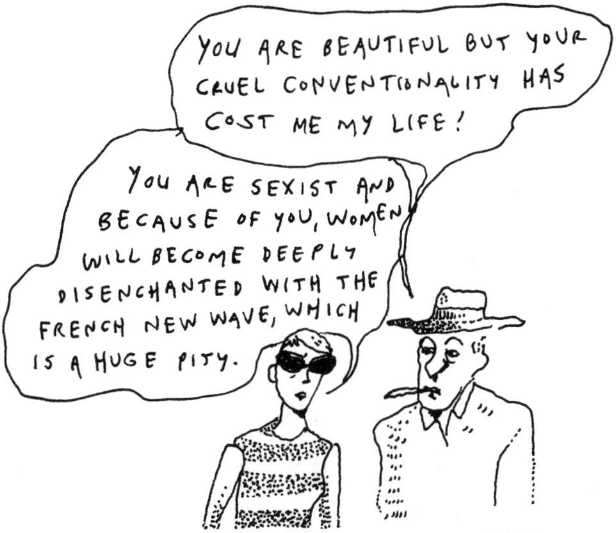
YOU ARE BEAUTIFUL BUT YOUR CRUEL CONVENTIONALITY HAS COST ME MY LIFE!
YOU ARE SEXIST AND BECAUSE OF YOU, WOMEN WILL BECOME DEEPLY DISENCHANTED WITH THE FRENCH NEW WAVE, WHICH IS A HUGE PITY.

IF WOMEN IN ART HAD VOICES

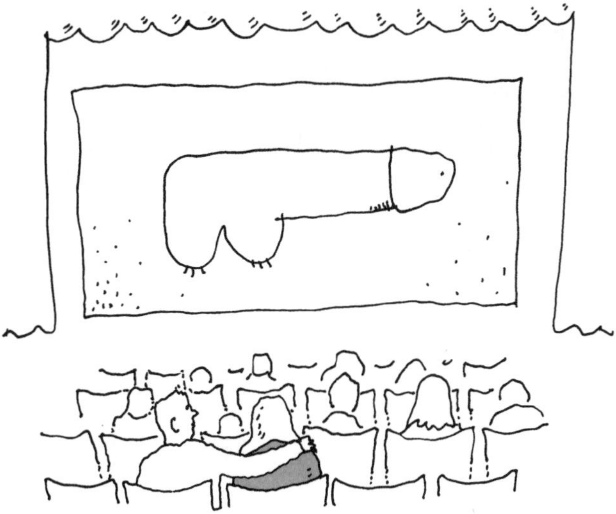

	THINGS YOU CAN DO AS A MAN	THINGS YOU CAN DO AS A WOMAN
GO TO A NOT-RICH COUNTRY ALONE	✓	
WIN A CURVEBALL NOBEL PRIZE FOR A REASON OTHER THAN BEING FEMALE	✓	
HAVE A RELIGIOUS AWAKENING AND JOIN AN OLD-FASHIONED COMMUNITY IN ANY CAPACITY BESIDES "SERVANT."	✓	
BIKE OR WALK AROUND QUIET AND LOVELY NEIGHBORHOODS AT NIGHT	✓	
TAKE MASOCHISTIC DELIGHT IN HOBBLING YOURSELF PHYSICALLY AND FINANCIALLY WITH SHOES/CLOTHES/MAKEUP/HAIR REMOVAL/PLASTIC SURGERY/ ETC.		✓ F!!!

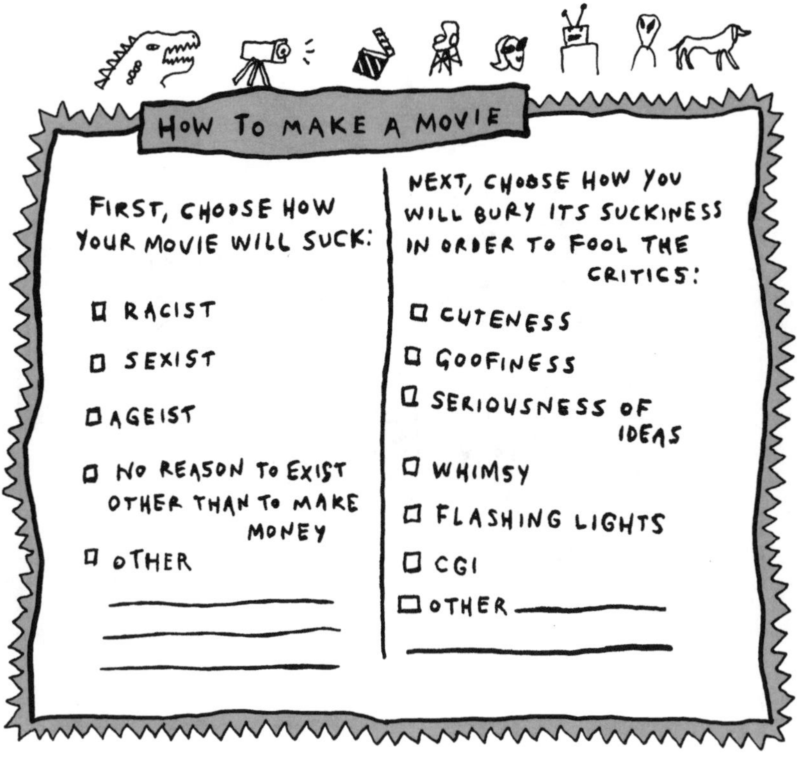
HOW TO MAKE A MOVIE
FIRST, CHOOSE HOW YOUR MOVIE WILL SUCK:
☐ RACIST
☐ SEXIST
☐ AGEIST
☐ NO REASON TO EXIST OTHER THAN TO MAKE MONEY
☐ OTHER
NEXT, CHOOSE HOW YOU WILL BURY ITS SUCKINESS IN ORDER TO FOOL THE CRITICS:
☐ CUTENESS
☐ GOOFINESS
☐ SERIOUSNESS OF IDEAS
☐ WHIMSY
☐ FLASHING LIGHTS
☐ CGI
☐ OTHER

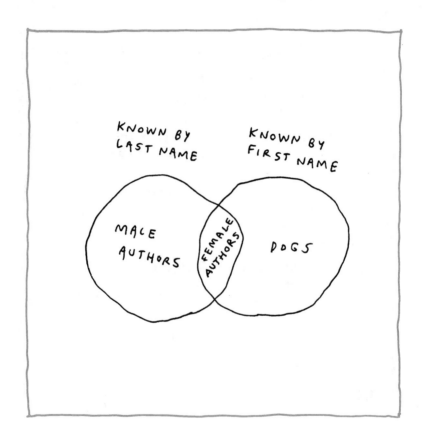

KNOWN BY
LAST NAME

KNOWN BY
FIRST NAME

MALE
AUTHORS

FEMALE
AUTHORS

DOGS

GREAT WOMEN of HISTORY

THE TRUTH ABOUT HARRIET TUBMAN

- NO SENSE OF HUMOR
- NOT PRETTY
- PEDANTIC
- DIDN'T KNOW HOW TO HAVE FUN OR RELAX
- NOT A RENAISSANCE WOMAN
- NOT SOMEONE YOU'D WANT TO HAVE A DRINK WITH

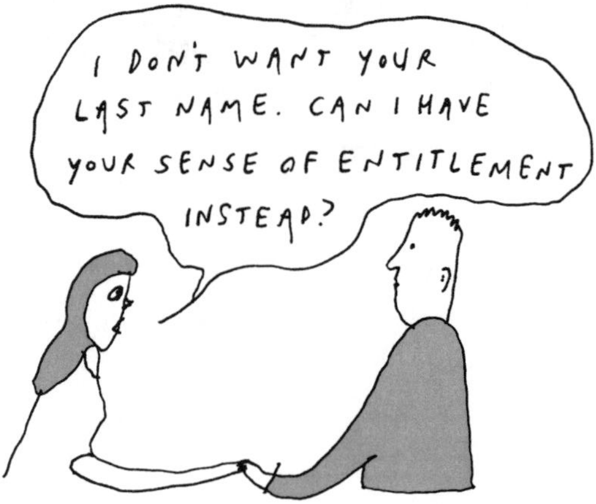
I DON'T WANT YOUR LAST NAME. CAN I HAVE YOUR SENSE OF ENTITLEMENT INSTEAD?

IF GREEN EGGS AND HAM
HAD A FEMALE NARRATOR

WELL, THEY DO LOOK
DELICIOUS AND IT WAS SO
KIND OF YOU TO MAKE THEM
FOR ME, BUT I HAD A HUGE
LUNCH AND I'M NOT VERY
HUNGRY RIGHT NOW.

OH, YOU'D LIKE TO KNOW IF
I'D EAT THEM IN A TRAIN?
OK, IN THAT CASE, SURE;
IF YOU INSIST.

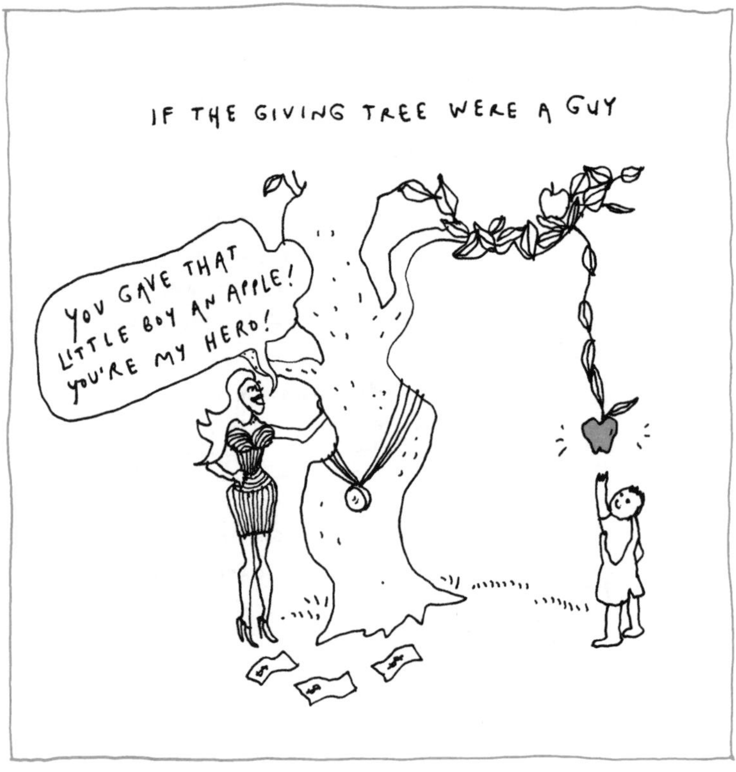
IF THE GIVING TREE WERE A GUY
YOU GAVE THAT LITTLE BOY AN APPLE! YOU'RE MY HERO!

HOW TO BE A NEAT FREAK WITHOUT CLEANING UP AFTER YOUR ROOMMATES

1. MOVE THE DIRT.

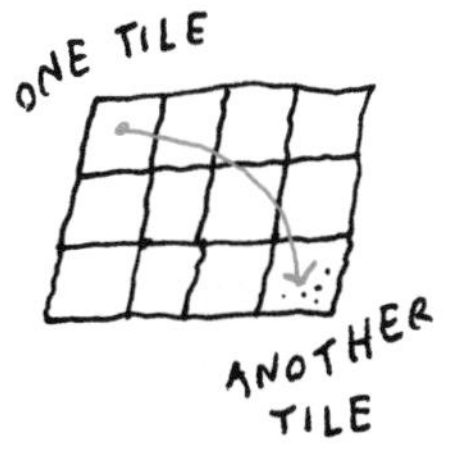
ONE TILE
ANOTHER TILE

2. ADD NEW DIRT OF YOUR OWN.

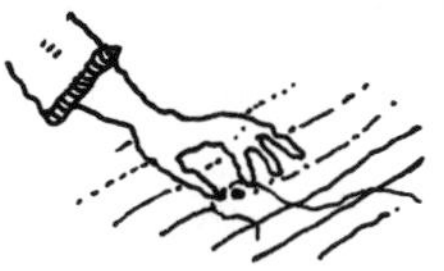

3. PRETEND IT IS A DIRT MUSEUM.

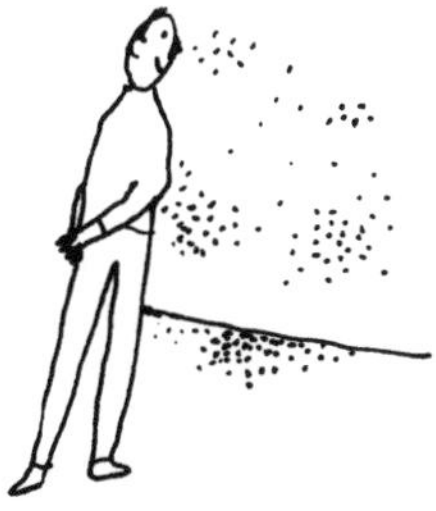

THE MANTRA OF "I AM NOT THE MAID"

- I AM NOT CLEANING THE SINK FOR THE TWELFTH DAY IN A ROW.

- IF YOU ALL KEEP LEAVING THE DOOR UNLOCKED, I WILL STOP LOCKING IT FOR YOU.

- NEXT TIME I BUY MORE DISH SOAP, I'M KEEPING IT IN MY ROOM, FOR ME ONLY.

- ALSO, TRASH BAGS.

- IF YOU EAT MY FOOD, I EAT YOURS.

WOMEN MAKING EXCUSES FOR MEN

THE TRAGEDY OF THE SIXTY-YEAR-OLD WOMAN IS THE TRAGEDY OF THE TWENTY-YEAR-OLD WOMAN IS THE TRAGEDY OF THE

OBJECTIFIED   IGNORED

THEORY #2 OF RUSSIAN DOLLS

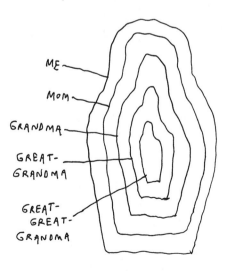

ME
MOM
GRANDMA
GREAT-
GRANDMA
GREAT-
GREAT-
GRANDMA

TOO OLD TO BE   TOO OLD TO BE BLAMED
SEEN AS SEXUAL   FOR HITTING ON EVERYONE

I'VE GOT IT!
LET'S BLAME
THE MOTHER!

I NEED TO FIGURE OUT WHO I AM BEFORE I CAN HELP SOCIETY BULLDOZE ME.

WHY DON'T YOU THINK ABOUT SOMEONE* OTHER THAN YOURSELF FOR ONCE?**

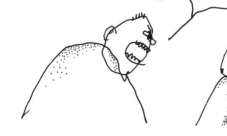

* ME

** EXCLUSIVELY

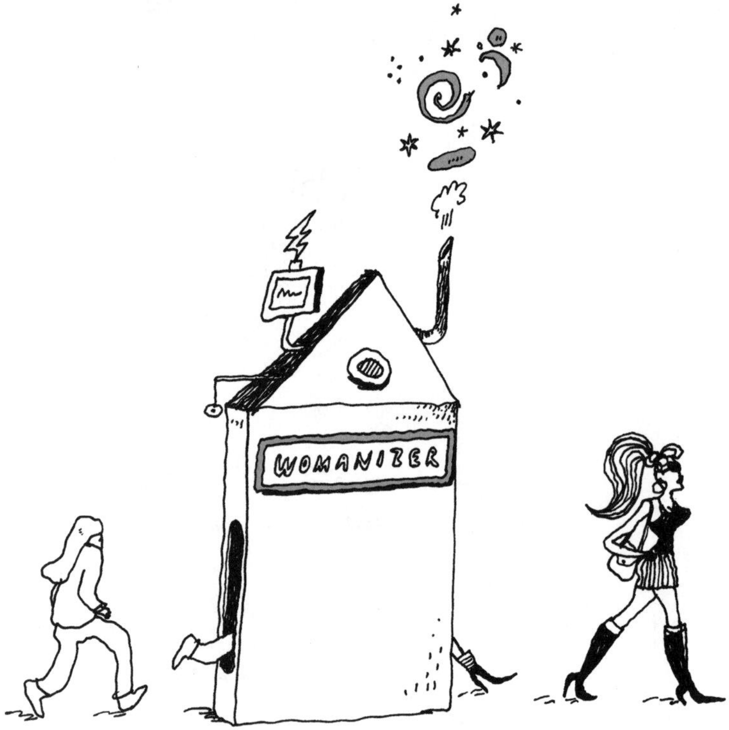
WOMANIZER

ISSUES OF CHOICE

GENDER RACE GENDER AND RACE CLASS

ARE YOU A VEGETABLE FOR MORAL REASONS?

HOW WE'RE SOCIALIZED

SELFLESS   SELF

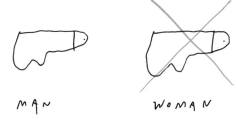

MAN   WOMAN

WHITE PERSON   BLACK PERSON

MALE	FEMALE
DOCTOR	DANCER
LAWYER	WHORE
POSTMAN	MOM
DENTIST	
CHEF	
SOLDIER	
POLITICIAN	
ANIMAL	
NARRATOR	
MATHEMATICIAN	
WRITER	
ARTIST	
DRIVER	
EXPLORER	
DAD	

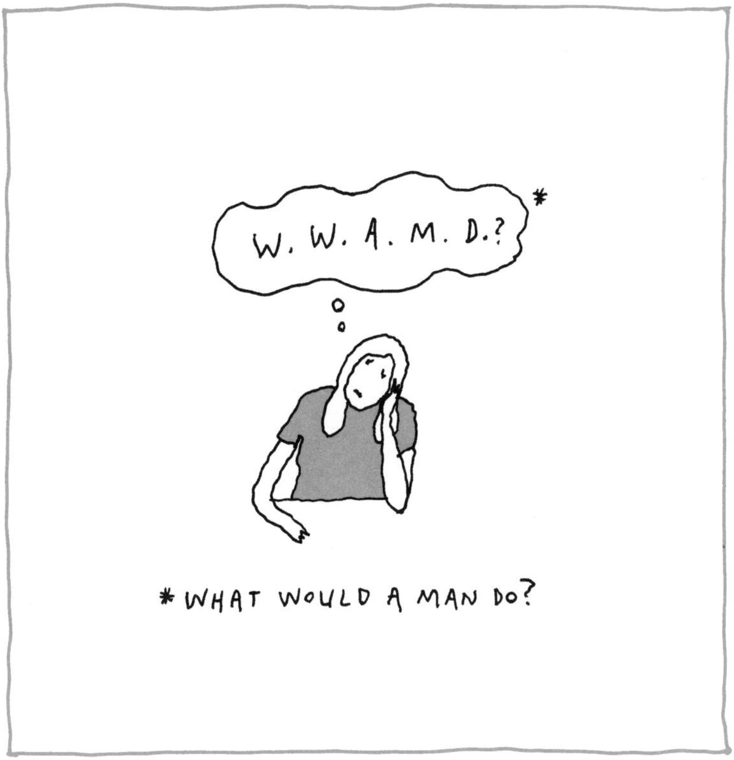
W. W. A. M. D.?*
* WHAT WOULD A MAN DO?

CONFLICTING IDENTITIES

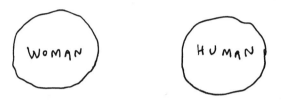

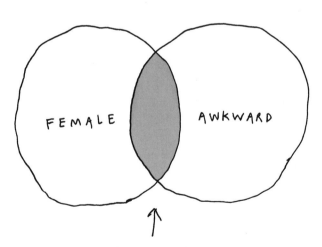

WOMAN
HUMAN

FEMALE
AWKWARD
HAVE VERY SPECIFIC NEEDS AND CANNOT ASSERT THEM

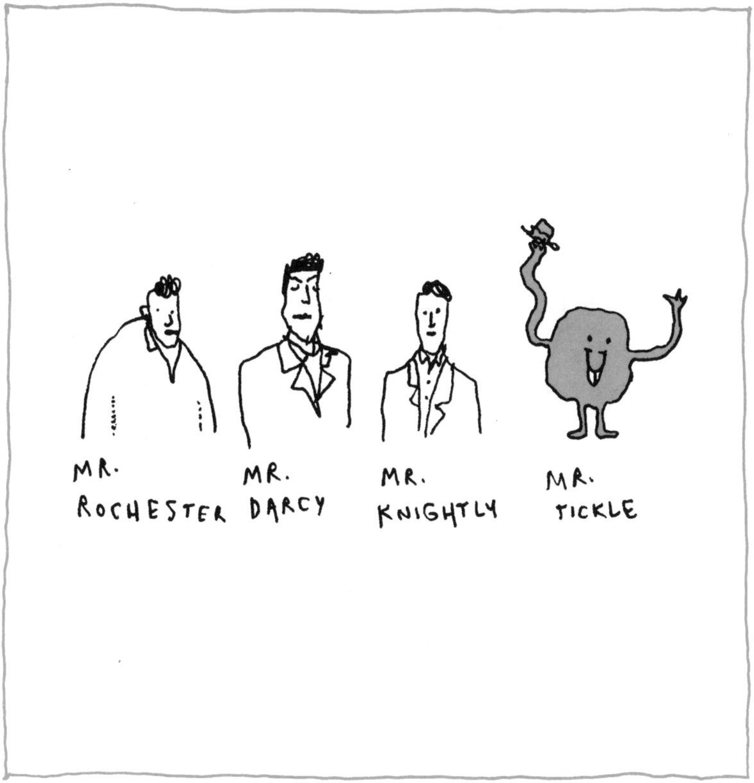
MR. ROCHESTER
MR. DARCY
MR. KNIGHTLY
MR. TICKLE

"FASCINATING"

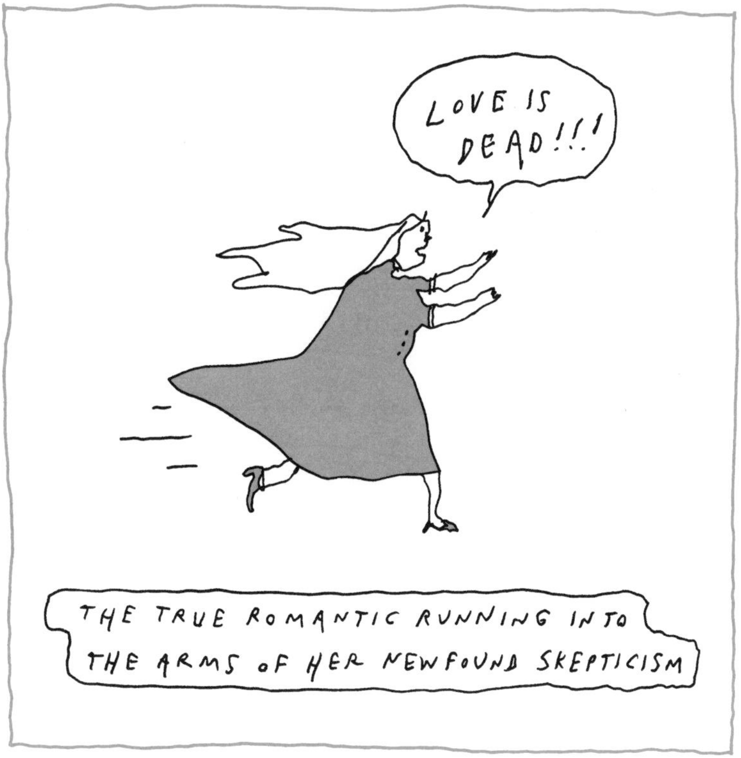
LOVE IS DEAD!!!
THE TRUE ROMANTIC RUNNING INTO THE ARMS OF HER NEWFOUND SKEPTICISM

THE PILL	MOOD SWINGS SPLOTCHES ON FACE MIGRAINES
CONDOMS	ANNOYING
ESTROGEN ONLY	PERIODS BETWEEN PERIODS
IUD	MAD SCIENCE EXPERIMENT
RYTHM METHOD	LIFE OF TERROR
PULL-OUT	"
ABSTINENCE	THEY WIN

GENTLY
PLACE

KICK

125

COMPARE/CONTRAST

1. SUPERMAN

2. SLEEPING BEAUTY

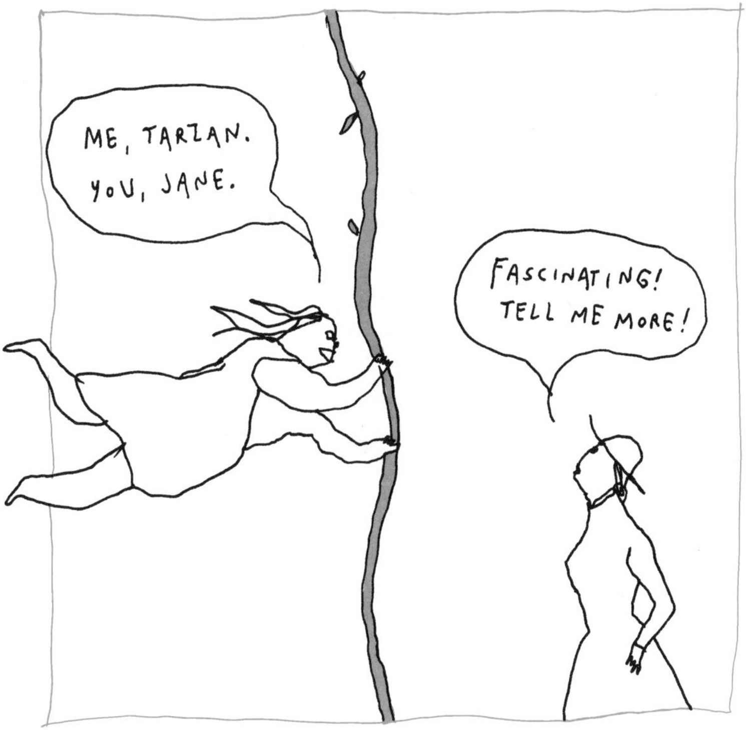
ME, TARZAN.
YOU, JANE.
FASCINATING!
TELL ME MORE!

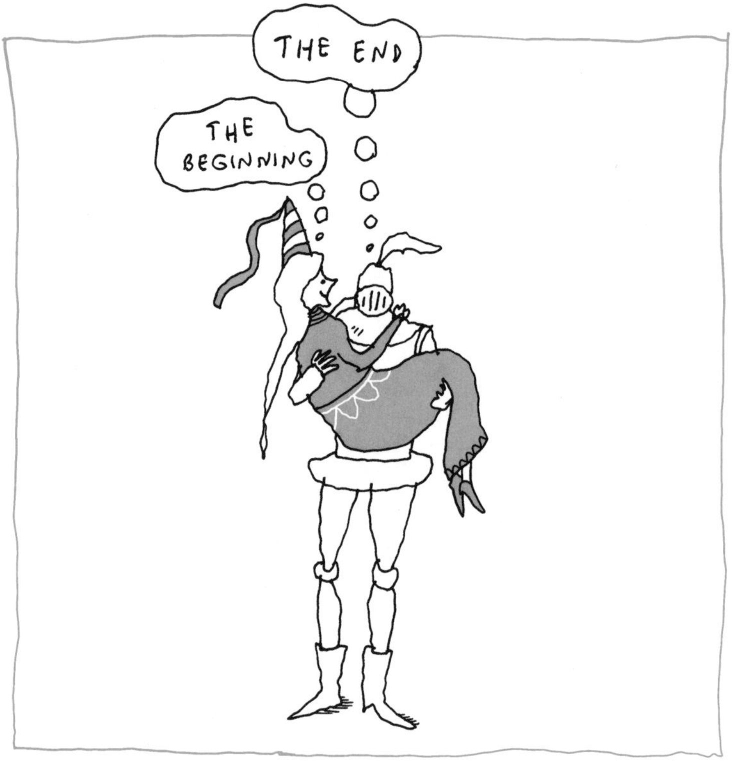
THE END
THE BEGINNING

TWO TYPES OF MANCHILD

1. PETER PAN   2. BEARDED
                       BABY

GAHHH! PEOPLE WHO UNDERSTAND AND ARTICULATE THEIR FEELINGS ARE SO COMPLICATED!!!

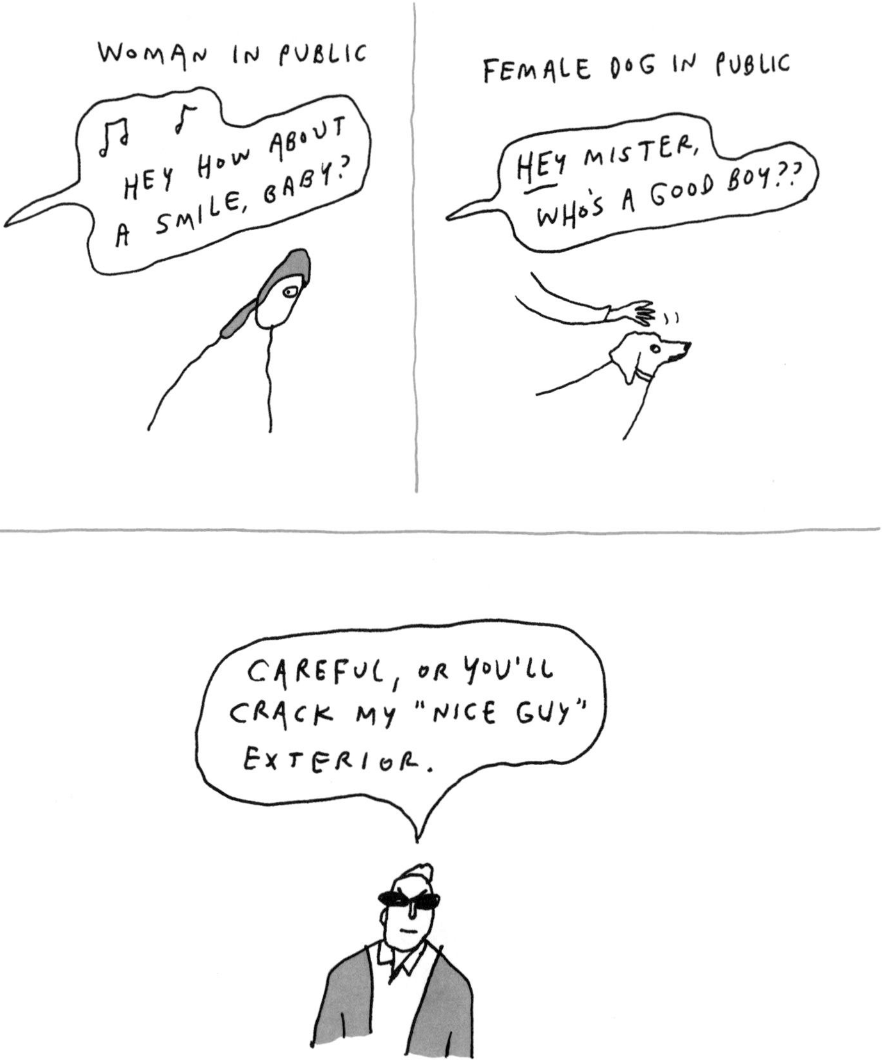
WOMAN IN PUBLIC
HEY HOW ABOUT A SMILE, BABY?
FEMALE DOG IN PUBLIC
HEY MISTER, WHO'S A GOOD BOY??
CAREFUL, OR YOU'LL CRACK MY "NICE GUY" EXTERIOR.

I DO NOT LIKE YOU SAM I AM.
I DO NOT LIKE YOU WHEN YOU TEXT.
I DO NOT WANT A "HEY, WHAT'S UP?"
I DO NOT WANT A LONGER NOTE.
I DO NOT WANT A RANDOM CALL.
I DO NOT WANT TO BE SURPRISED
    WHEN YOU SHOW UP AT MY EVENTS.
I DO NOT WANT TO MEET FOR LUNCH.
I DO NOT WANT TO MEET FOR TEA.
I DO NOT WANT TO READ YOUR BOOK.
I DO NOT WANT YOUR MOVIE RECS.
I DO NOT WANT THE GIFTS YOU SENT.
I DO NOT WANT TO HEAR YOU SAY
    YOU'RE SHOCKED THAT I'D REACT THIS WAY.
I DO NOT WANT TO LISTEN HOW
    YOU'RE ACTUALLY THE NICEST GUY
       AND HAVE TO ANSWER, "YES, YOU ARE."
I DO NOT WANT TO SECOND-GUESS
    IF I WAS BEING CLEAR ENOUGH,
       AND YET IT'S ALL I EVER SEEM TO DO.
I'M SORRY I OFFENDED YOU.

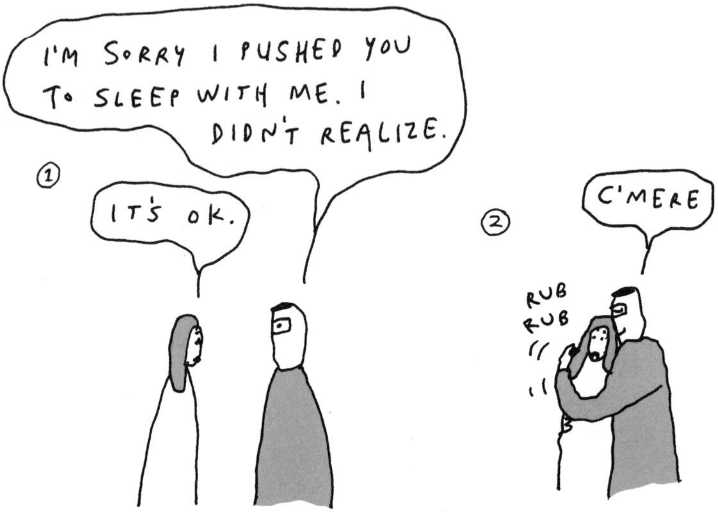
I'M SORRY I PUSHED YOU TO SLEEP WITH ME. I DIDN'T REALIZE.
1
IT'S OK.
2
C'MERE
RUB RUB

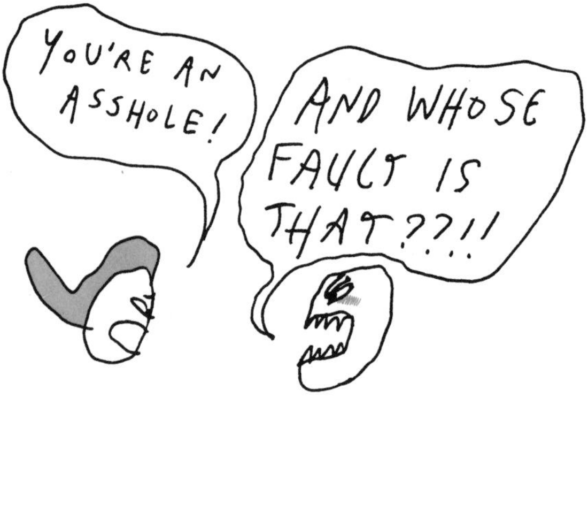
YOU'RE AN ASSHOLE!
AND WHOSE FAULT IS THAT??!!

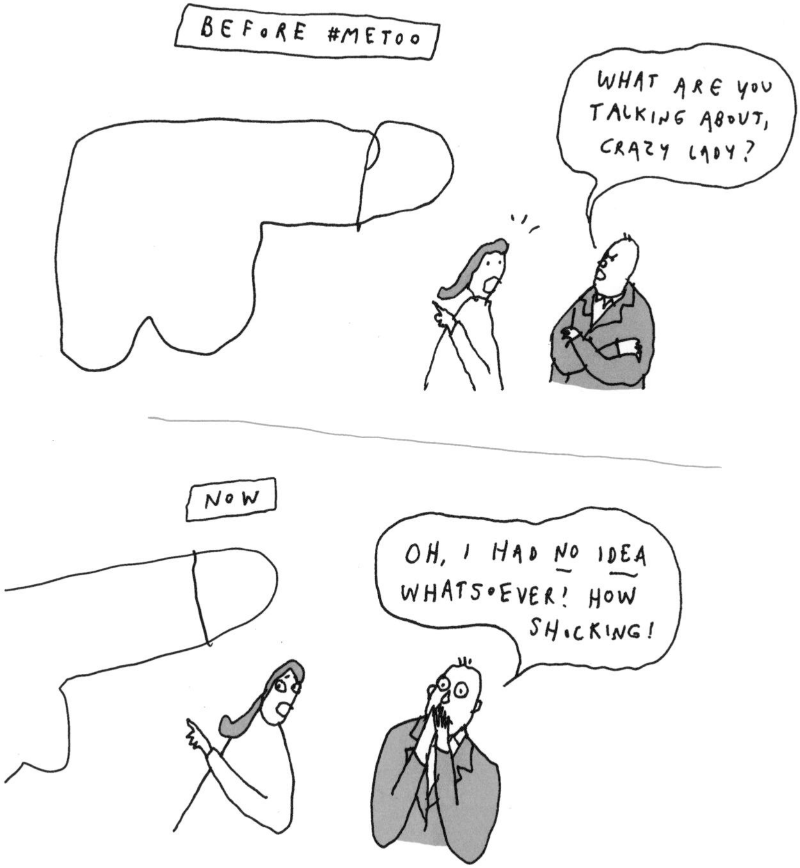
BEFORE #METOO
WHAT ARE YOU TALKING ABOUT, CRAZY LADY?
NOW
OH, I HAD NO IDEA WHATSOEVER! HOW SHOCKING!

"HE ASSAULTED ME."
"NO I DIDN'T."

LET ME JUST REOPEN THAT WOUND FOR YOU, SWEETIE.

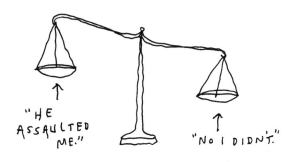

(NOV 8TH, 2016)

①

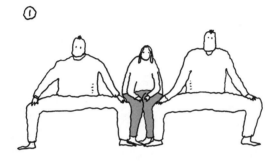

②

NOV. 9TH

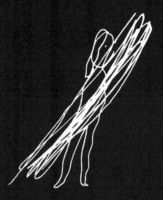

WE HAD BEEN HOPEFUL.

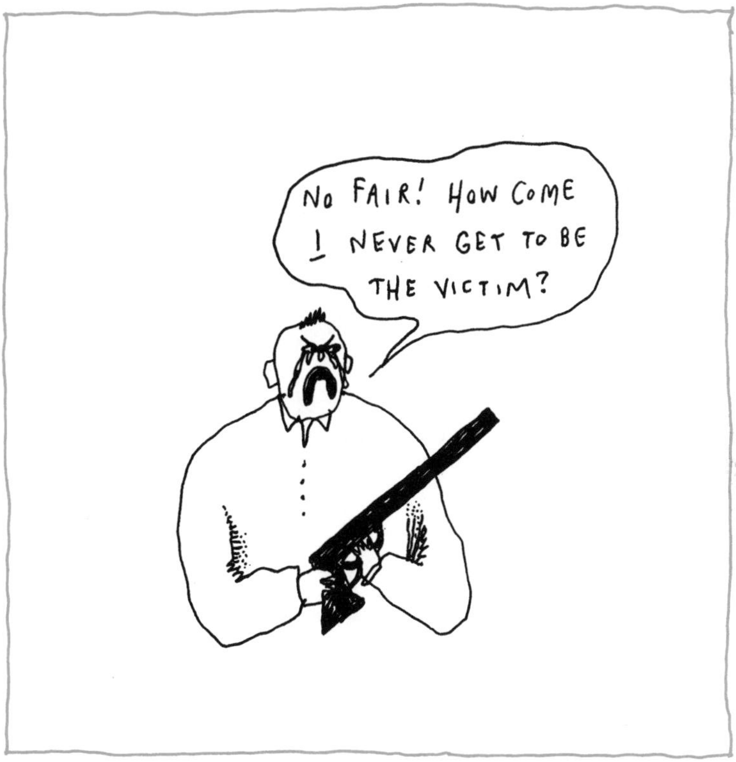
NO FAIR! HOW COME I NEVER GET TO BE THE VICTIM?

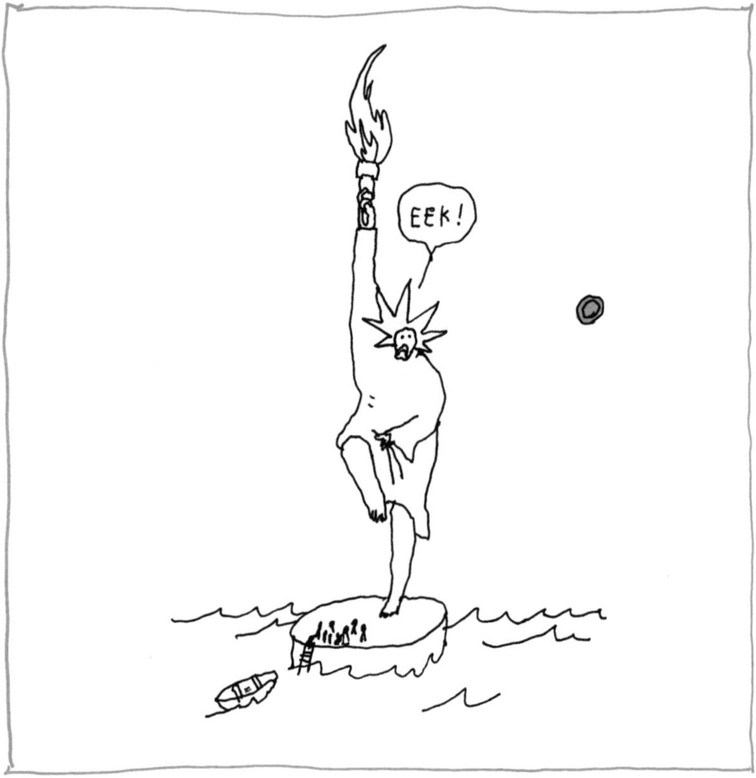
EEK!

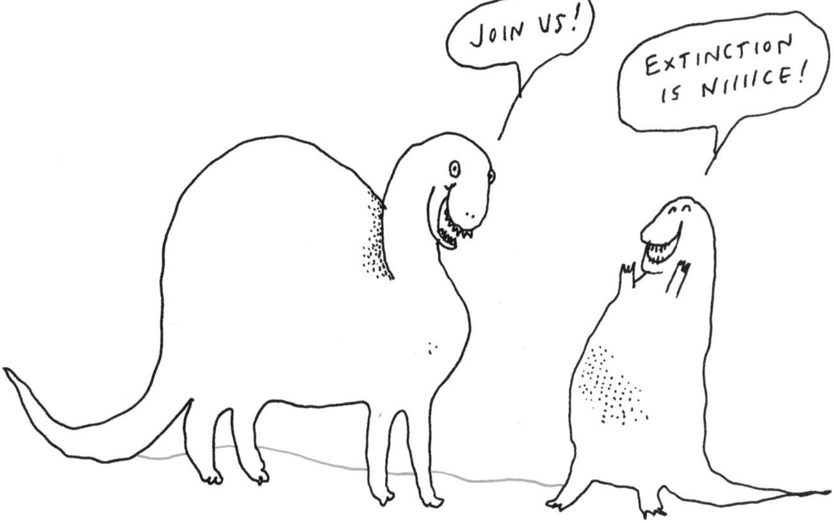
JOIN US!
EXTINCTION IS NIIIICE!

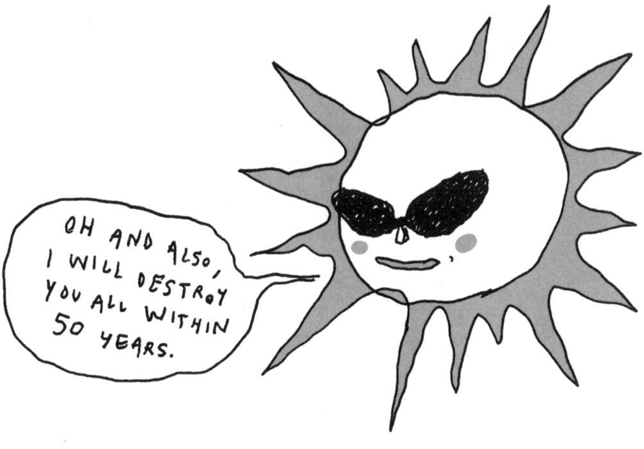
OH AND ALSO, I WILL DESTROY YOU ALL WITHIN 50 YEARS.

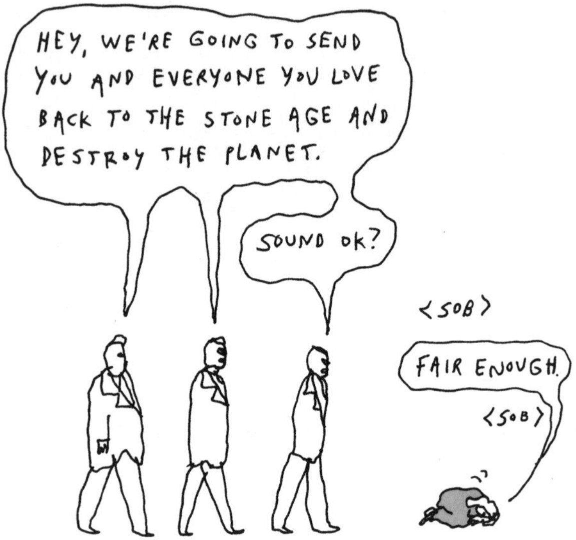
HEY, WE'RE GOING TO SEND YOU AND EVERYONE YOU LOVE BACK TO THE STONE AGE AND DESTROY THE PLANET.
SOUND OK?
<SOB>
FAIR ENOUGH.
<SOB>

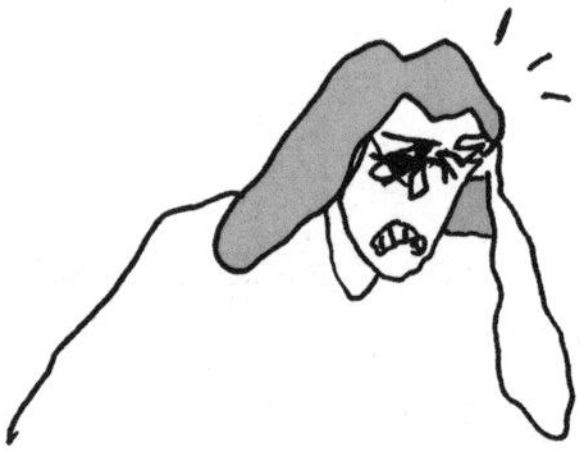

HEADACHE FROM
TRYING TO EMPATHIZE

THE MARXISTS VS.
THE FEMINISTS

OUR EVOLVEDNESS IS
IS OUR ACHILLES' HEEL.

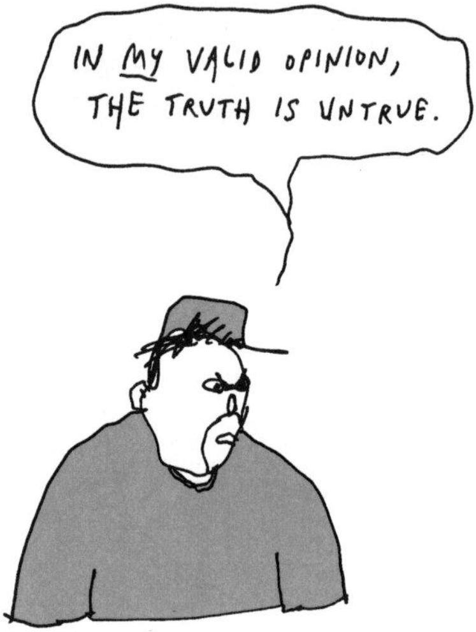
IN MY VALID OPINION, THE TRUTH IS UNTRUE.

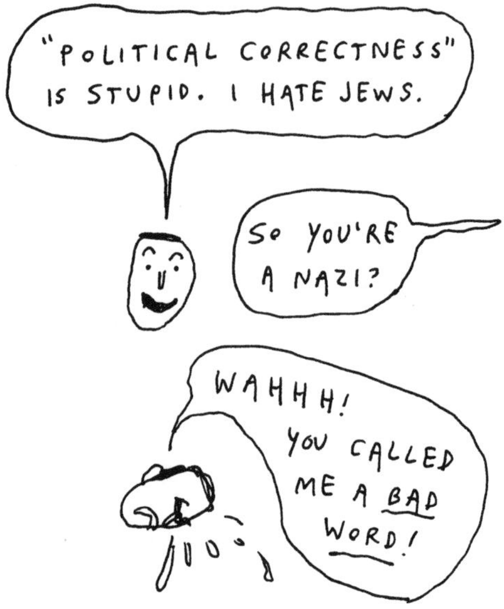
"POLITICAL CORRECTNESS" IS STUPID. I HATE JEWS.
SO YOU'RE A NAZI?
WAHHH! YOU CALLED ME A BAD WORD!

TROLL PHRASEBOOK

HELLO	SUCK IT
I FEEL IGNORED.	YOU THINK YOU'RE SUCH A SPECIAL LITTLE SNOWFLAKE, DON'T YOU.
I FEEL SO HELPLESS IN THE FACE OF RISING TOTALITARIANISM.	THIS POST IS DEMEANING TO FEMALE FRIENDSHIP. SHOCKED AND DISAPPOINTED. UNFOLLOWING NOW.
YOU HAVE NO IDEA HOW HARD IT IS RAISING A TWO-YEAR-OLD IN THIS CITY, ESPECIALLY WITH JAKE AS "COPARENT."	AND YOU CLAIM TO BE EMPATHETIC. DISGUSTING.
I REGRET HAVING PAID AN ARM AND A LEG FOR A SO-CALLED "BFA."	$125 FOR THIS GARBAGE? YOU MUST BE ROLLING IN IT, CONGRATS.
I HATE MYSELF FOR HATING MYSELF FOR HATING MYSELF.	YOUR FOLLOWERS ARE LIKE TRAINED MONKEYS. WHAT A SELF-CONGRATULATORY CIRCLE-JERK ROFL.
MY PARENTS NEVER THOUGHT I HAD BRAINS OR BEAUTY. BUT LOOK AT ME NOW: RETIRED FROM A 40-YEAR CAREER, A HUSBAND WHO IS A PILLAR IN THE COMMUNITY, A SUMMER HOUSE, AS MANY VACATIONS AS YOU PLEASE, AN INTELLIGENT BOOK CLUB, SEASON TICKETS TO THE THEATER, AND THREE GORGEOUS GRANDCHILDREN.	SOME JOKES ARE FUNNY. THIS ONE, MY FRIEND, IS NOT.

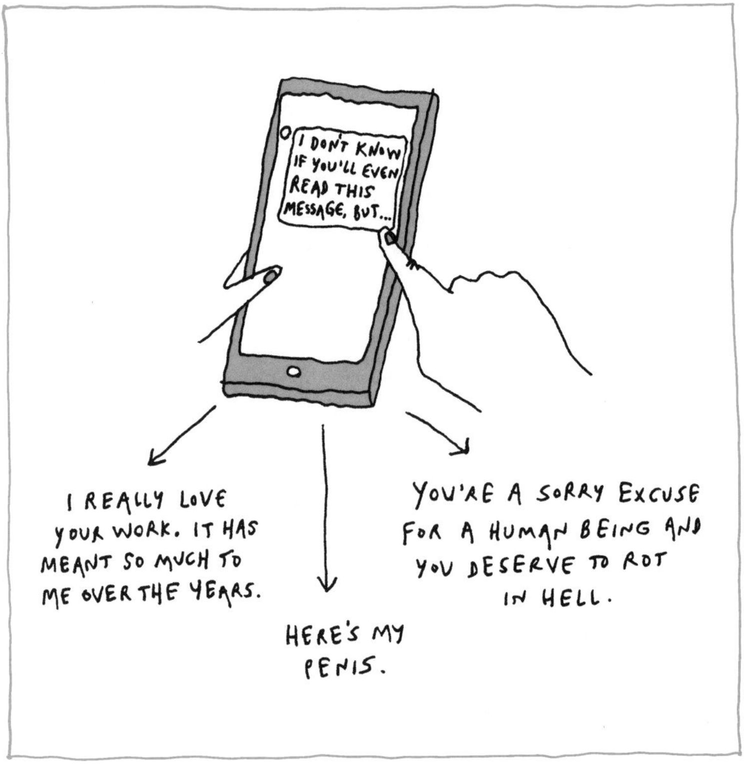
I DON'T KNOW IF YOU'LL EVEN READ THIS MESSAGE, BUT...
I REALLY LOVE YOUR WORK. IT HAS MEANT SO MUCH TO ME OVER THE YEARS.
HERE'S MY PENIS.
YOU'RE A SORRY EXCUSE FOR A HUMAN BEING AND YOU DESERVE TO ROT IN HELL.

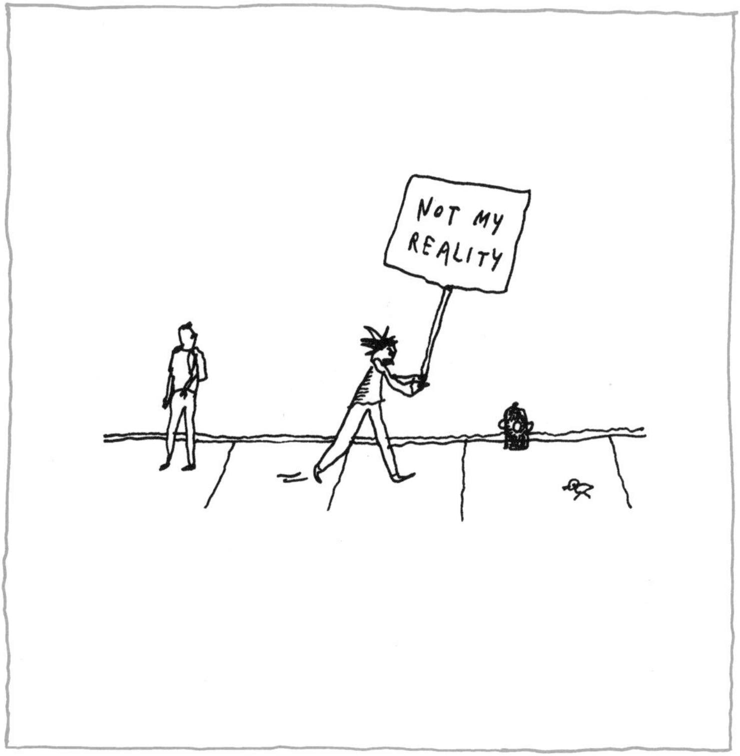
NOT MY
REALITY

1
POWER TO THE PEOPLE!!!
2
THANKS!

TAKE ME TO YOUR- HA! HA! HA!- TO YOUR- HA! HA!- EXCUSE ME. TO YOUR "LEADER."

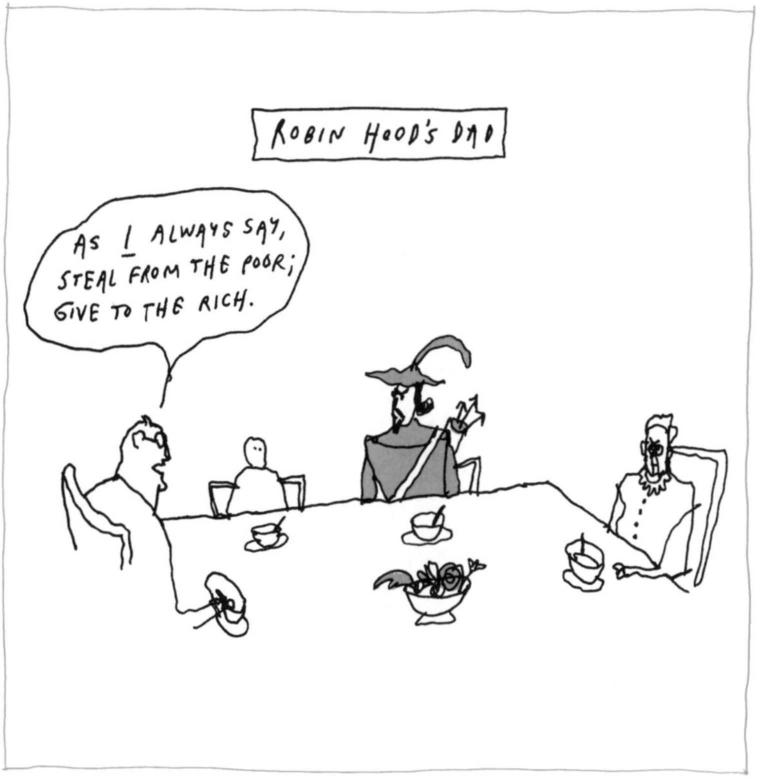
ROBIN HOOD'S DAD
AS I ALWAYS SAY, STEAL FROM THE POOR; GIVE TO THE RICH.

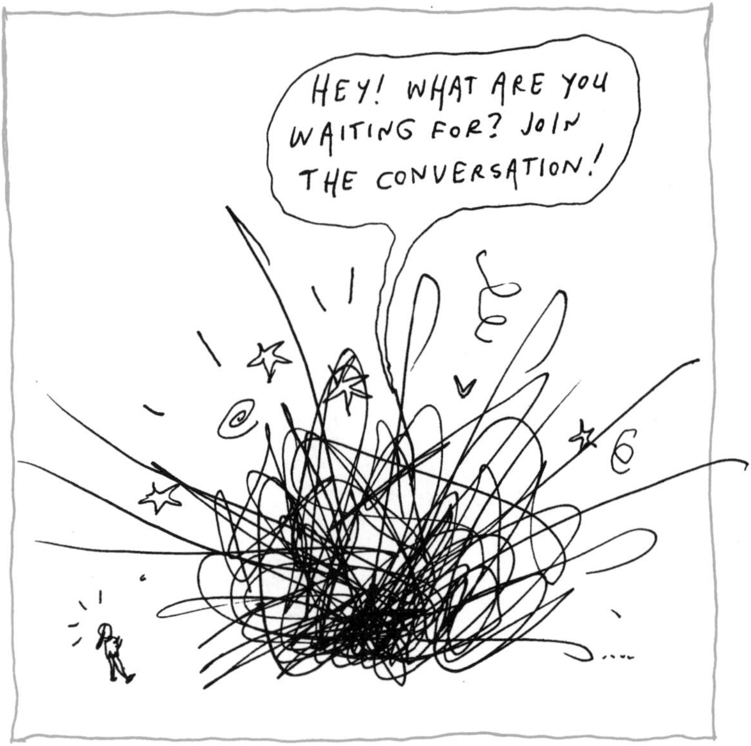
HEY! WHAT ARE YOU WAITING FOR? JOIN THE CONVERSATION!

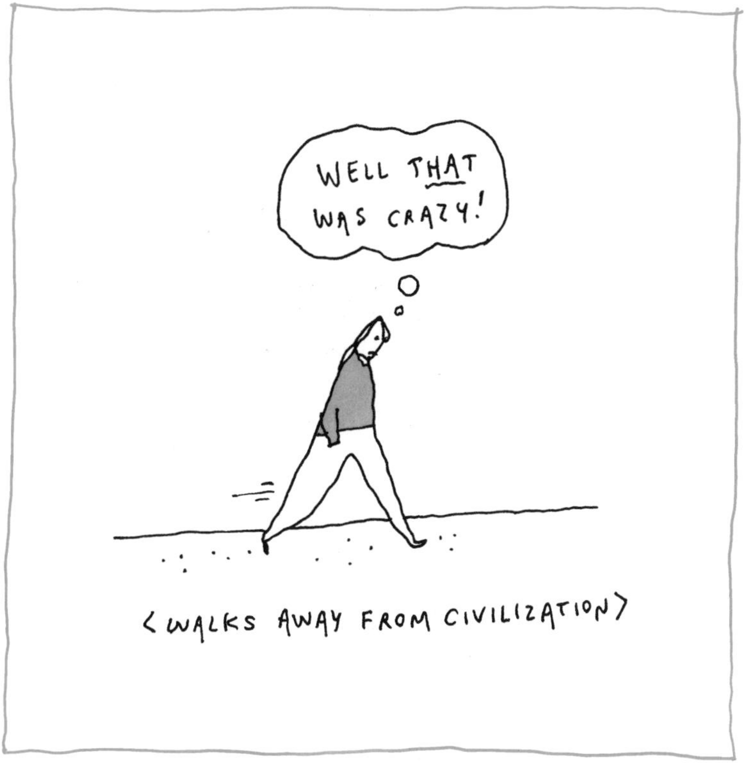
WELL THAT WAS CRAZY!
<WALKS AWAY FROM CIVILIZATION>

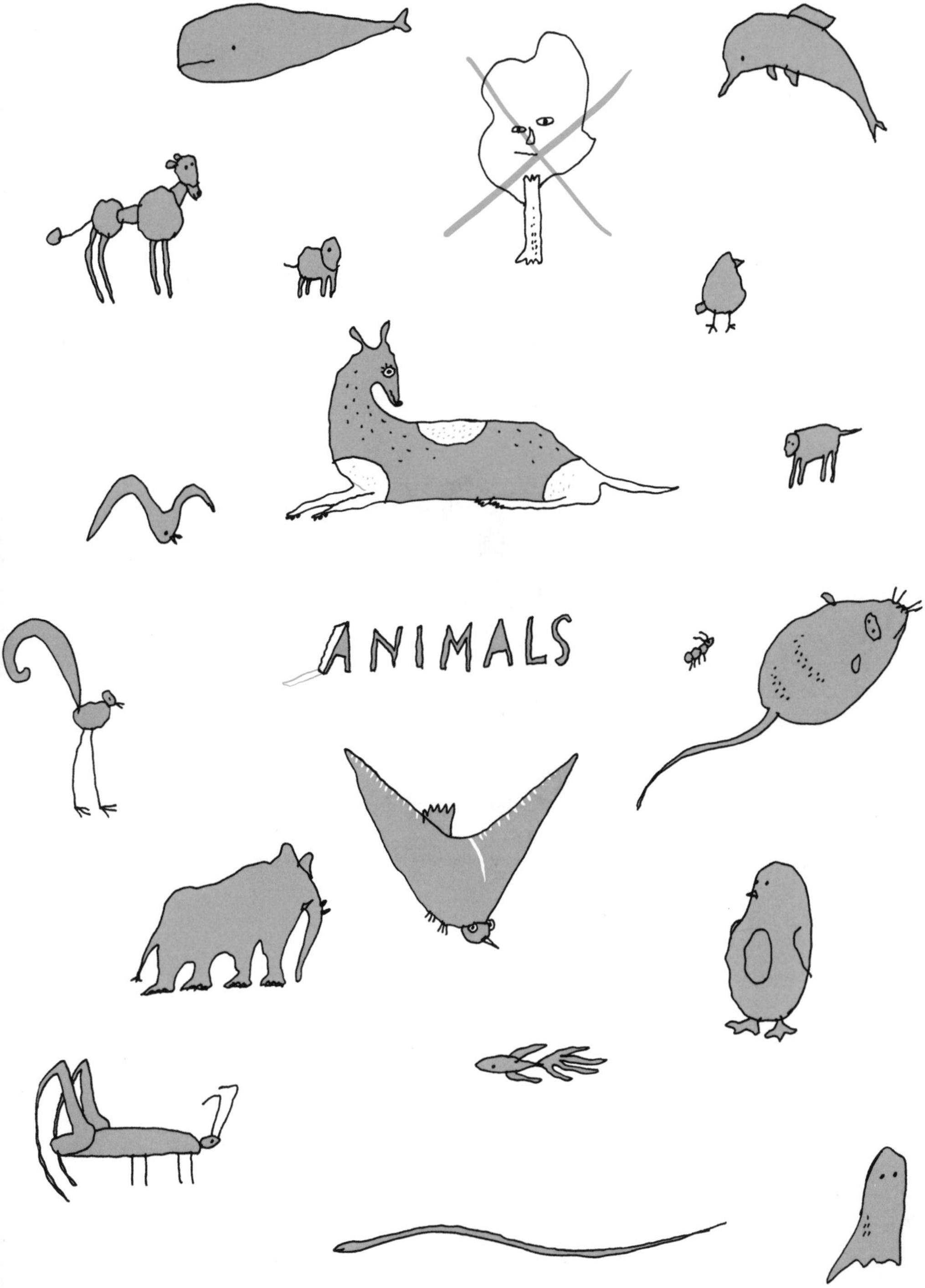
ANIMALS

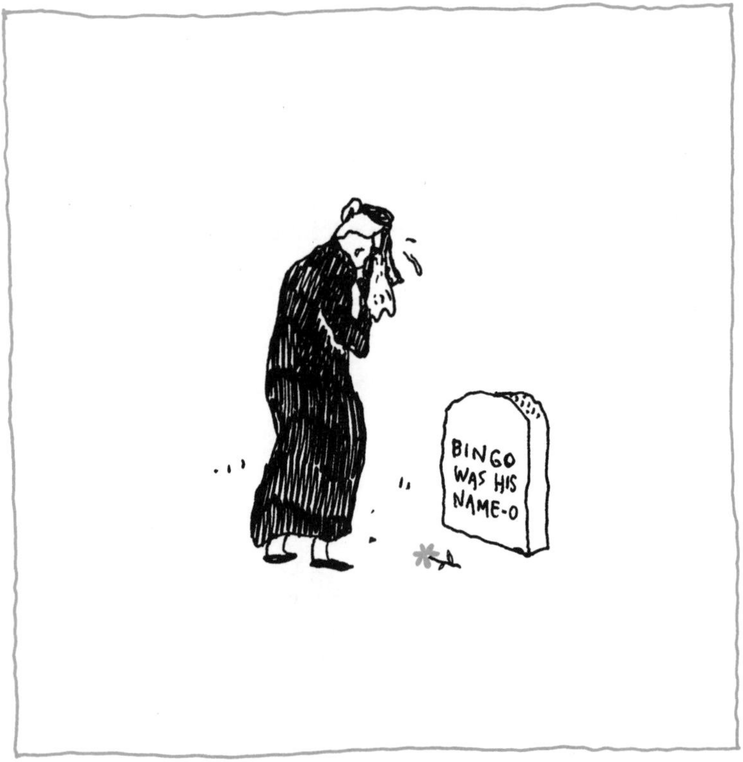
BINGO
WAS HIS
NAME-O

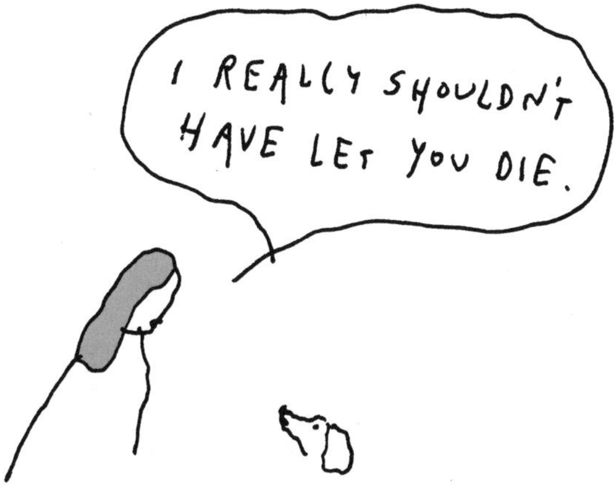
I REALLY SHOULDN'T HAVE LET YOU DIE.

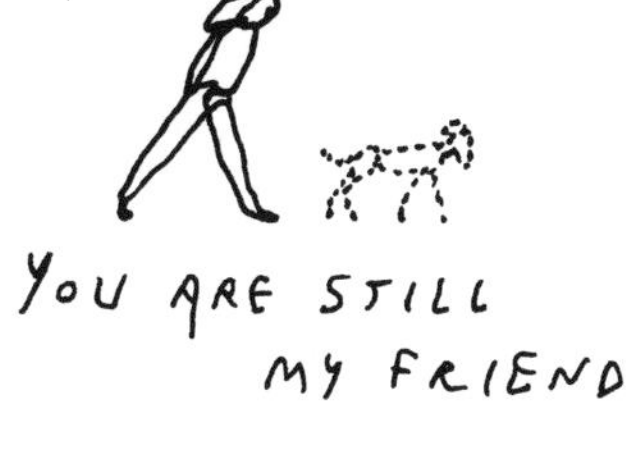
YOU ARE STILL
MY FRIEND

WHAT DEODORANT LOOKS LIKE TO A DOG

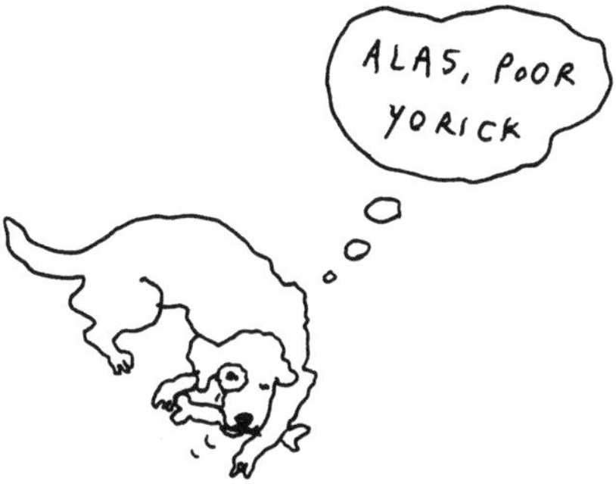
ALAS, POOR YORICK

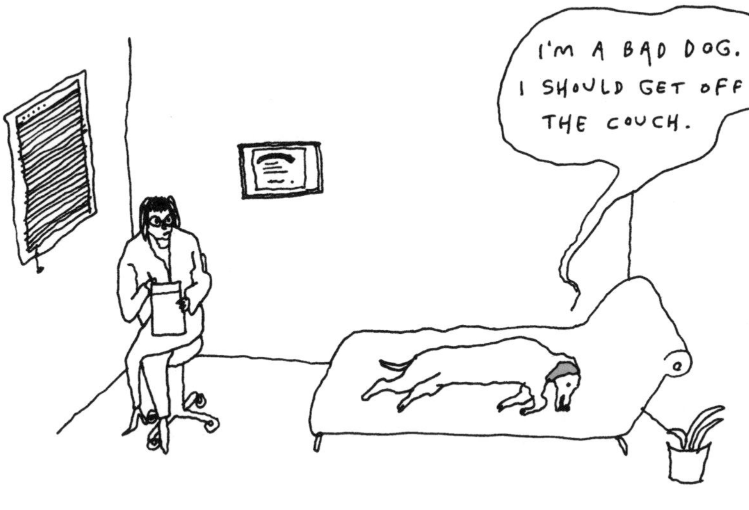
I'M A BAD DOG. I SHOULD GET OFF THE COUCH.

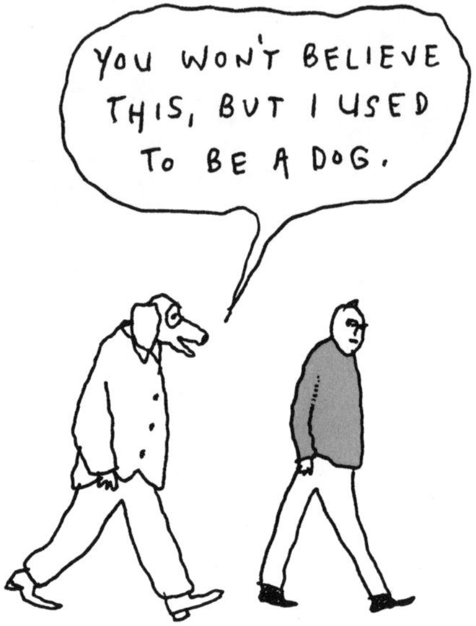
YOU WON'T BELIEVE THIS, BUT I USED TO BE A DOG.

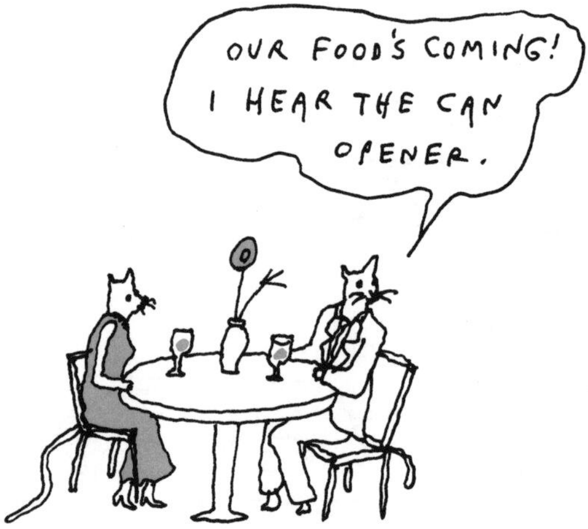
OUR FOOD'S COMING! I HEAR THE CAN OPENER.

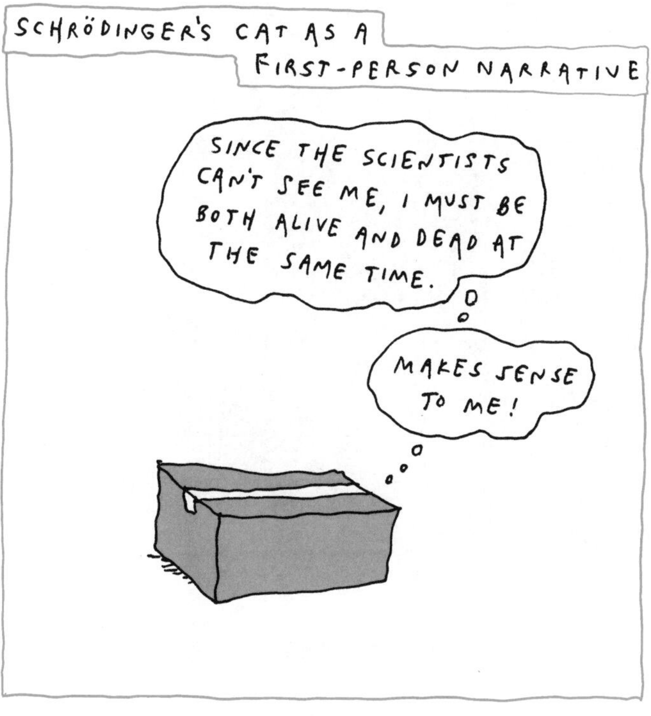
SCHRÖDINGER'S CAT AS A FIRST-PERSON NARRATIVE
SINCE THE SCIENTISTS CAN'T SEE ME, I MUST BE BOTH ALIVE AND DEAD AT THE SAME TIME.
MAKES SENSE TO ME!

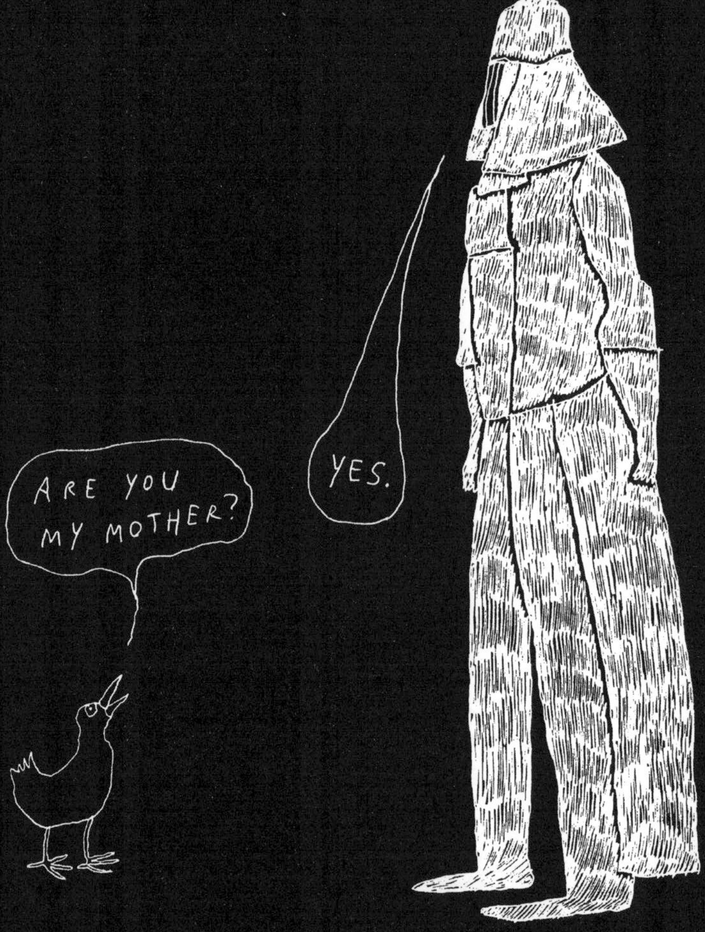
ARE YOU MY MOTHER?
YES.

BIRD PRISON

SPARE →

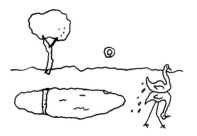

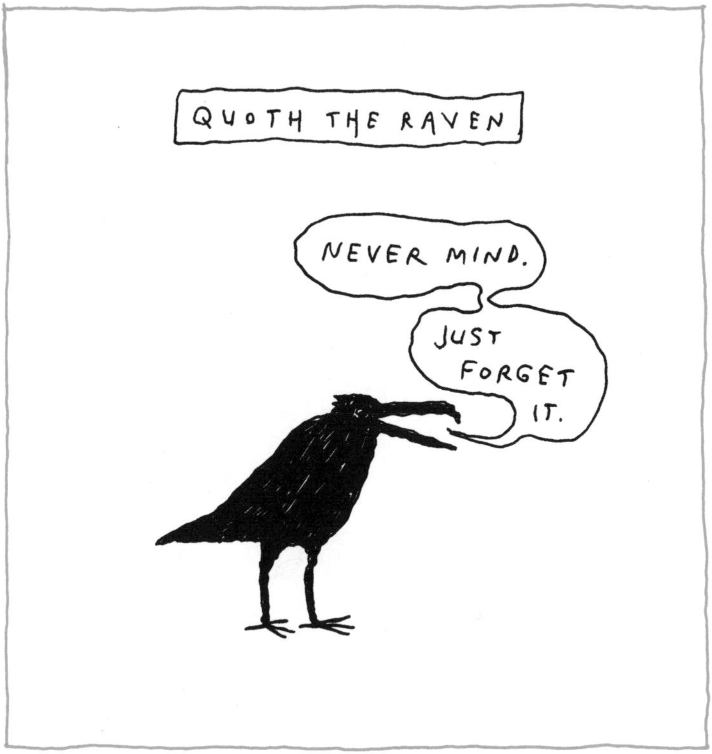
QUOTH THE RAVEN
NEVER MIND.
JUST FORGET IT.

YOU BROKE IT!

HEY. THAT'S MY SORROW YOU'RE SINGING ABOUT.

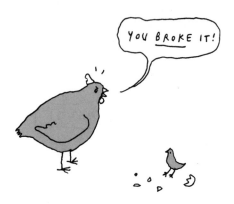

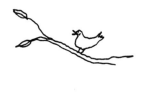

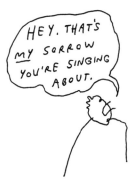

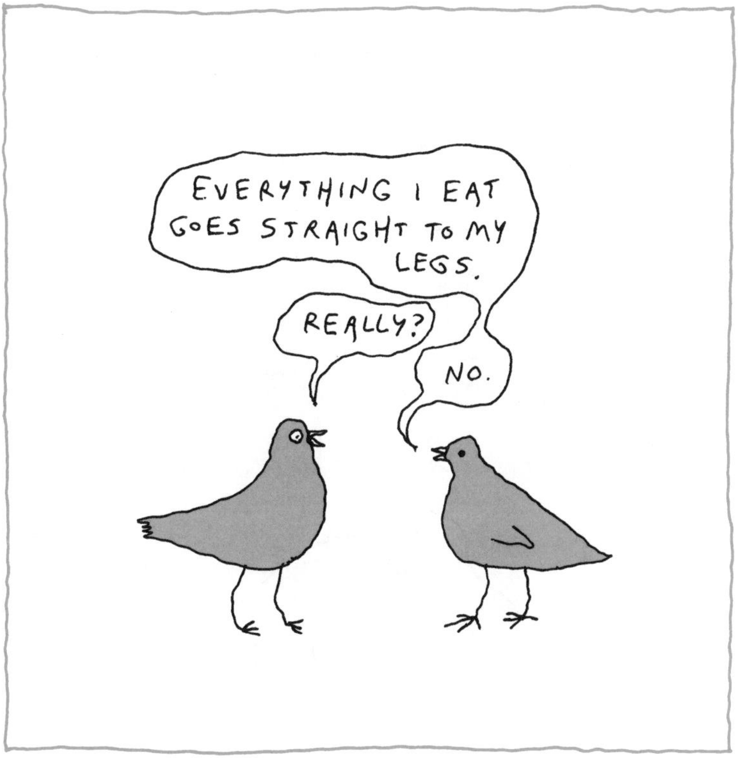
EVERYTHING I EAT GOES STRAIGHT TO MY LEGS.
REALLY?
NO.

NUDE DESCENDING A CURB

ONE · DOZEN · EGGS

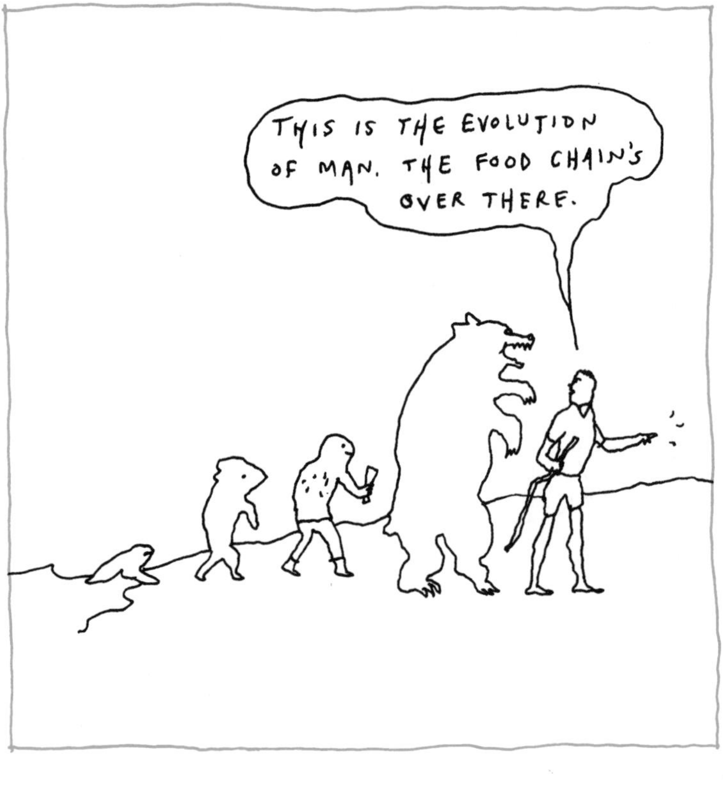
THIS IS THE EVOLUTION OF MAN. THE FOOD CHAIN'S OVER THERE.

THE DEVOLUTION OF FISH

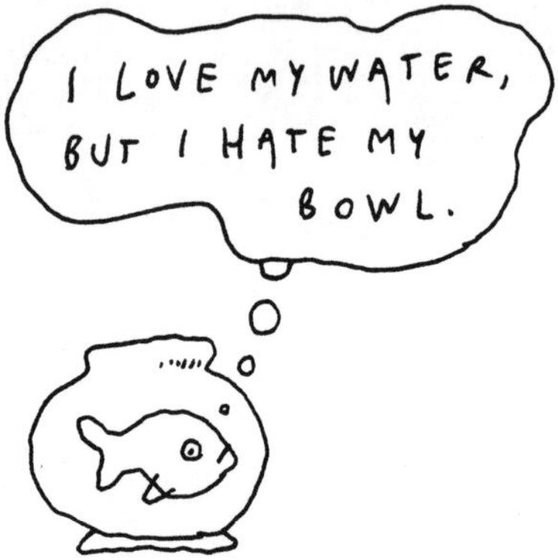
I LOVE MY WATER, BUT I HATE MY BOWL.

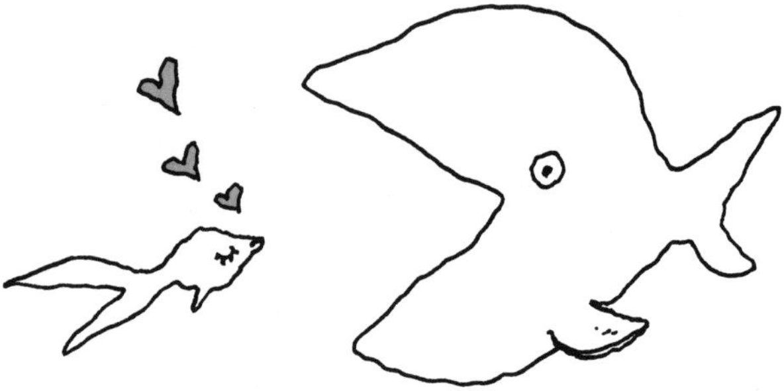

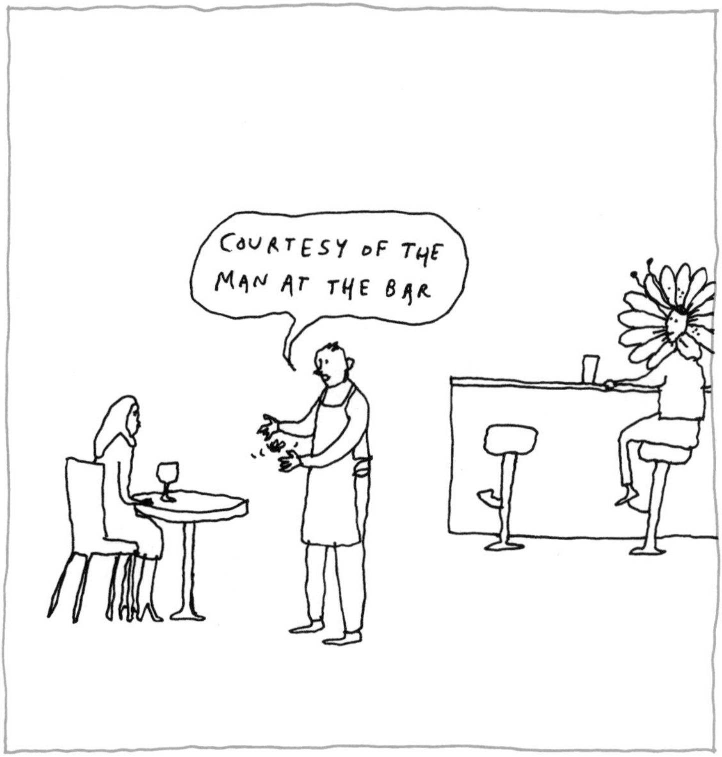
COURTESY OF THE MAN AT THE BAR

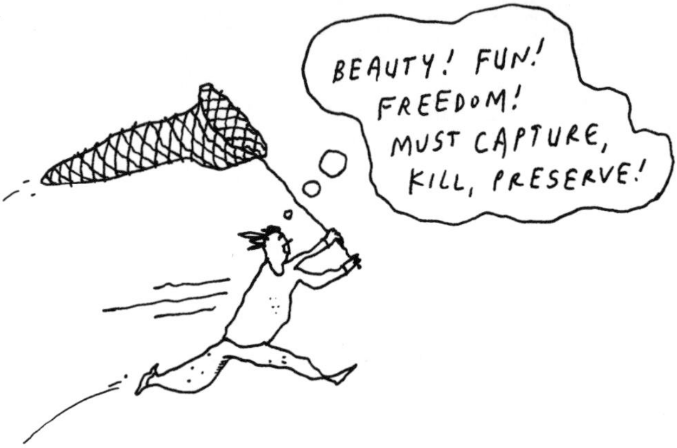
BEAUTY! FUN!
FREEDOM!
MUST CAPTURE,
KILL, PRESERVE!

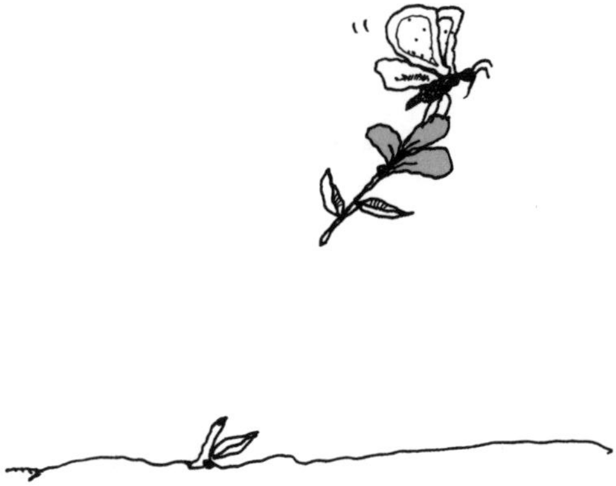

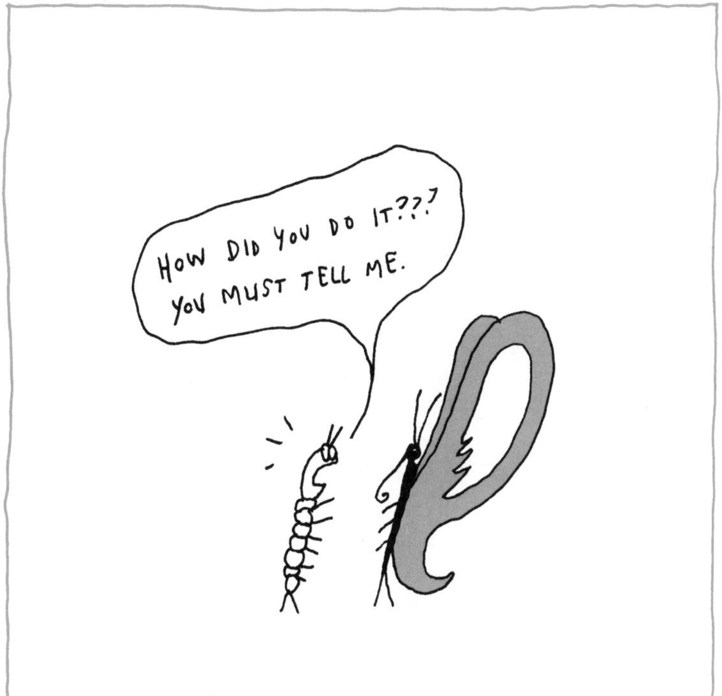
HOW DID YOU DO IT???
YOU MUST TELL ME.

HUMANE BUTTERFLY NET

WHAT A SNAIL WOULD LOOK LIKE
WITHOUT ITS SHELL

OUR HEROINE COMES OUT
OF HER SHELL;
SHE IS A SLUG NOW.

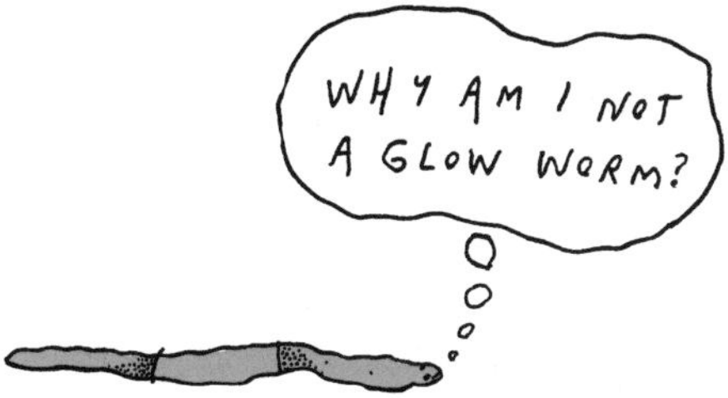
WHY AM I NOT A GLOW WORM?

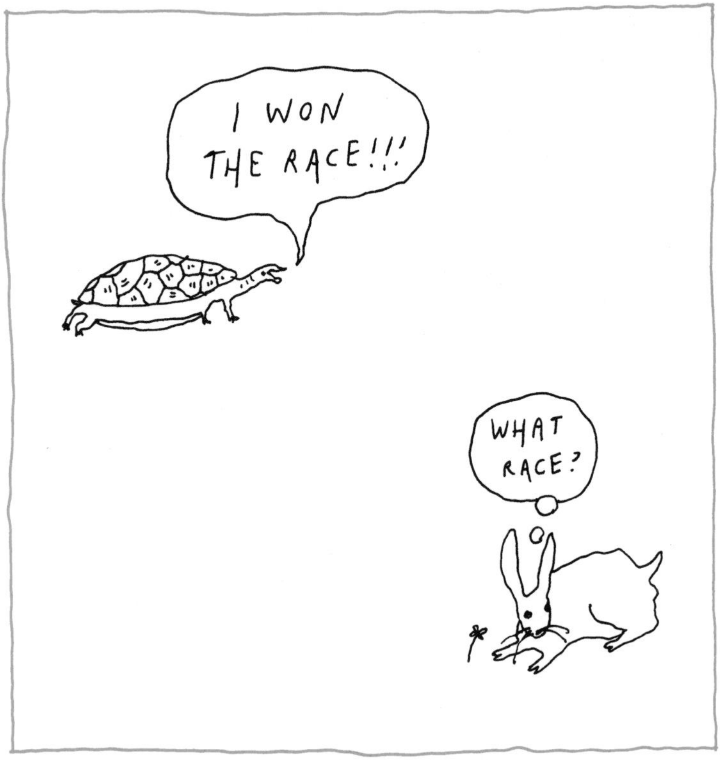
I WON THE RACE!!!
WHAT RACE?

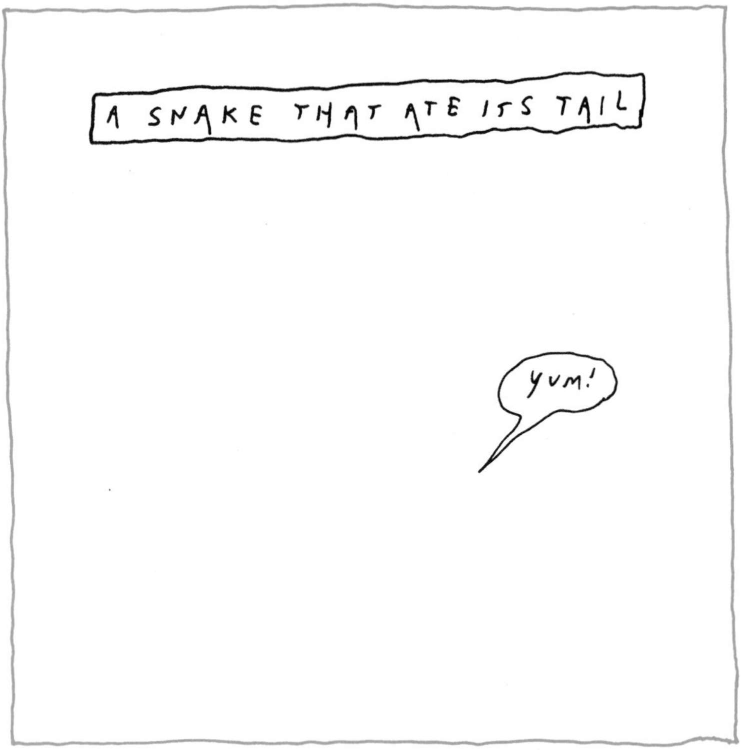
A SNAKE THAT ATE ITS TAIL
yum!

A SNAKE THAT ATE BABAR

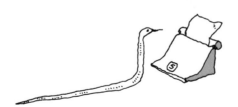

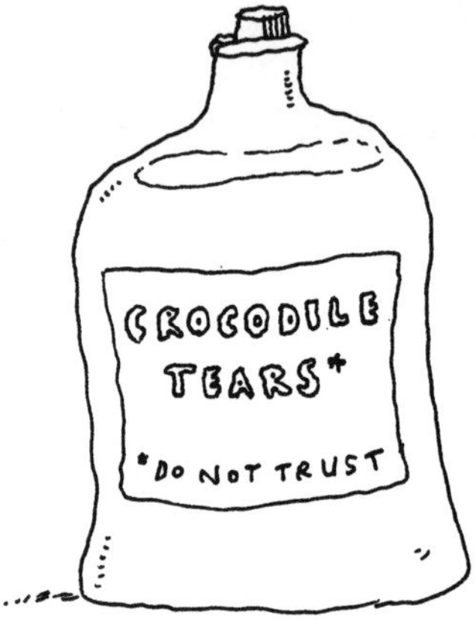
CROCODILE
TEARS*
*DO NOT TRUST

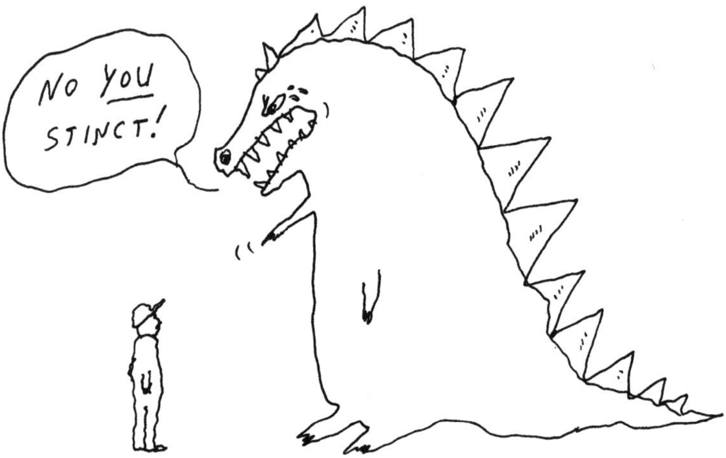
NO YOU
STINCT!

GIVE A MAN A FISH
HERE
BOY OH BOY, I'LL EAT FOR A DAY!
TEACH A MAN TO FISH
NOM NOM NOM
UTTERLY STILL AND SILENT OCEANS

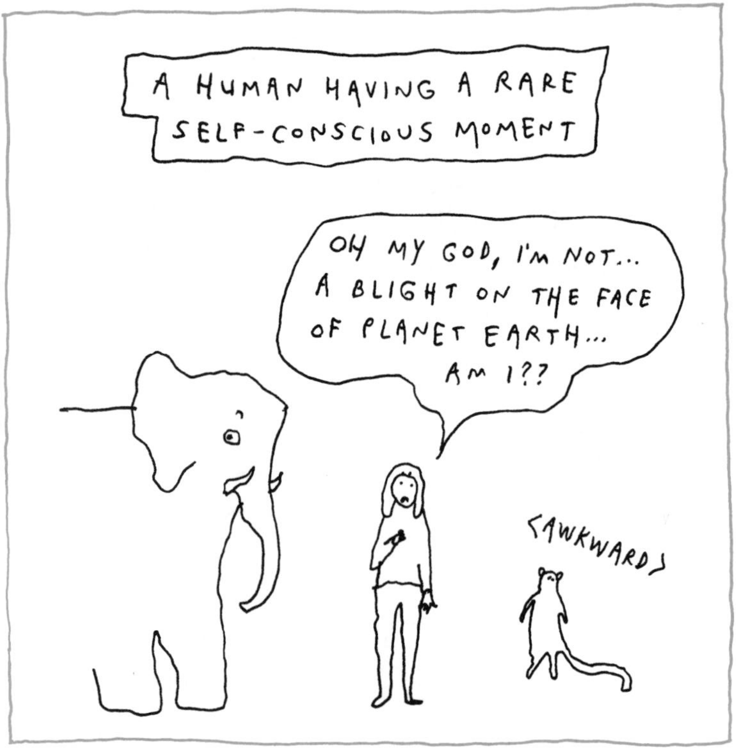
A HUMAN HAVING A RARE SELF-CONSCIOUS MOMENT
OH MY GOD, I'M NOT... A BLIGHT ON THE FACE OF PLANET EARTH... AM I??
<AWKWARD>

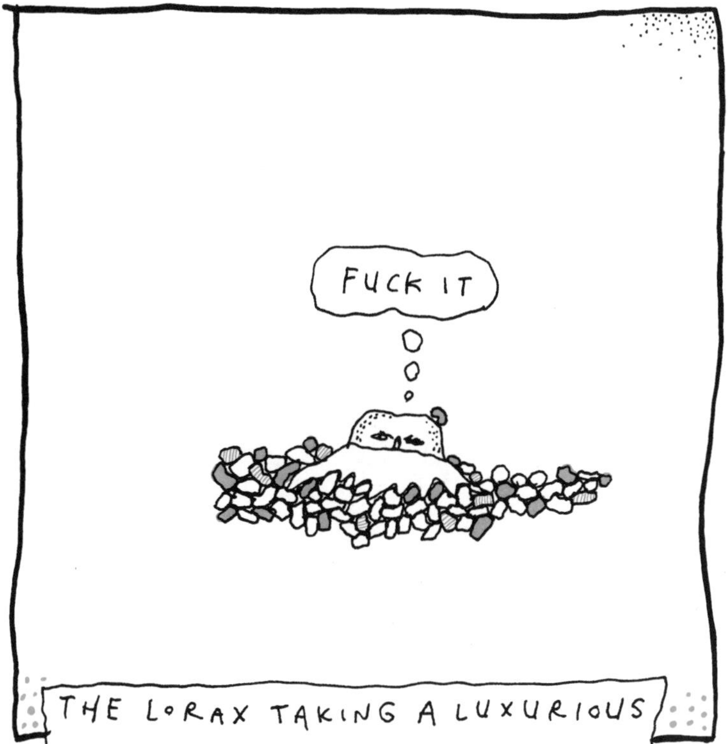
FUCK IT

THE LORAX TAKING A LUXURIOUS BATH IN STYROFOAM PELLETS

ART

&

MYTH-MAKING

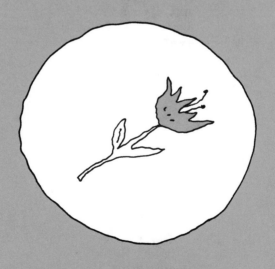

WORKER

HOBBYIST

GENIUS

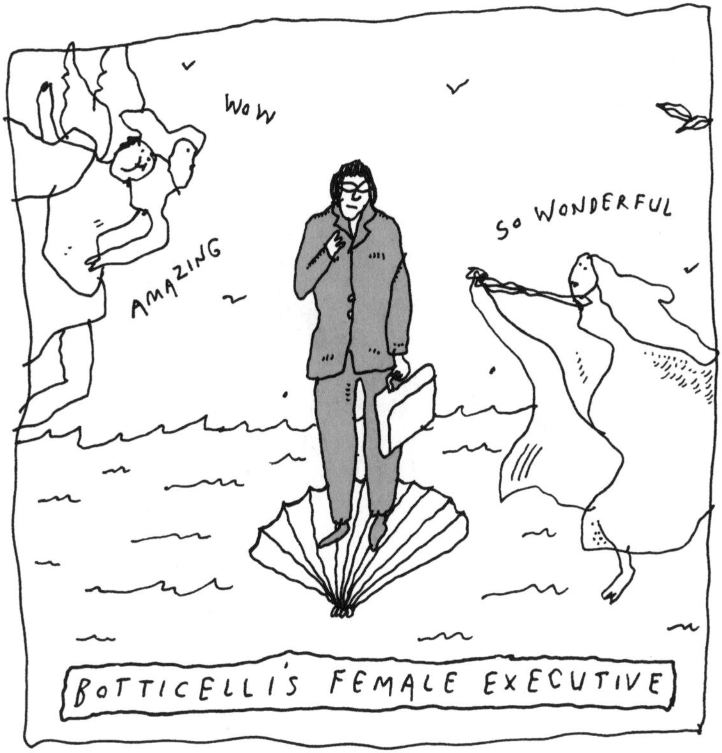
WOW
AMAZING
SO WONDERFUL
BOTTICELLI'S FEMALE EXECUTIVE

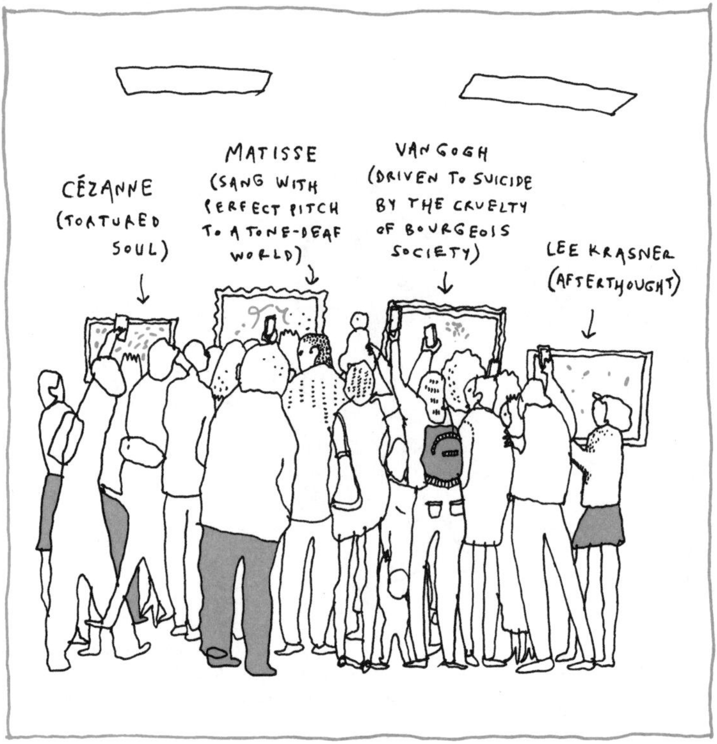

CÉZANNE
(TORTURED SOUL)
MATISSE
(SANG WITH PERFECT PITCH TO A TONE-DEAF WORLD)
VAN GOGH
(DRIVEN TO SUICIDE BY THE CRUELTY OF BOURGEOIS SOCIETY)
LEE KRASNER
(AFTERTHOUGHT)

MONA LISA FROWN

THE YAWN

A PERSON PRACTICING
THE ART OF TACT

THIS IS LIFE. IF YOU
CAN'T DRAW IT, YOU ARE
NOT A REAL ARTIST.

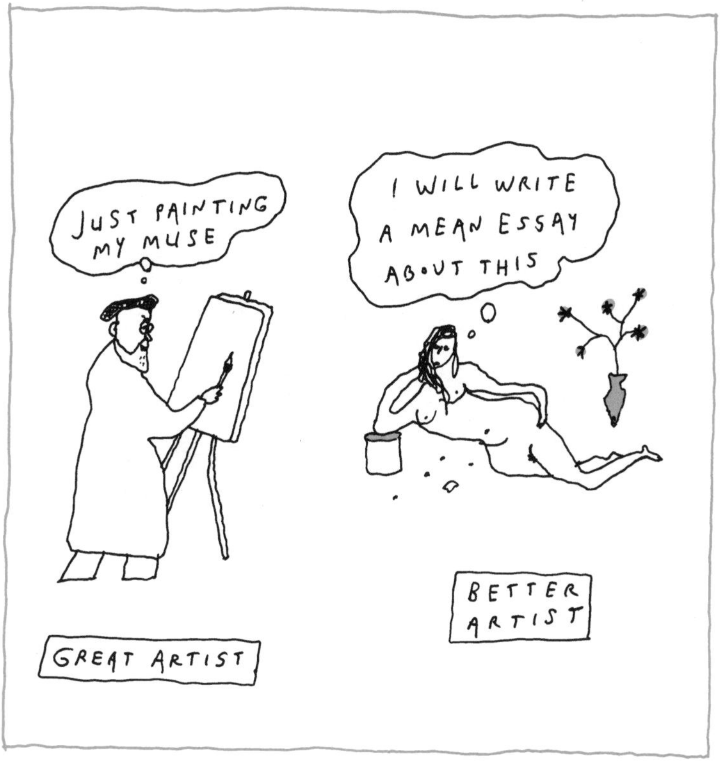
JUST PAINTING MY MUSE
GREAT ARTIST
I WILL WRITE A MEAN ESSAY ABOUT THIS
BETTER ARTIST

DISCERNING
NUMEROUS

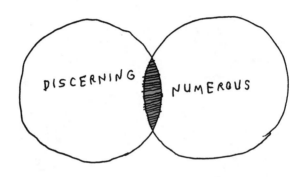

KEY

▤ = THE IDEAL AUDIENCE

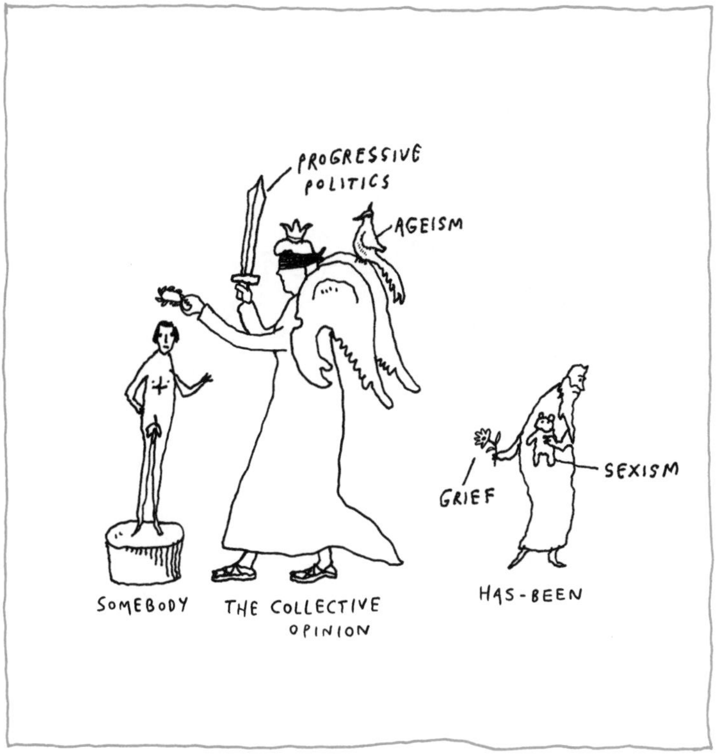
PROGRESSIVE POLITICS
AGEISM
SEXISM
GRIEF
SOMEBODY
THE COLLECTIVE OPINION
HAS-BEEN

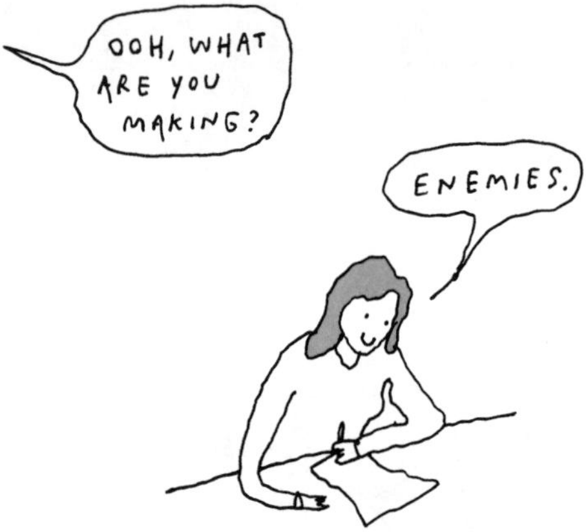
OOH, WHAT ARE YOU MAKING?
ENEMIES.

1. CREATE A MONSTER.
2. RUN.

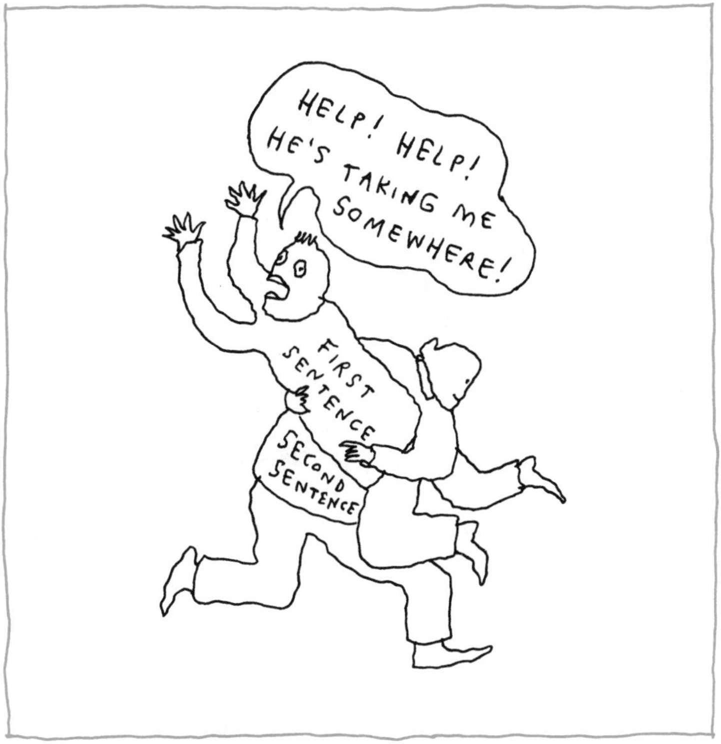
HELP! HELP! HE'S TAKING ME SOMEWHERE!
FIRST SENTENCE
SECOND SENTENCE

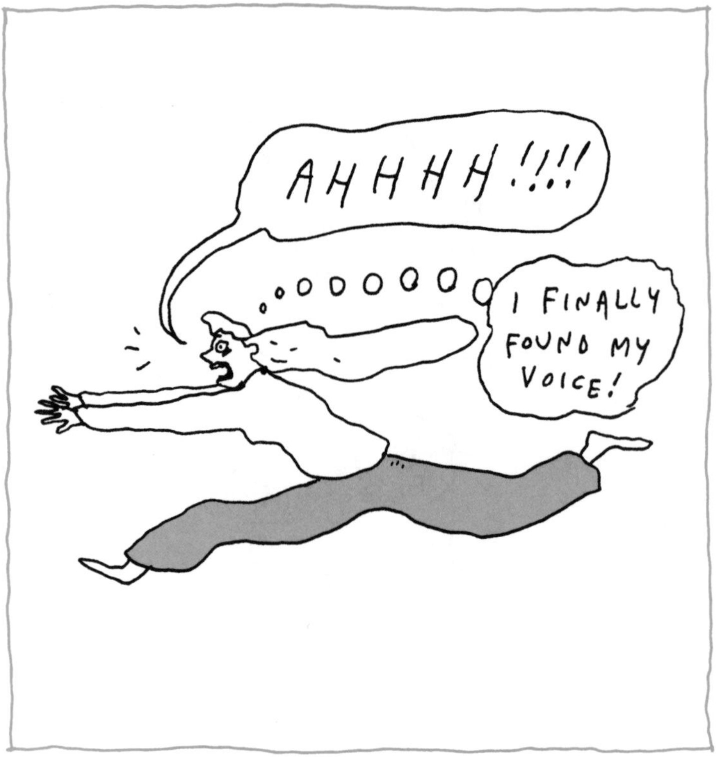
AHHHH!!!!
I FINALLY FOUND MY VOICE!

1% INSPIRATION
95% NAUSEA
4% PERSPIRATION

WHEN YOU'RE DRAWING SOMETHING YOU THINK YOU SHOULD DRAW
PEA BRAIN
RUSTY MACHINERY
CLUNK
WHEN THERE IS SOMETHING THAT WANTS TO BE DRAWN AND YOU WERE MADE TO DRAW IT

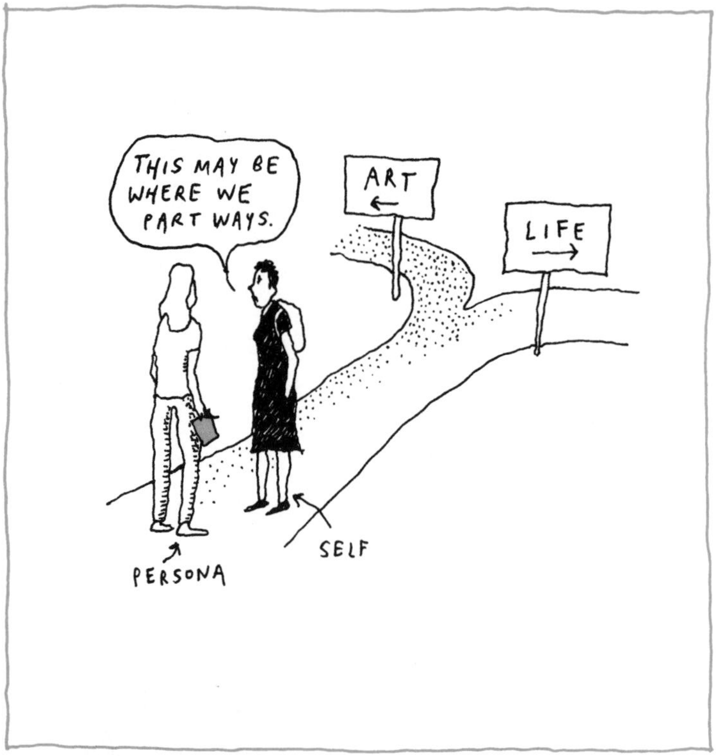
THIS MAY BE WHERE WE PART WAYS.
ART ←
LIFE →
PERSONA
SELF

TWO WAYS TO MAKE ART

① THROW TIGHTROPES
INTO THE AIR AND WALK
ON THEM VERY QUICKLY
SO YOU DON'T FALL.

② INHERIT A MANSION.
REMOVE ALL THE PARTS
YOU DON'T REALLY,
REALLY, REALLY LIKE.

THE COMICS WORLD
DEAD ARTIST
LIVING ARTIST
EDITOR
NONPROFIT ADMINISTRATOR
INSANE PERSON
HOPEFUL
AN ARTIST WHO THINKS SHE'S A NOBODY
A NOBODY WHO THINKS SHE'S AN ARTIST
SCHOLAR
BUTT-KISSER
FAMOUS PERSON

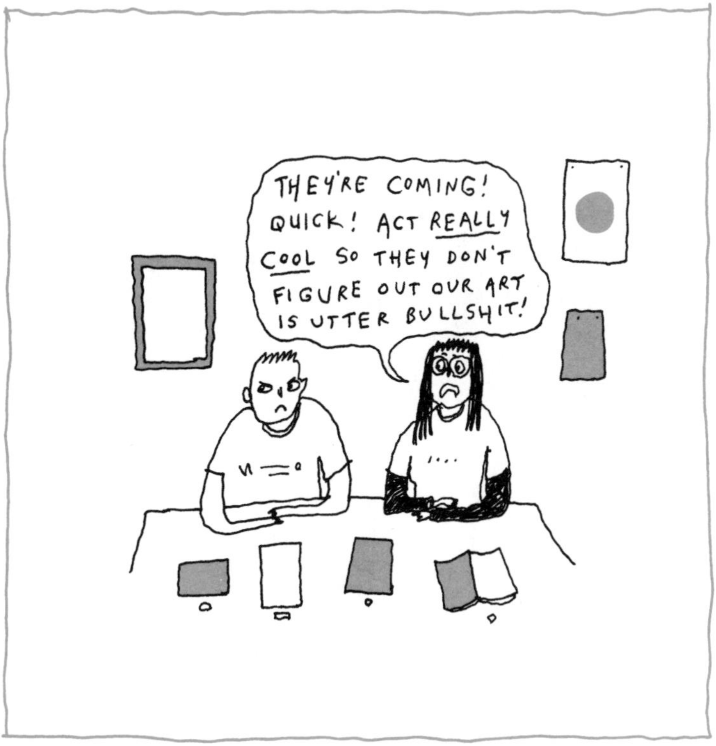
THEY'RE COMING! QUICK! ACT REALLY COOL SO THEY DON'T FIGURE OUT OUR ART IS UTTER BULLSHIT!

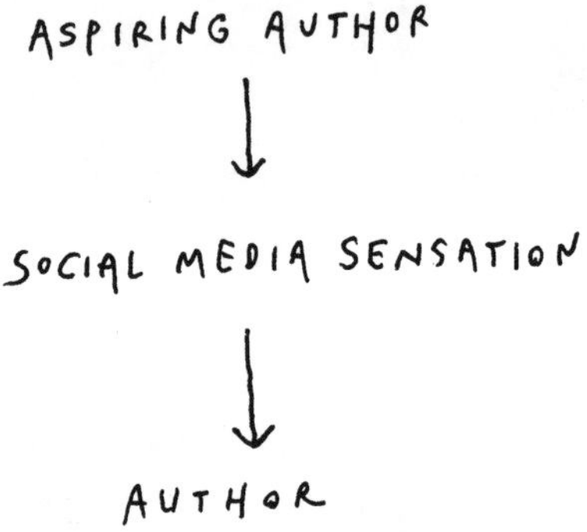
ASPIRING AUTHOR
SOCIAL MEDIA SENSATION
AUTHOR

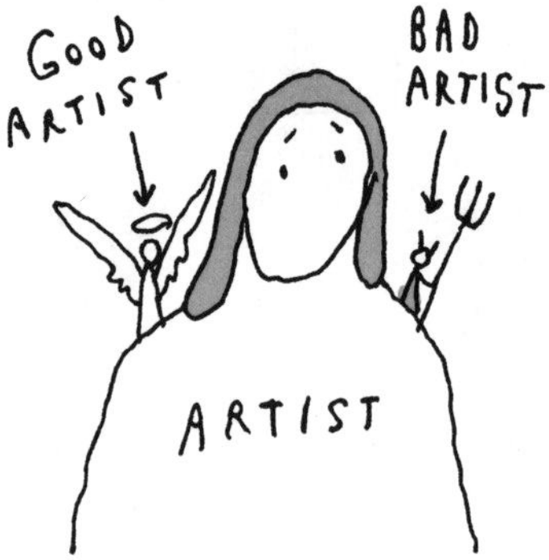
GOOD ARTIST
BAD ARTIST
ARTIST

PAIN $>$ SELF-MADE ORIGIN STORY $\rightarrow$ GOOD ARTIST

PAIN $<$ SELF-MADE ORIGIN STORY $\rightarrow$ PRETENTIOUS ASS

UP & COMING IN THE ARTS

READING NEWS
(INCONSOLABLE,
NUMB TEARS)

READING HOROSCOPE
(RELIGIOUS, "EVERY-
ONE IS CONNECTED"
TEARS)

READING POETRY
("I'M GONNA DIE
ONE DAY" TEARS)

READING CHILDREN'S
BOOK ("WHERE DID IT
ALL GO" TEARS)

ON READING PROUST VERY SLOWLY

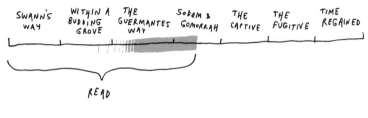

SWANN'S WAY   WITHIN A BUDDING GROVE   THE GUERMANTES WAY   SODOM & GOMORRAH   THE CAPTIVE   THE FUGITIVE   TIME REGAINED

READ

⬤ = STILL REMEMBER

NEVER READ NABOKOV   LOVES NABOKOV   HATES NABOKOV   LOVES NABOKOV FOR THE WRONG REASONS

FUCK   MARRY   KILL   MIGHT KILL YOU

MOOD OF ART: IDEALISTIC AND OBSCURE

MOOD OF MEME: WIDE-EYED

MOOD OF COMICS: CAN-DO

MOOD OF NOVELS: WEARY

MOOD OF JOURNALISM: THOROUGH, EARNEST

MOOD OF CARTOONS: DAPPER GENT

MOOD OF RELIGION: MYSTERIOUS, MAD

MOOD OF THE PAST: NOSTALGIC

MOOD OF THE FUTURE: NULL

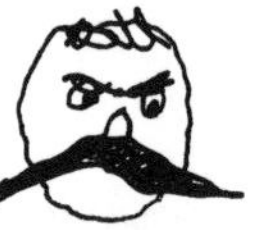

☐ DICTATOR

☐ PHILOSOPHER

☐ MUPPET

A GIANT PLAYING THE BASS

A CRITIQUE OF THE MAN SINGING
"CAT'S IN THE CRADLE" IN THE PARK
(OR, WHY I CAN'T HAVE FUN)

- NO SHAME
- POINTLESS MORALISM
- NO ORIGINALITY
- ASKS HIMSELF THE WRONG
  QUESTIONS, IF ANY

THE PIANO LESSON

FACT

EAT MODERATELY AND STICK
TO YOUR EXERCISE REGIMEN
TO MAINTAIN A HEALTHY WEIGHT.

MYTH

FOR HALF THE YEAR, PERSEPHONE
MUST RESIDE IN THE UNDERWORLD
AS THE BRIDE OF HADES. FOR THESE
MONTHS, DEMETER GRIEVES, PLANTS
DIE, AND A COLD FROST COVERS THE
EARTH.

<u>STORIES</u>	<u>LIES</u>
GOD	CHRONOLOGY
ART	CITIES
THE INDIVIDUAL	THE COLLECTIVE

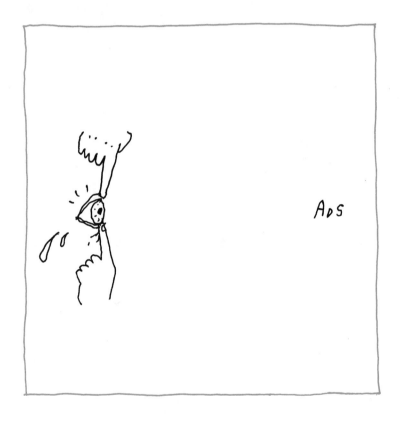

AoS

A HERO GOES ON A JOURNEY
SO LONG, SUCKERS!
A STRANGER COMES TO TOWN
WHY, HELLO!

ONCE UPON A TIME
HAPPILY EVER AFTER

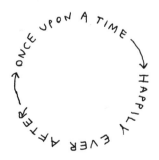

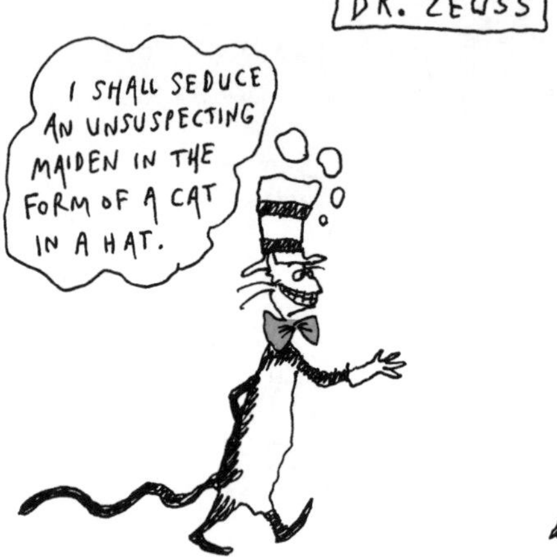
DR. ZEUSS
I SHALL SEDUCE AN UNSUSPECTING MAIDEN IN THE FORM OF A CAT IN A HAT.

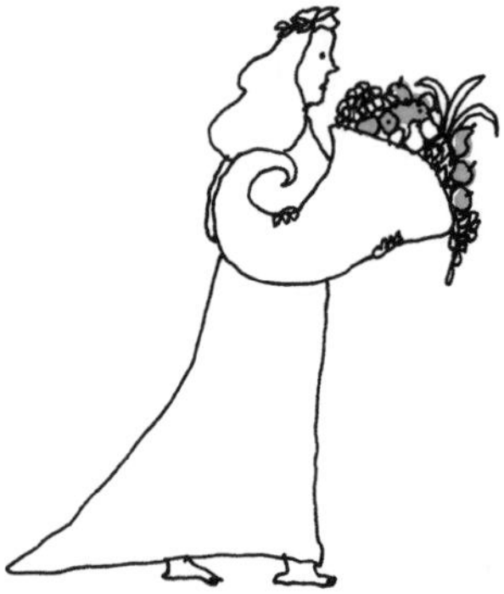

NAME: LADY BOUNTIFUL

#1 FEAR: BOUNTY HUNTERS

TWO PHILOSOPHIES

1. GOD IS LOVE.

2. FOOD IS LOVE.

GOD AND NOAH/ABRAHAM/ISAAC/
JACOB/JOSEPH/MOSES

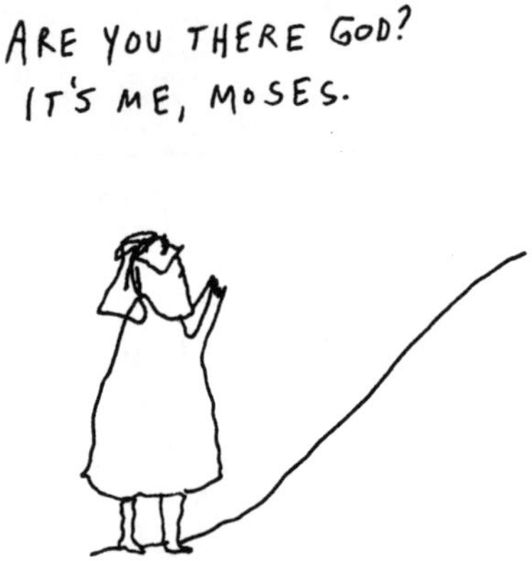
ARE YOU THERE GOD?
IT'S ME, MOSES.

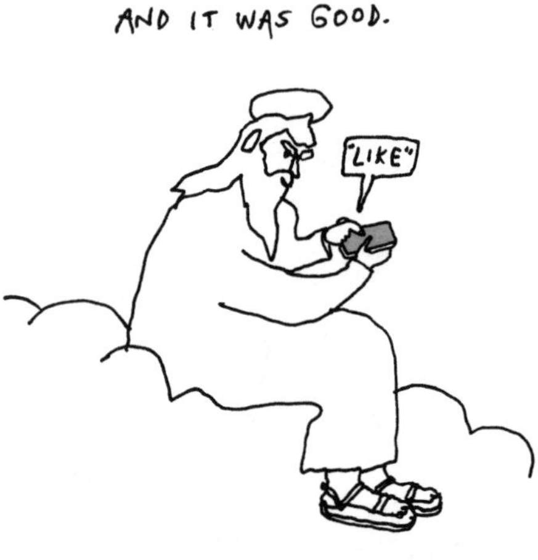
AND IT WAS GOOD.
"LIKE"

GOD COMING OUT TO NOAH

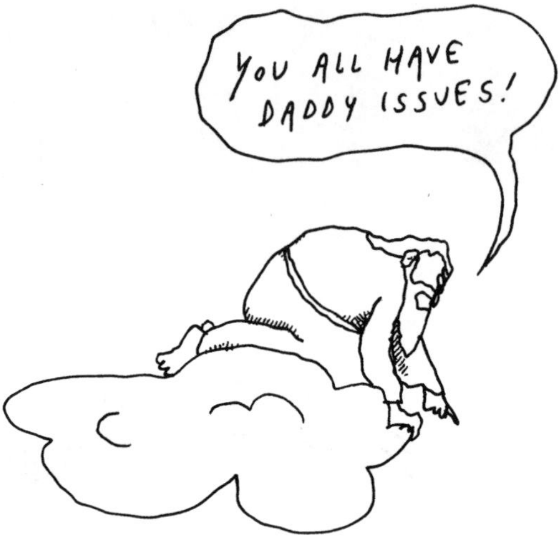
YOU ALL HAVE DADDY ISSUES!

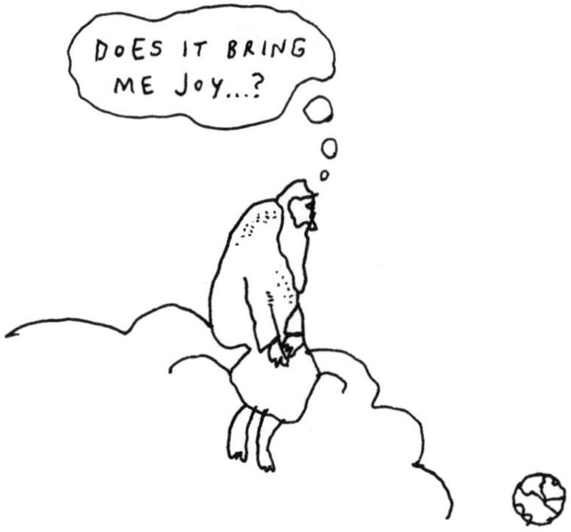
DOES IT BRING ME JOY...?

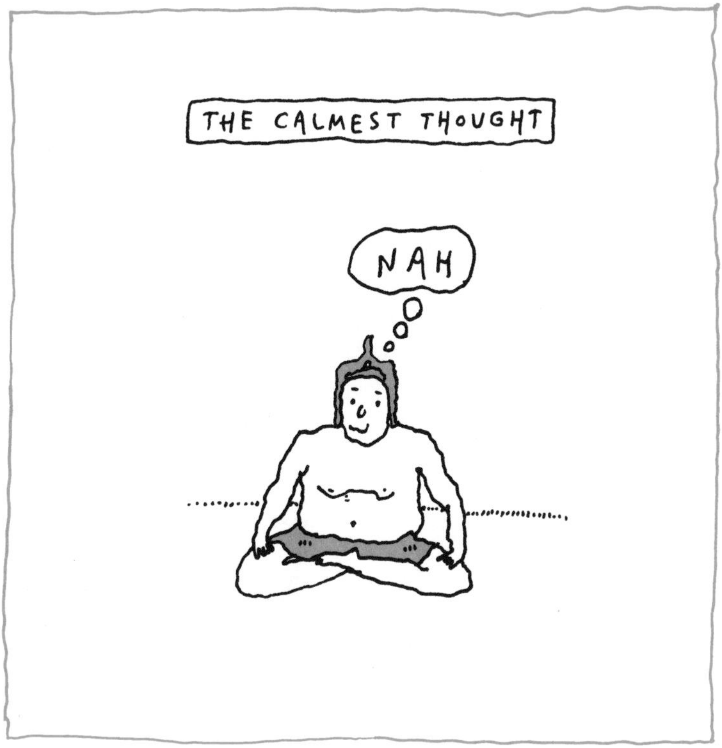
THE CALMEST THOUGHT
NAH

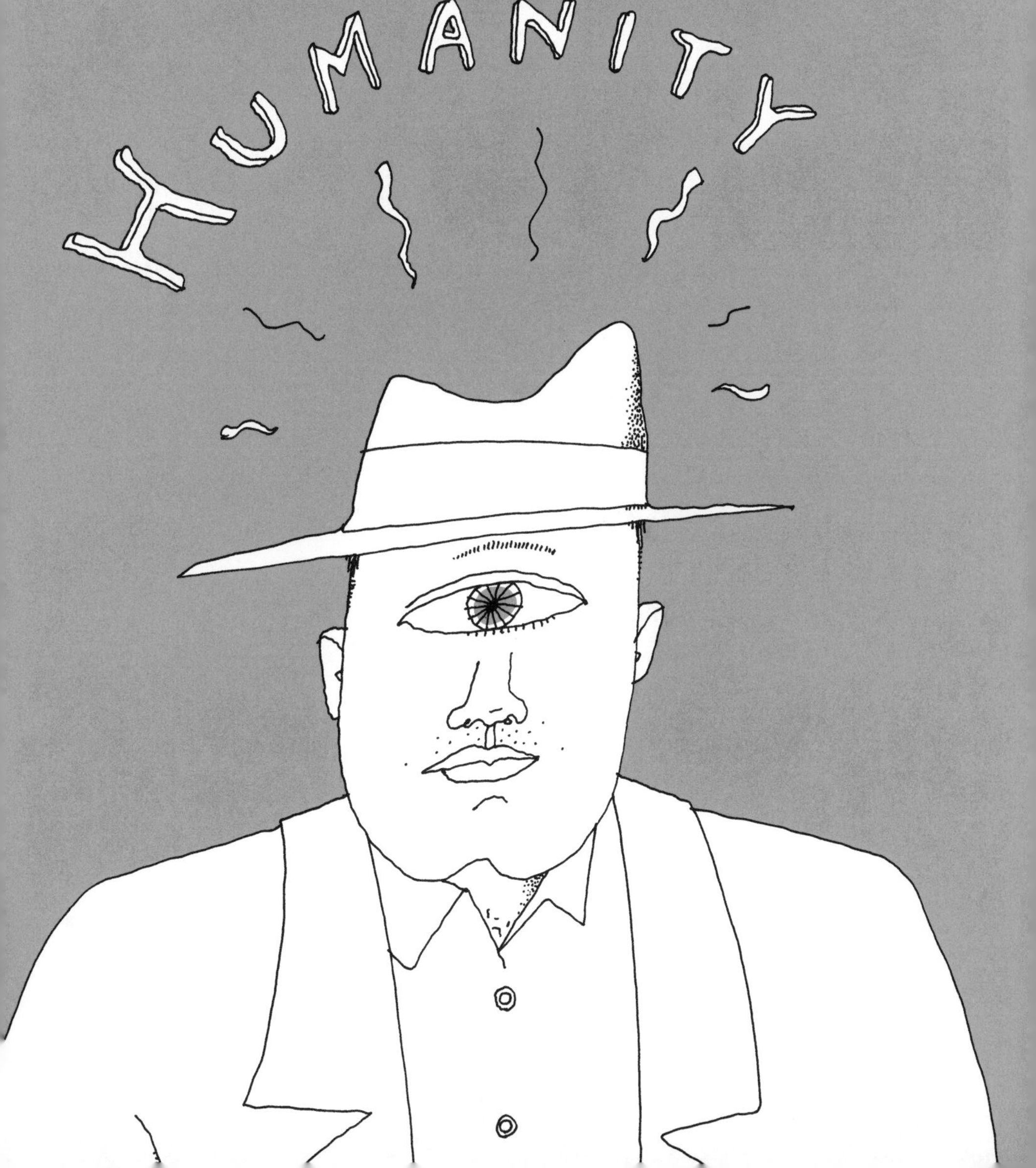
HUMANITY

THE TRUMPET

THE PUFF

THE ENGINE

THE SUBTLE PICK

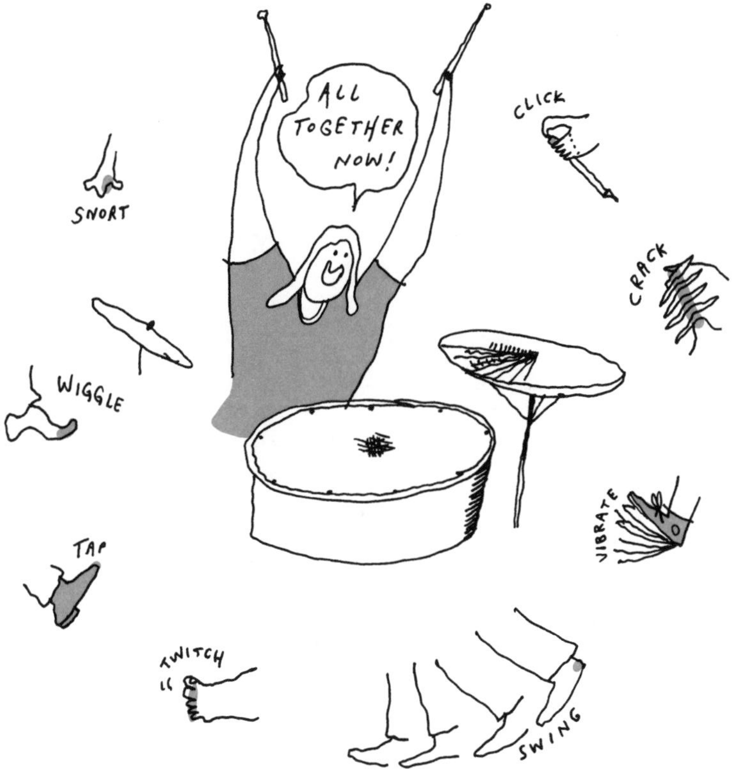
ALL TOGETHER NOW!
CLICK
SNORT
CRACK
WIGGLE
VIBRATE
TAP
TWITCH
SWING

<ANNOYINGLY>
SORRY I ANNOYED YOU!

HELL
SNORT SNORT

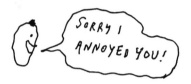

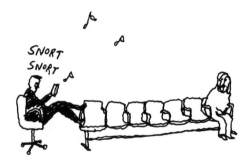

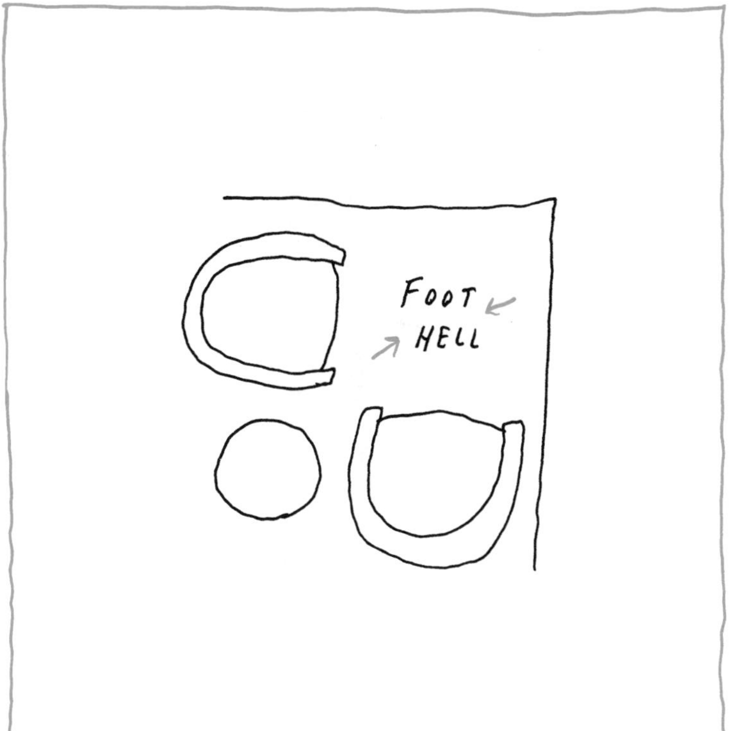
FOOT
HELL

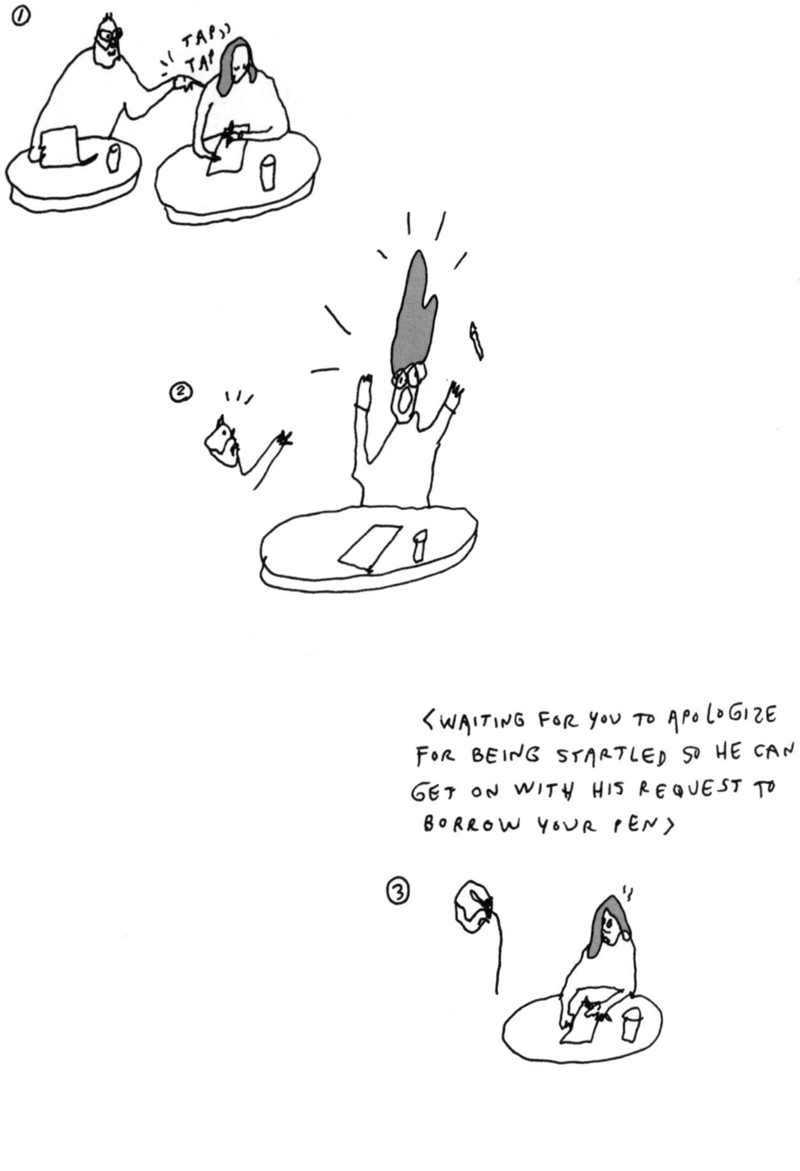
TAP TAP
<WAITING FOR YOU TO APOLOGIZE FOR BEING STARTLED SO HE CAN GET ON WITH HIS REQUEST TO BORROW YOUR PEN>

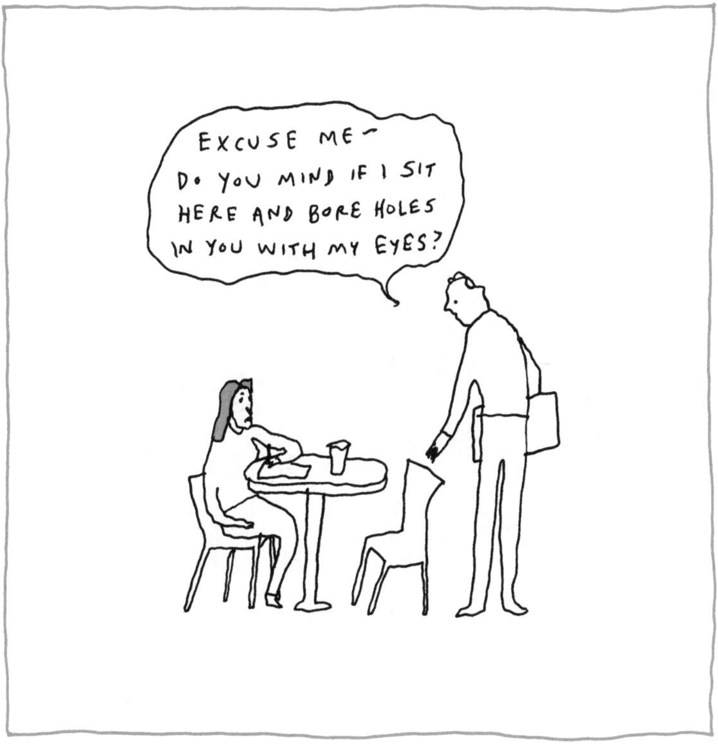
EXCUSE ME-
DO YOU MIND IF I SIT
HERE AND BORE HOLES
IN YOU WITH MY EYES?

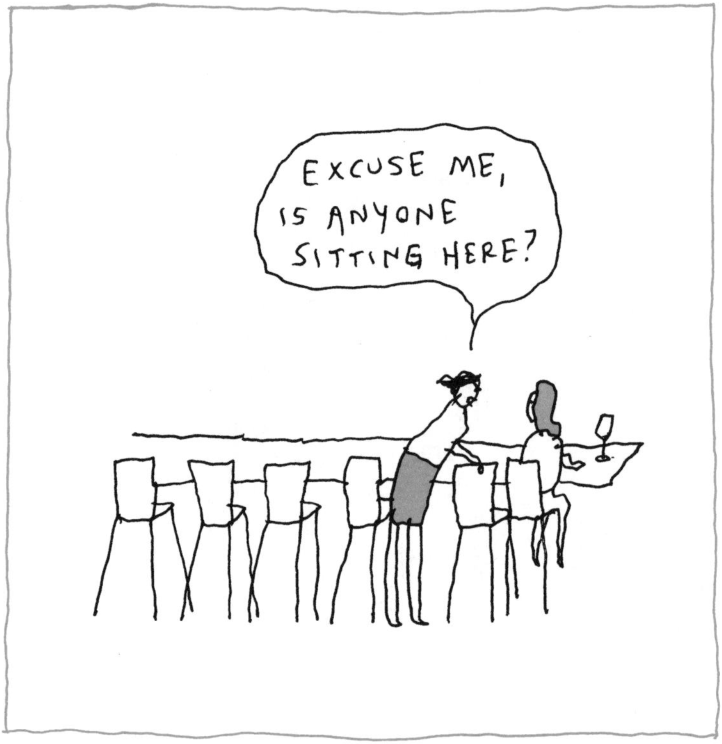
EXCUSE ME,
IS ANYONE
SITTING HERE?

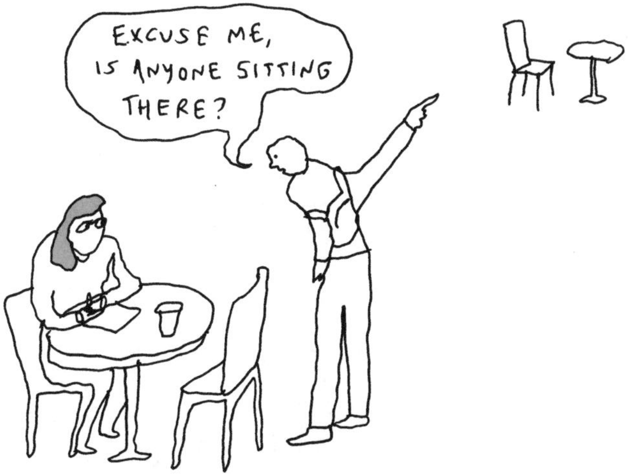
EXCUSE ME,
IS ANYONE SITTING
THERE?

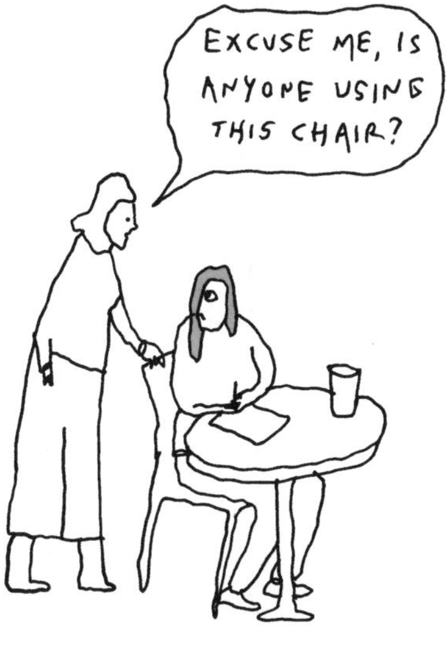
EXCUSE ME, IS
ANYONE USING
THIS CHAIR?

1
EXCUSE ME.
WAIT HERE
2
??
WAIT HERE

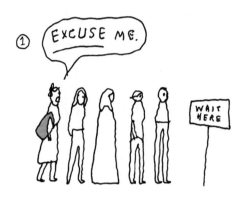

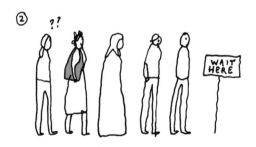

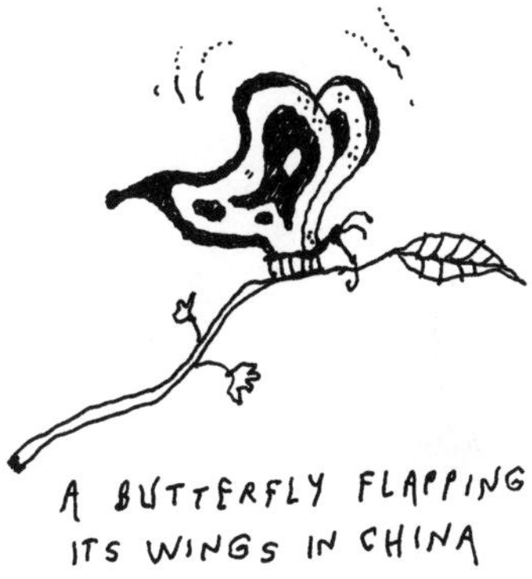
A BUTTERFLY FLAPPING
ITS WINGS IN CHINA

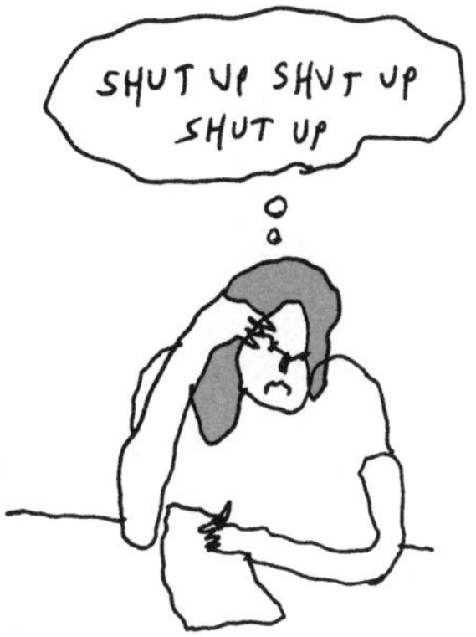
SHUT UP SHUT UP
SHUT UP

DEMON FOOT

I'M NOT PEEING TILL SHE LEAVES
I'M NOT LEAVING TILL SHE PEES.
SMOOTH SMOOTH

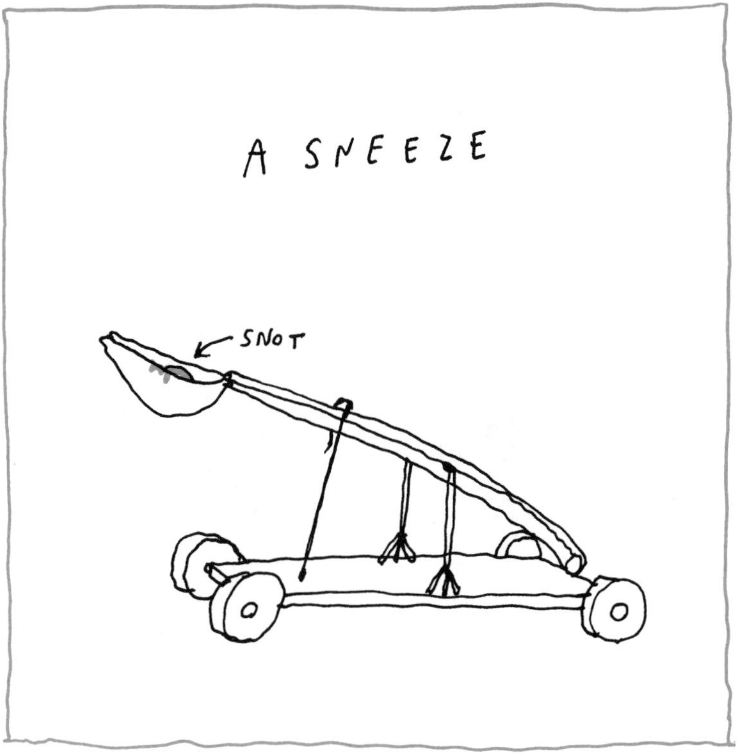
A SNEEZE
SNOT

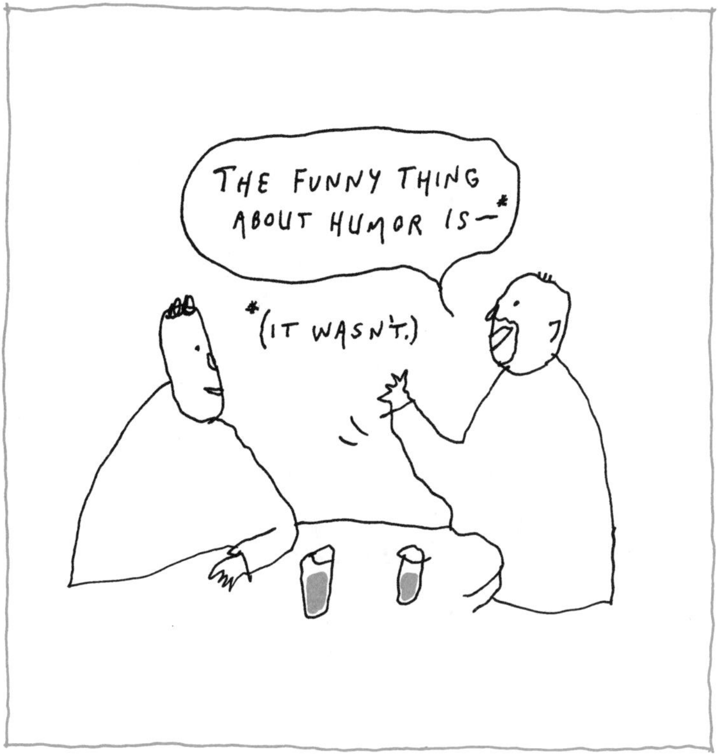
THE FUNNY THING ABOUT HUMOR IS—*
*(IT WASN'T.)

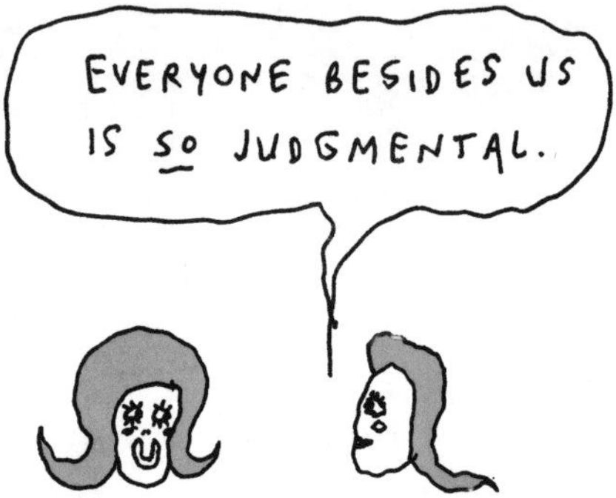
EVERYONE BESIDES US IS SO JUDGMENTAL.

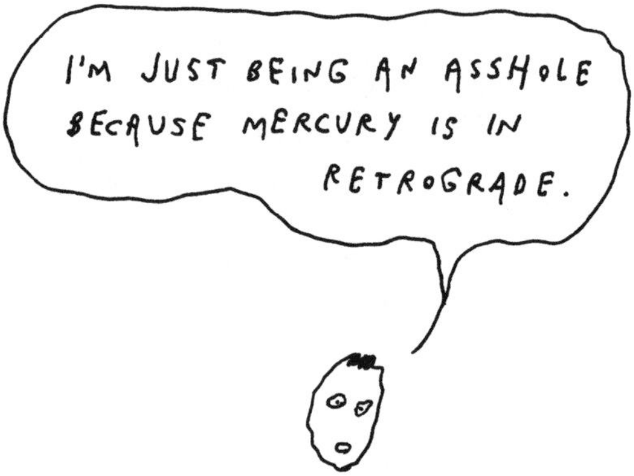
I'M JUST BEING AN ASSHOLE BECAUSE MERCURY IS IN RETROGRADE.

NEW AGE ASSHOLE

OVERHEARD IN THE MILKTOAST CAFÉ

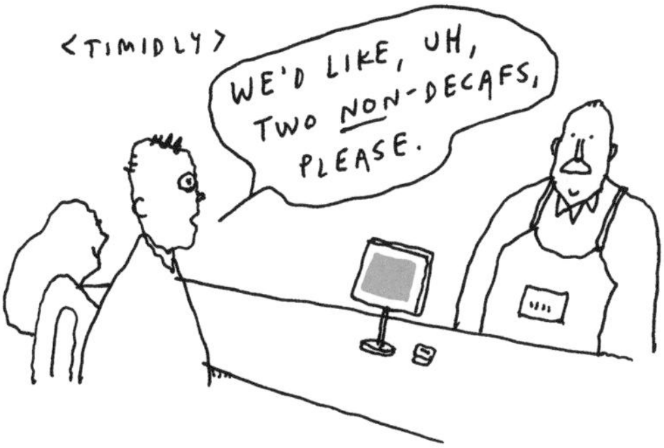
<TIMIDLY>
WE'D LIKE, UH, TWO NON-DECAFS, PLEASE.

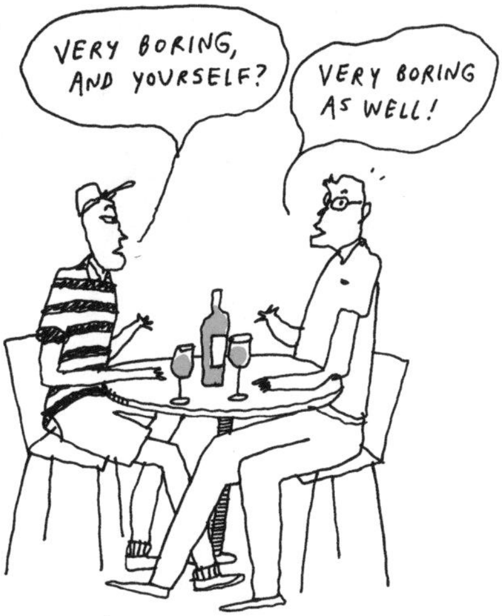
VERY BORING, AND YOURSELF?
VERY BORING AS WELL!

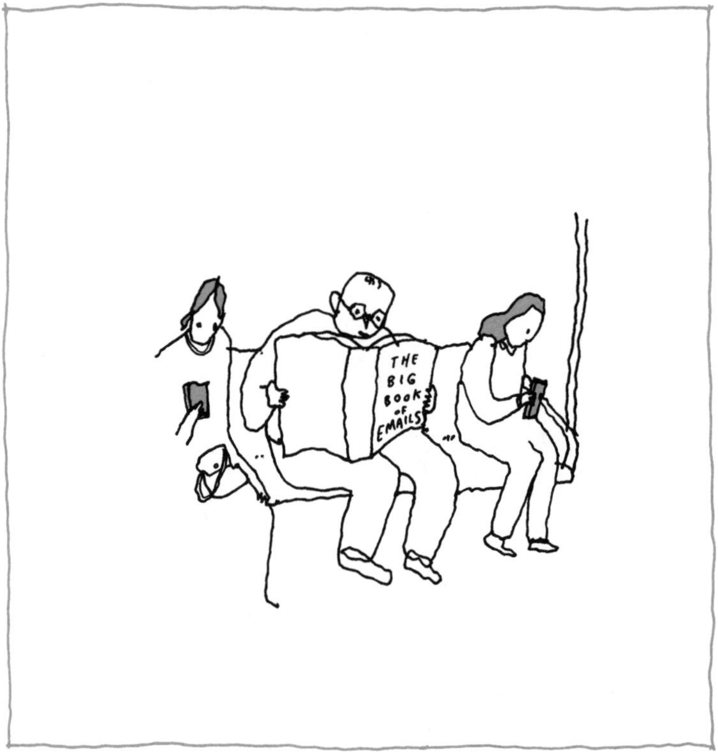
THE
BIG
BOOK
OF
EMAILS

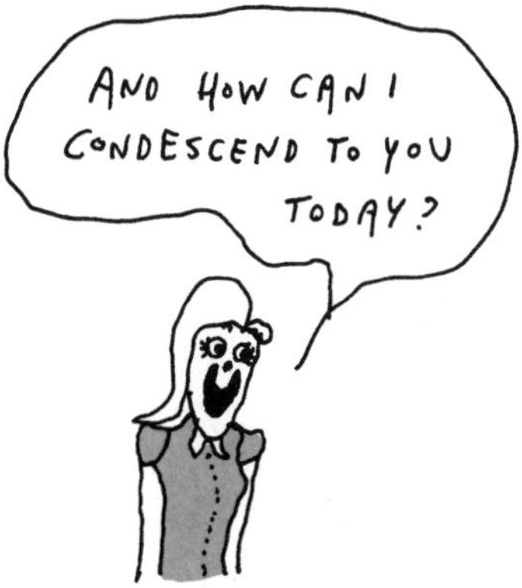
AND HOW CAN I CONDESCEND TO YOU TODAY?

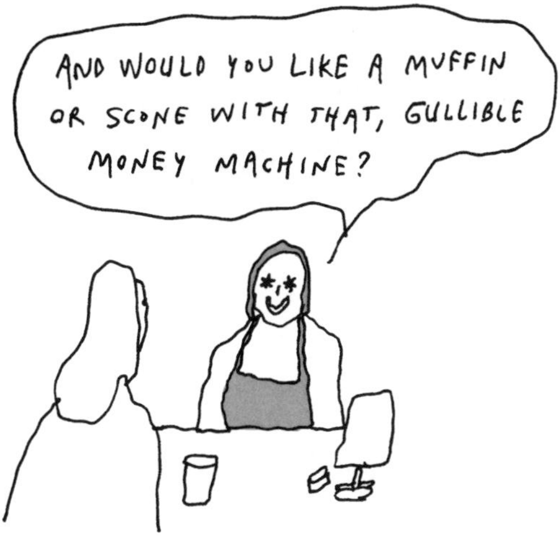
AND WOULD YOU LIKE A MUFFIN OR SCONE WITH THAT, GULLIBLE MONEY MACHINE?

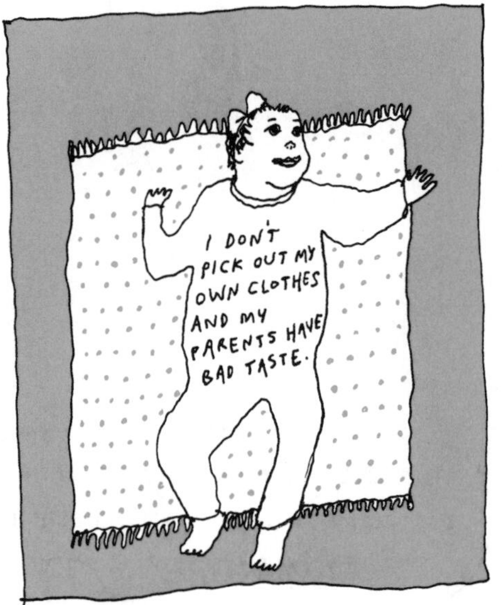
I DON'T PICK OUT MY OWN CLOTHES AND MY PARENTS HAVE BAD TASTE.
♡10

	WHEN PEOPLE ARE MEAN	WHEN PEOPLE ARE NICE
WHEN YOU EXPECT PEOPLE TO BE MEAN	YOU ARE RESIGNED	YOU ARE SUSPICIOUS
WHEN YOU EXPECT PEOPLE TO BE NICE	YOU ARE SHOCKED AND PRONE TO REACT	YOU ARE AT ONE WITH THE WORLD

KEY

□ = BAD

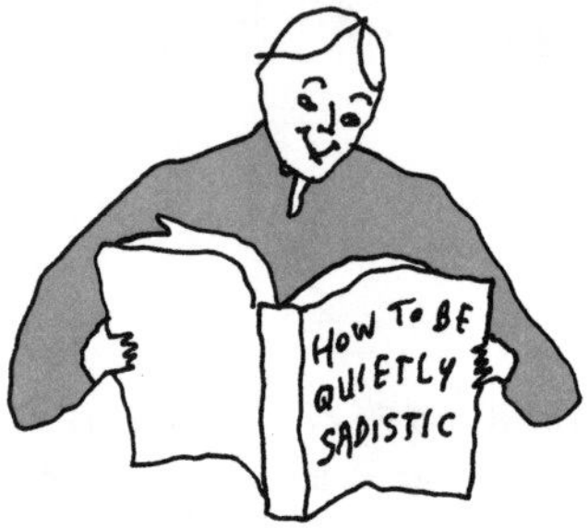
HOW TO BE
QUIETLY
SADISTIC

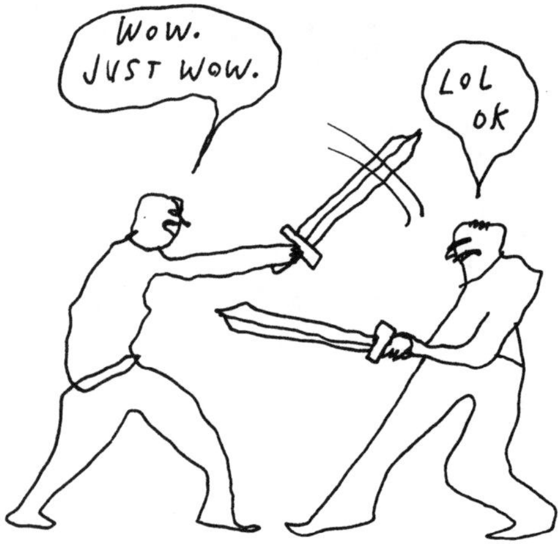
WOW.
JUST WOW.
LOL
OK

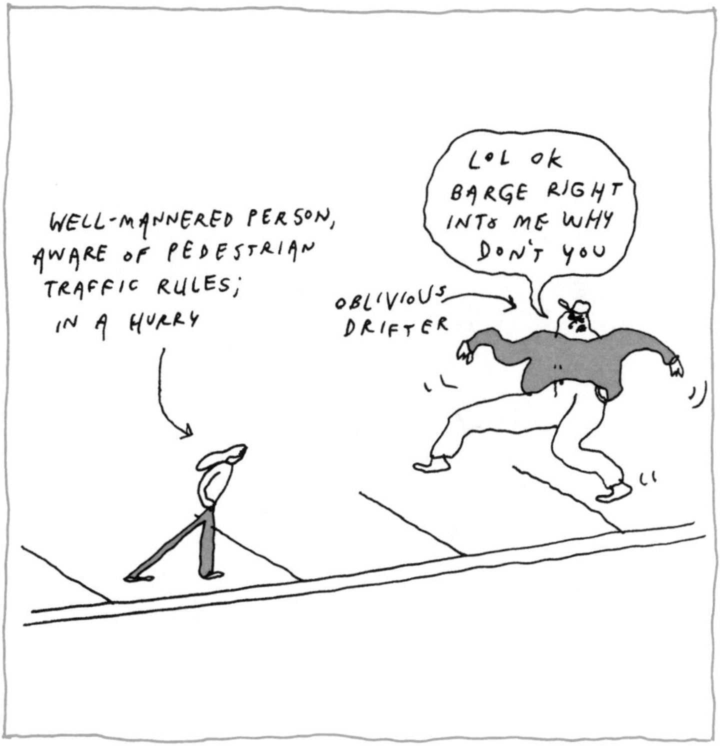
WELL-MANNERED PERSON, AWARE OF PEDESTRIAN TRAFFIC RULES; IN A HURRY
LOL OK BARGE RIGHT INTO ME WHY DON'T YOU
OBLIVIOUS DRIFTER

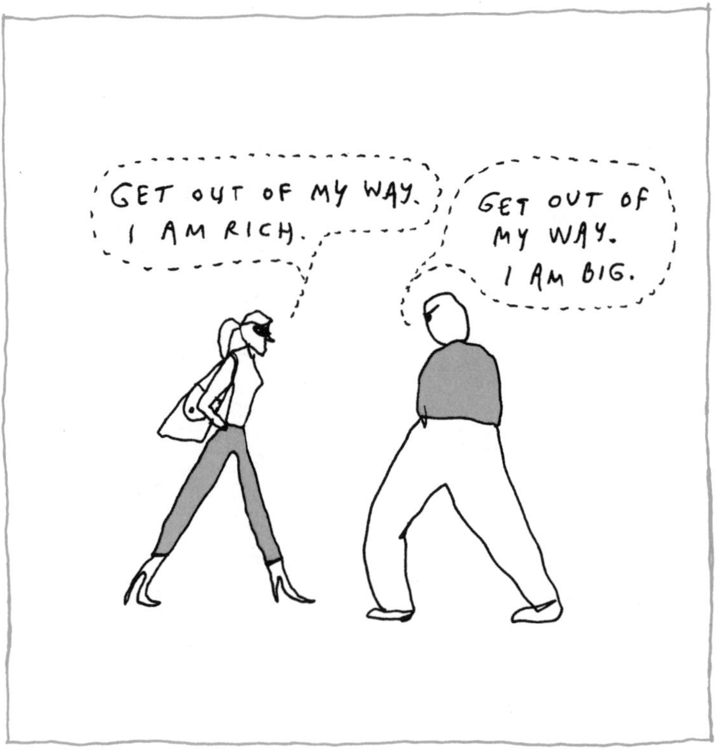
GET OUT OF MY WAY. I AM RICH.
GET OUT OF MY WAY. I AM BIG.

DOUCHES GAZING INTO INFINITY

FINALLY, A DRINK UMBRELLA THAT
ACTUALLY WORKS.

EXIT
DO NOT ENTER

12 AA
BATTERIES
-BATTERIES NOT INCLUDED!

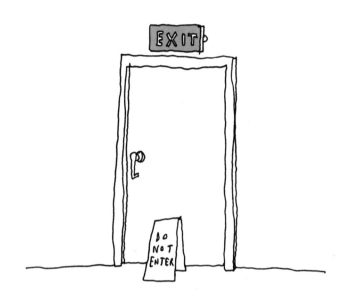

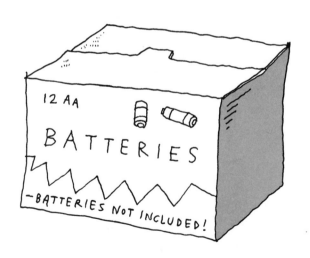

LOST AND FOUND

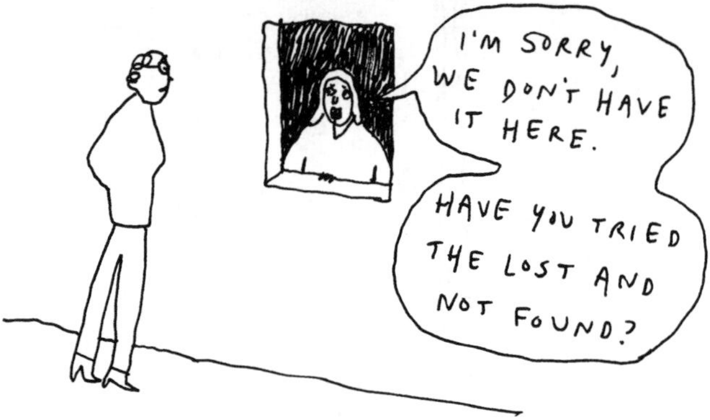
I'M SORRY, WE DON'T HAVE IT HERE.
HAVE YOU TRIED THE LOST AND NOT FOUND?

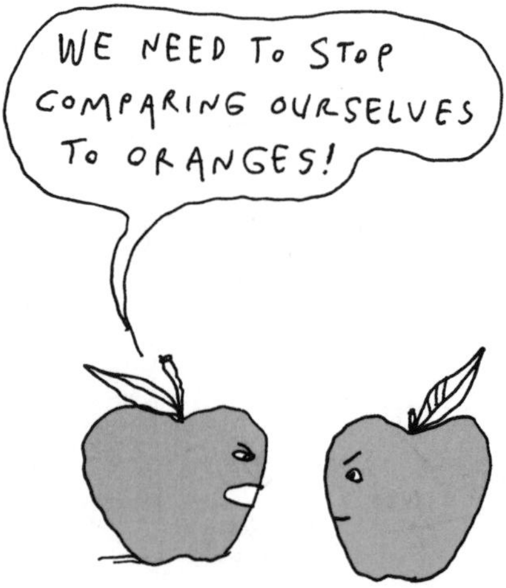
WE NEED TO STOP COMPARING OURSELVES TO ORANGES!

PONG-PONG

MA'AM, YOU MADE A TINY MISTAKE. WHAT PART OF "YOU HAVE THEREBY RELINQUISHED YOUR STATUS AS A HUMAN" DON'T YOU UNDERSTAND?

UNEXPECTED KINDNESS
BREATHTAKING CRUELTY

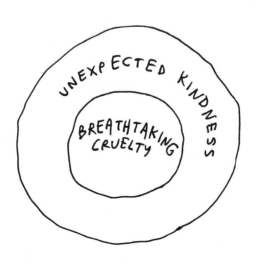

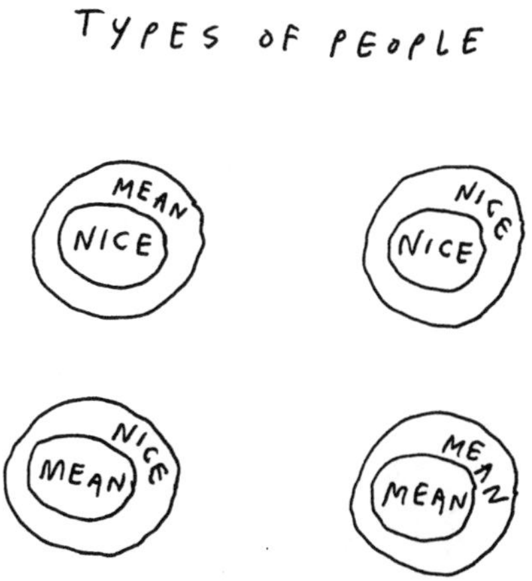
TYPES OF PEOPLE
MEAN
NICE
NICE
NICE
NICE
MEAN
MEAN
MEAN

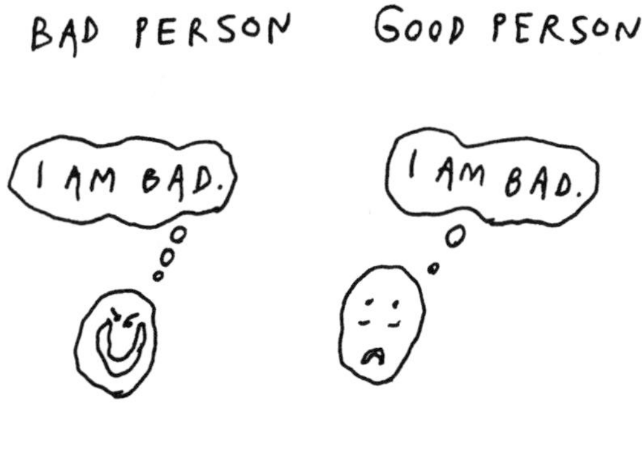
BAD PERSON
GOOD PERSON
I AM BAD.
I AM BAD.

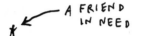

A FRIEND IN NEED

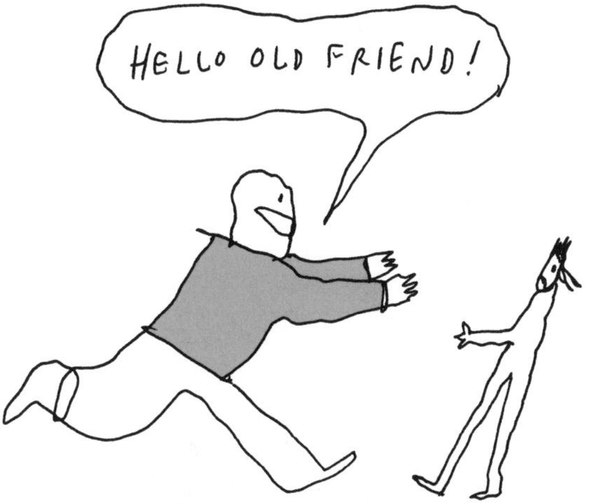
HELLO OLD FRIEND!

HELLO, COMPLETE STRANGER.

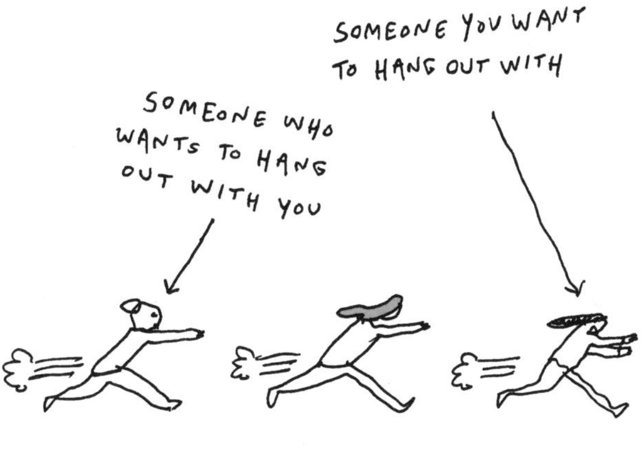
SOMEONE YOU WANT TO HANG OUT WITH
SOMEONE WHO WANTS TO HANG OUT WITH YOU

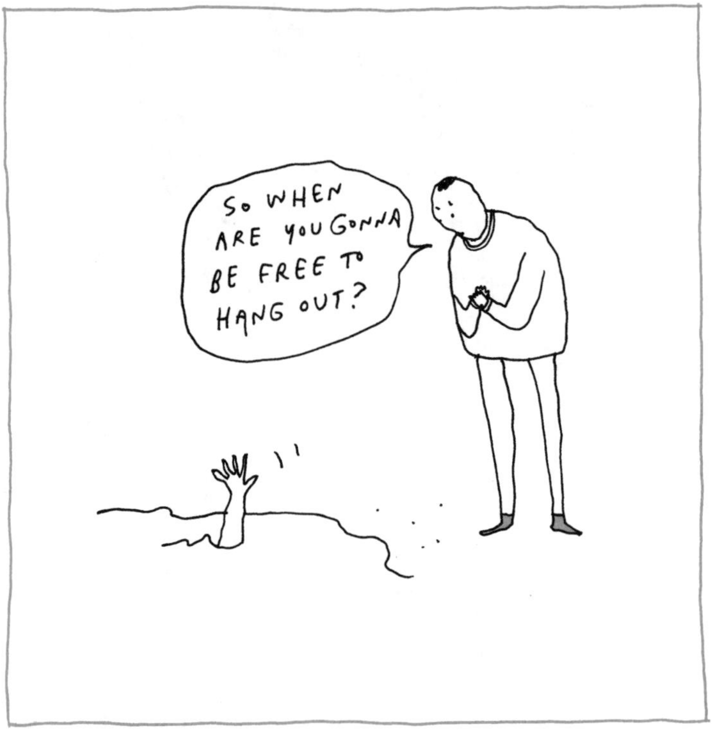
SO WHEN ARE YOU GONNA BE FREE TO HANG OUT?

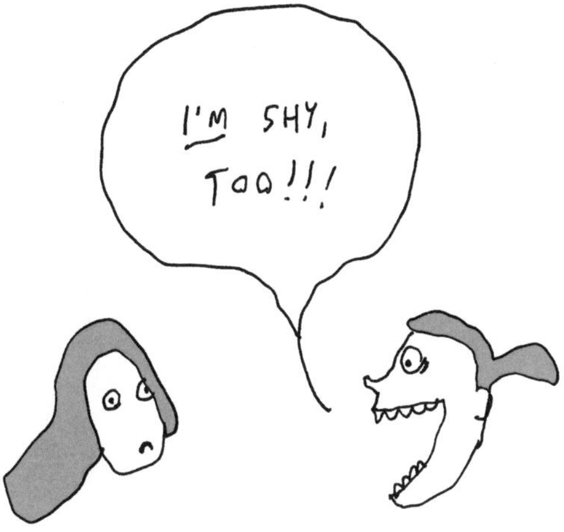
I'M SHY, TOO!!!

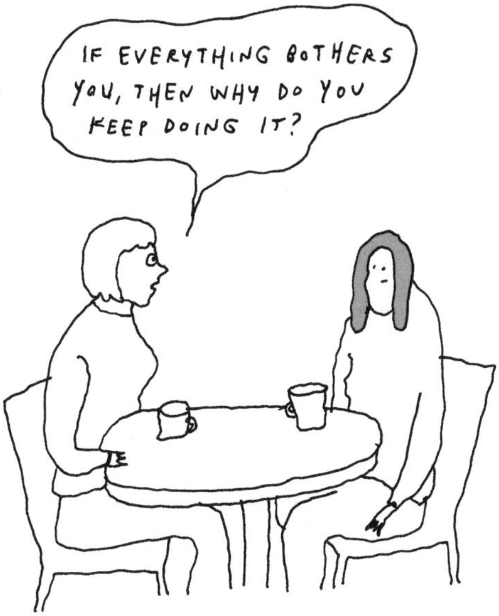
IF EVERYTHING BOTHERS YOU, THEN WHY DO YOU KEEP DOING IT?

YOU
THE PERSON
WHO QUIETLY
HATES YOU

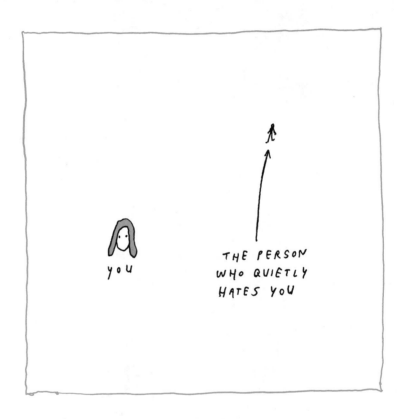

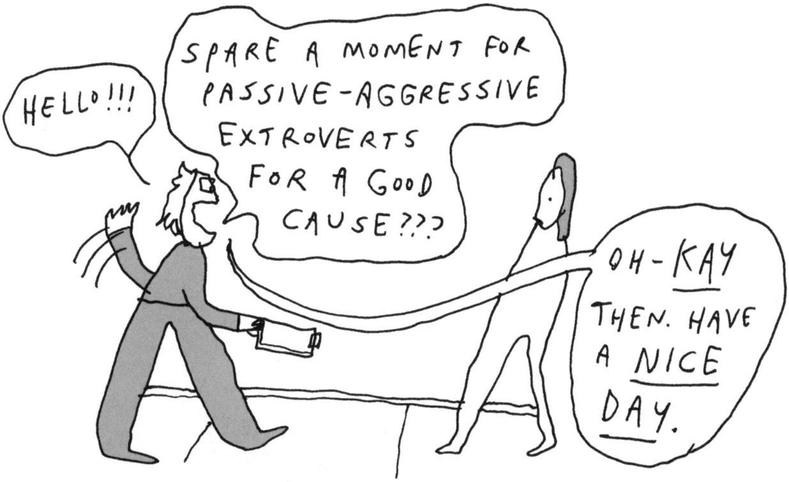
HELLO!!!
SPARE A MOMENT FOR PASSIVE-AGGRESSIVE EXTROVERTS FOR A GOOD CAUSE???
OH-KAY THEN. HAVE A NICE DAY.

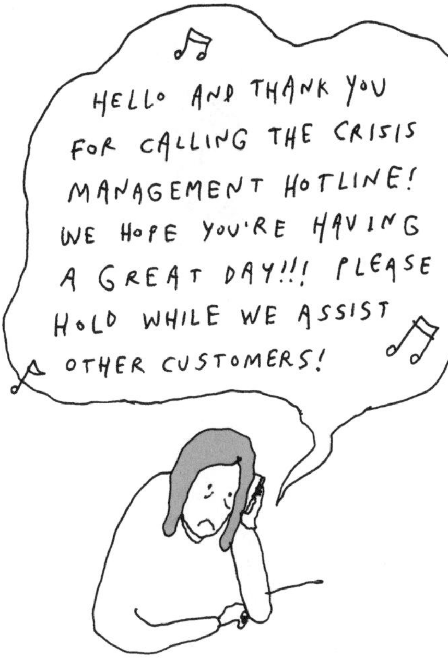
HELLO AND THANK YOU FOR CALLING THE CRISIS MANAGEMENT HOTLINE! WE HOPE YOU'RE HAVING A GREAT DAY!!! PLEASE HOLD WHILE WE ASSIST OTHER CUSTOMERS!

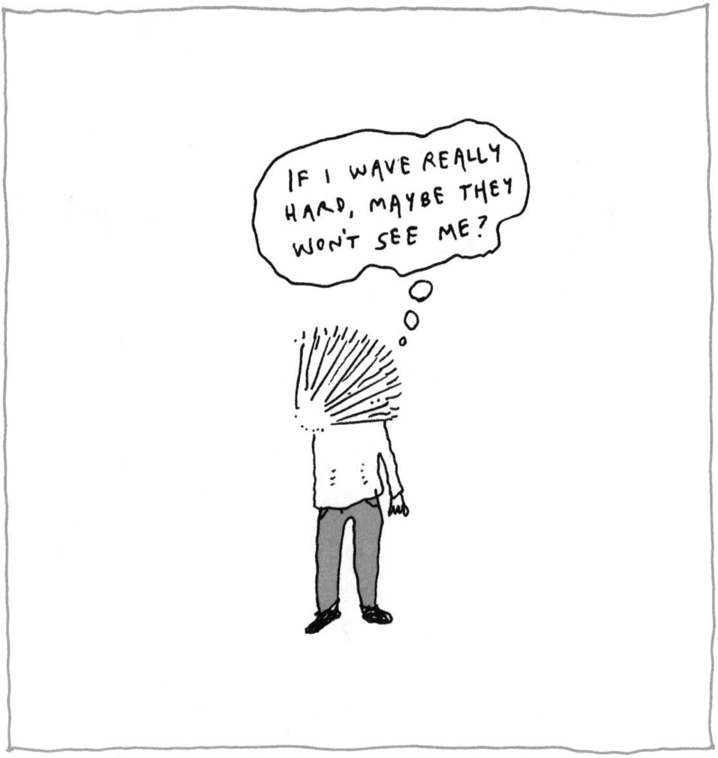
IF I WAVE REALLY HARD, MAYBE THEY WON'T SEE ME?

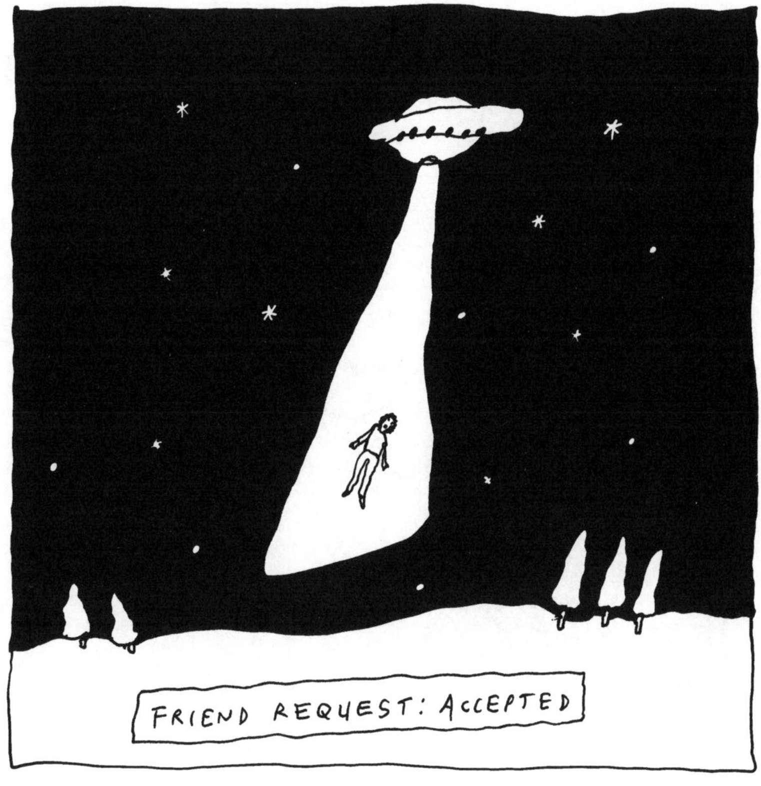
FRIEND REQUEST: ACCEPTED

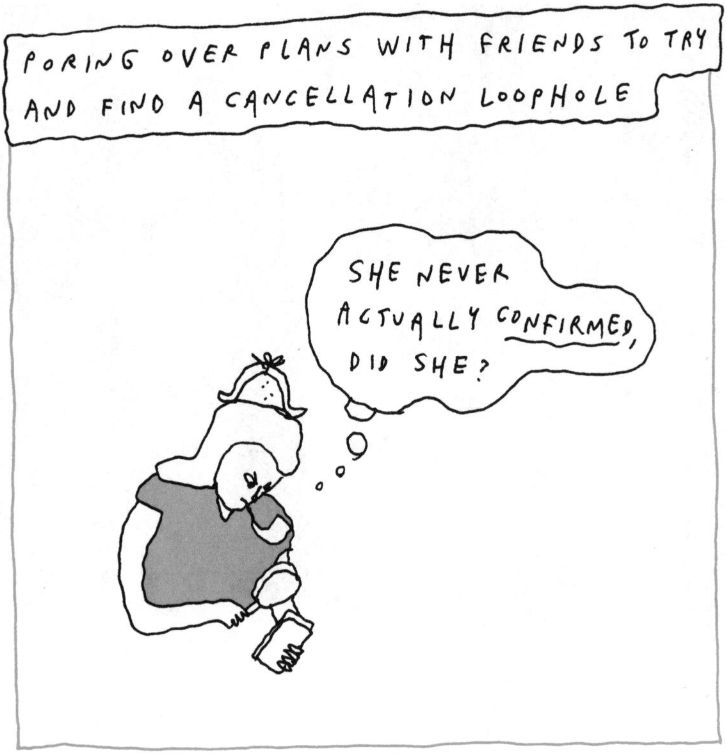
PORING OVER PLANS WITH FRIENDS TO TRY AND FIND A CANCELLATION LOOPHOLE
SHE NEVER ACTUALLY CONFIRMED, DID SHE?

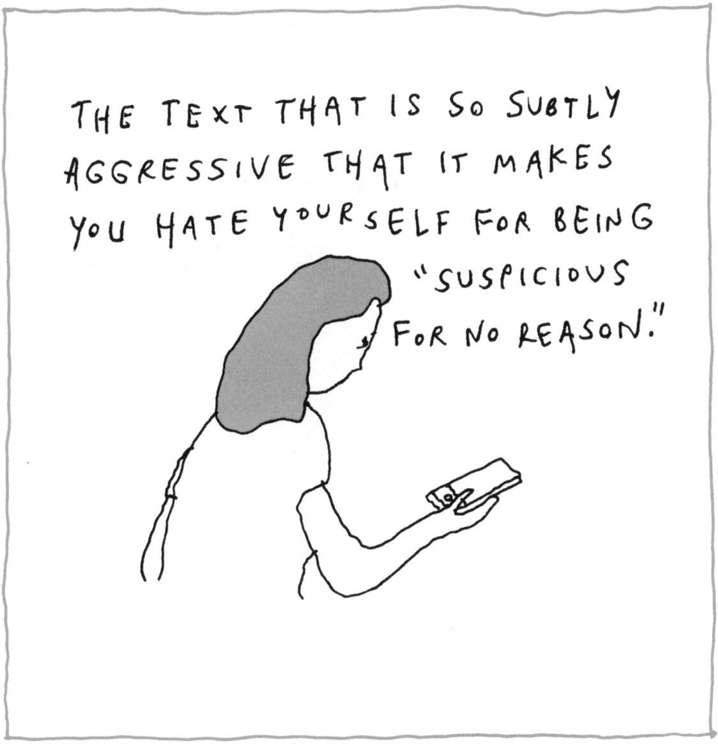
THE TEXT THAT IS SO SUBTLY AGGRESSIVE THAT IT MAKES YOU HATE YOURSELF FOR BEING "SUSPICIOUS FOR NO REASON."

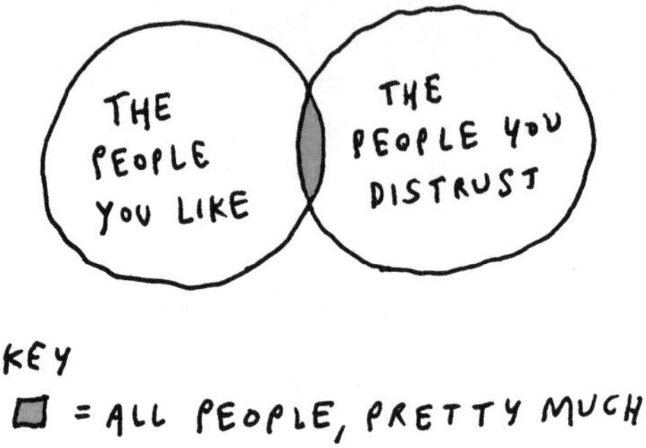
THE PEOPLE YOU LIKE
THE PEOPLE YOU DISTRUST
KEY
= ALL PEOPLE, PRETTY MUCH

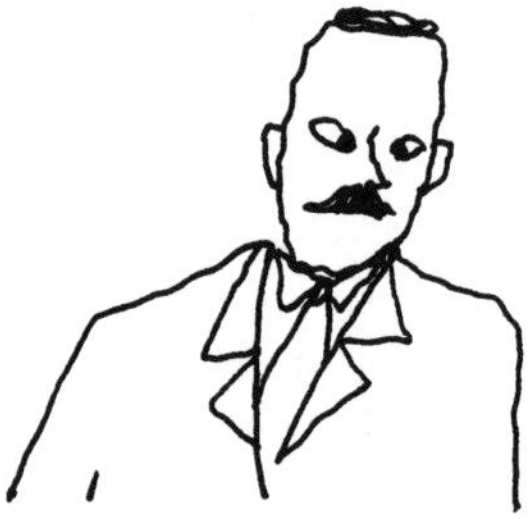

JOHN VENN, INVENTOR OF THE VENN DIAGRAM

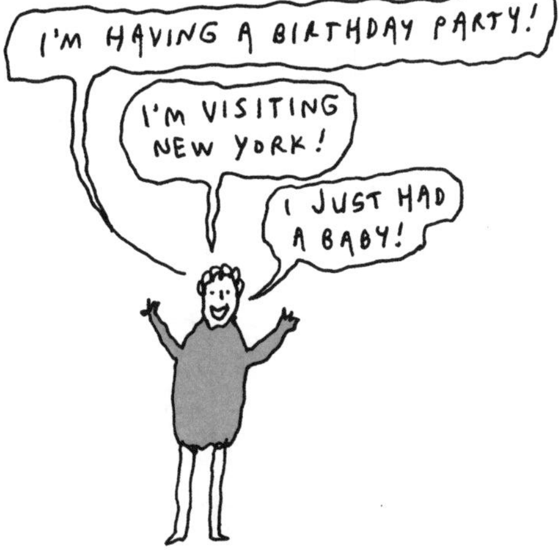
I'M HAVING A BIRTHDAY PARTY!
I'M VISITING NEW YORK!
I JUST HAD A BABY!

<EVERYONE>

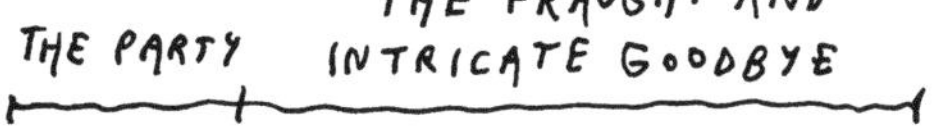
THE PARTY
THE FRAUGHT AND INTRICATE GOODBYE

	HORRIBLE	MEANINGFUL	WONDERFUL
ONE-ON-ONE DINNER WITH FRIEND			✓
MEET NEIGHBOR FOR QUICK WALK		✓	
POWER LUNCH NEAR RANDOM ACQUAINTANCE'S OFFICE	✓		
BRIDAL SHOWER IN NEW JERSEY	✓		
LOW-KEY FAMILY GATHERING		✓	
MEET OUT-OF-TOWN FRIENDS NEAR MIDTOWN	✓		
INTENSIVE FAMILY GATHERING	✓		
FIRST DATE			✓
SECOND DATE		✓	
THIRD DATE	✓		
PARTY WITH SPARKLY PEOPLE			✓
PARTY WITH DULL PEOPLE	✓		
A DRINK WITH A FEW FRIENDS			✓
BRUNCH WITH SEVEN FRIENDS	✓		
MEETING WITH A STRANGER, 4 P.M.			✓
BEING STUCK IN AN ELEVATOR WITH A TALKATIVE NEIGHBOR, 8 A.M.	✓		

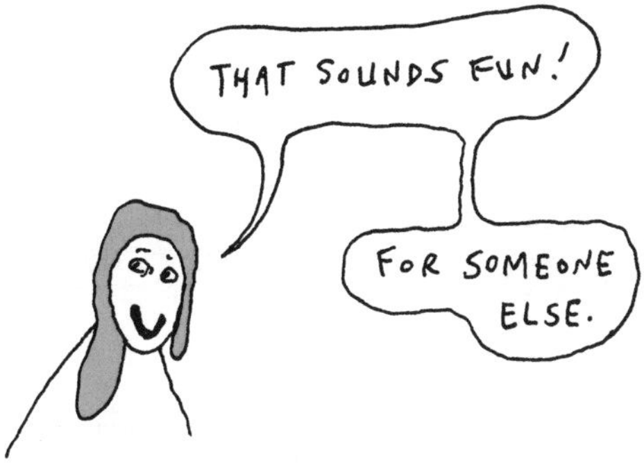
THAT SOUNDS FUN!
FOR SOMEONE ELSE.

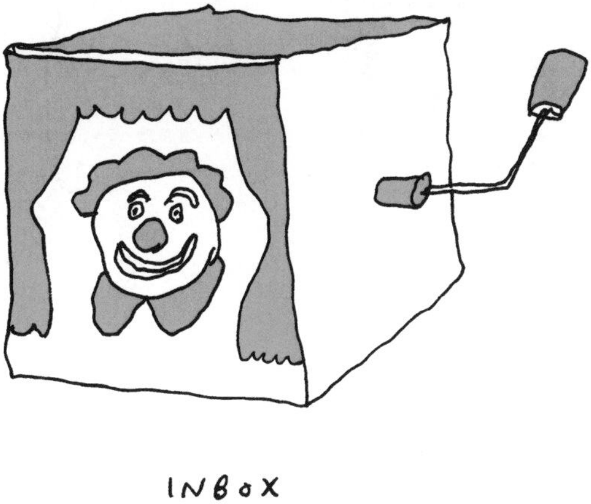

INBOX

TOOLS FOR KEEPING FRIENDS AT BAY

SOFT STICK

CLOAK
OF EVASIVENESS

BAD TYPES OF FRIENDLY

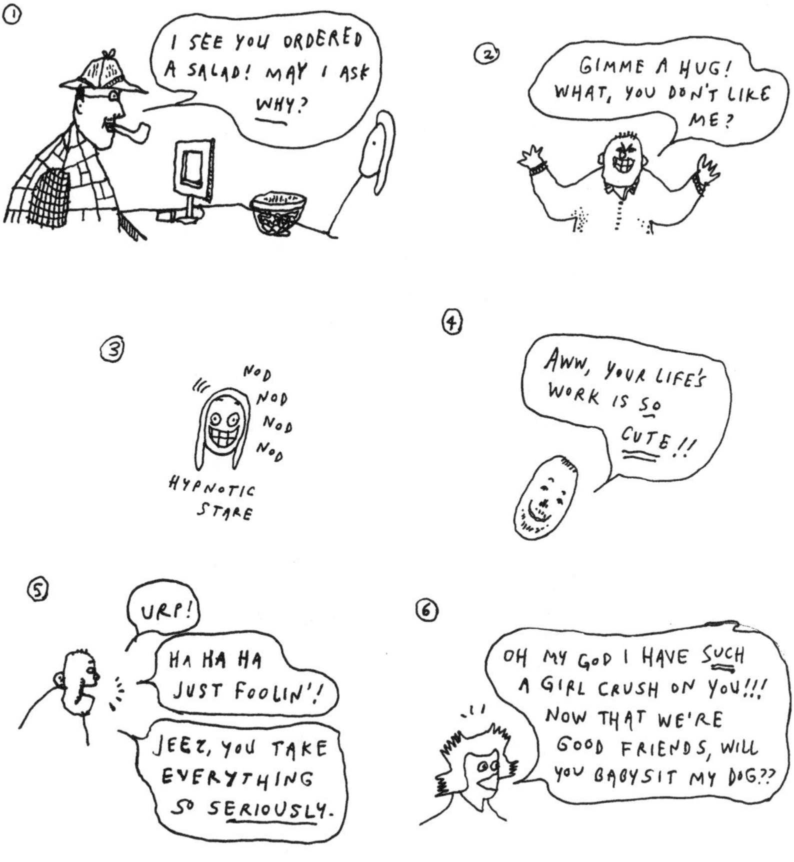

①
I SEE YOU ORDERED A SALAD! MAY I ASK WHY?
②
GIMME A HUG! WHAT, YOU DON'T LIKE ME?
③
NOD NOD NOD NOD
HYPNOTIC STARE
④
AWW, YOUR LIFE'S WORK IS SO CUTE!!
⑤
URP!
HA HA HA JUST FOOLIN'!
JEEZ, YOU TAKE EVERYTHING SO SERIOUSLY.
⑥
OH MY GOD I HAVE SUCH A GIRL CRUSH ON YOU!!! NOW THAT WE'RE GOOD FRIENDS, WILL YOU BABYSIT MY DOG??

FRIENDS

- THE REALLY SPECIAL ONE YOU
  FEEL GUILTY TOWARD BECAUSE
  YOU'RE NOT A GREAT FRIEND
- THE SUBTLY JEALOUS ONE
- THE ONE WHO WANTS YOU ON
  THEIR ROSTER
- THE ONE YOU WANT ON YOUR ROSTER
- THE ONE WHO VALUES FRIENDSHIP
  IN A WAY YOU DON'T UNDERSTAND,
  NOT HAVING HAD MANY FRIENDS IN
  YOUR FORMATIVE YEARS
- THE EXTROVERT WHO THINKS YOU'RE
  RUDE FOR TRYING TO CHANGE PLANS
- THE INTROVERT WHO TRIES HARD
  AND THINKS YOU SHOULD, TOO
- THE WOMAN WHO HAS A CRUSH ON YOU
- THE MAN WHO HAS A CRUSH ON YOU
- THE MAN YOU HAVE A CRUSH ON
- THE MAN WHO KNOWS YOU ONCE HAD
  A CRUSH ON HIM
- THE MAN WHO ONCE HAD A CRUSH ON
  YOU AND STILL WANTS SOMETHING,
  SO YOU FEEL GUILTY WHEN YOU
  GO HOME

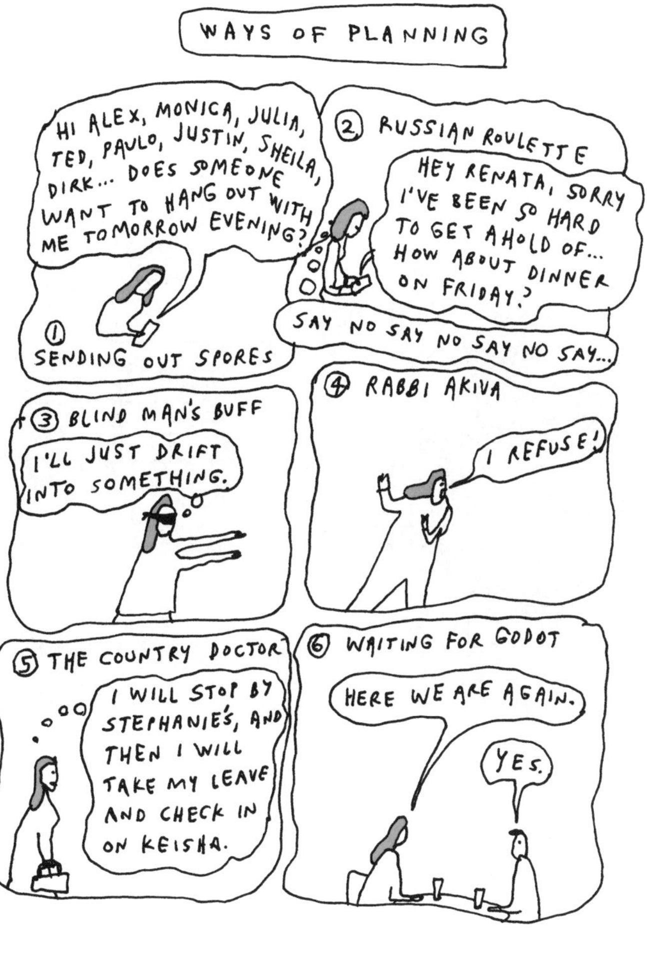
WAYS OF PLANNING
HI ALEX, MONICA, JULIA, TED, PAULO, JUSTIN, SHEILA, DIRK... DOES SOMEONE WANT TO HANG OUT WITH ME TOMORROW EVENING?
① SENDING OUT SPORES
② RUSSIAN ROULETTE
HEY RENATA, SORRY I'VE BEEN SO HARD TO GET AHOLD OF... HOW ABOUT DINNER ON FRIDAY?
SAY NO SAY NO SAY NO SAY...
③ BLIND MAN'S BUFF
I'LL JUST DRIFT INTO SOMETHING.
④ RABBI AKIVA
I REFUSE!
⑤ THE COUNTRY DOCTOR
I WILL STOP BY STEPHANIE'S, AND THEN I WILL TAKE MY LEAVE AND CHECK IN ON KEISHA.
⑥ WAITING FOR GODOT
HERE WE ARE AGAIN.
YES.

THE COMING WEEK
FIT ME IN!!
PLANS
LAST-MINUTE INVITATION

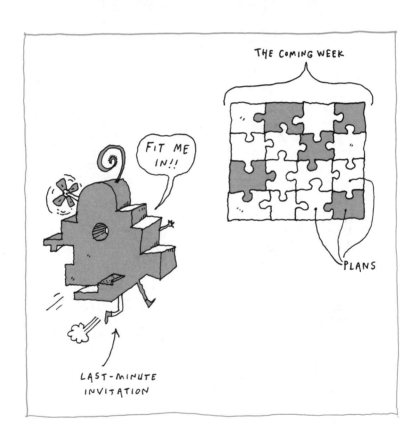

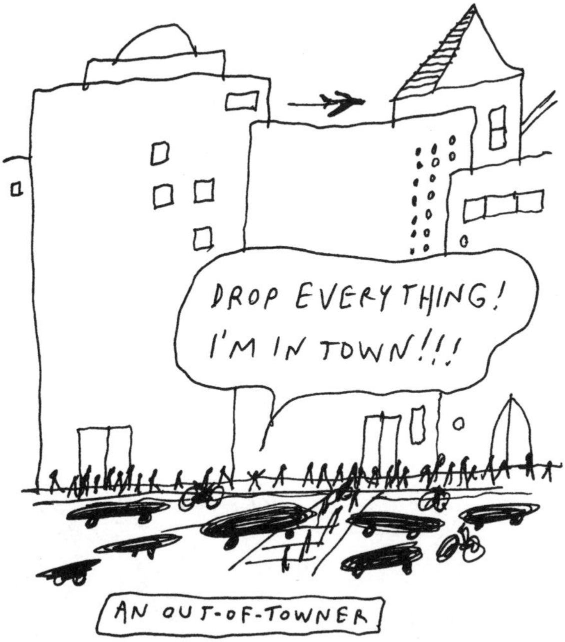
DROP EVERYTHING! I'M IN TOWN!!!
AN OUT-OF-TOWNER

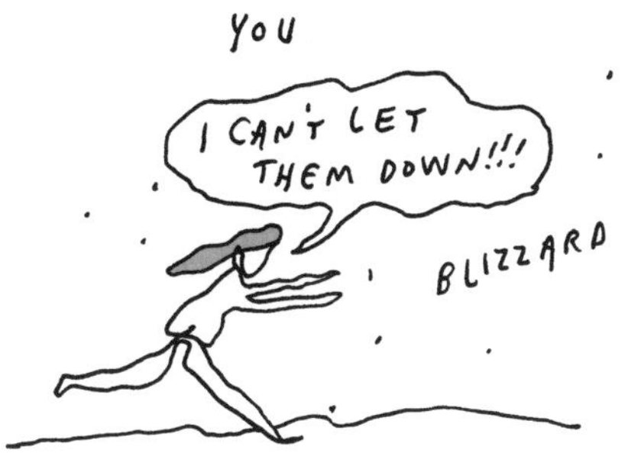
YOU
I CAN'T LET THEM DOWN!!!
BLIZZARD

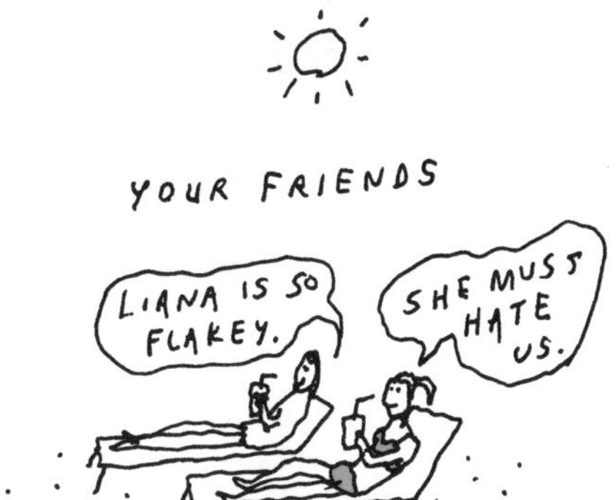
YOUR FRIENDS
LIANA IS SO FLAKEY.
SHE MUST HATE US.

PHASES OF OVERWHELM
1. EASY BREEZY
OH, HI! I HAVE NOTHING GOING ON, LET'S HANG OUT!
2. TERSE
THANKS.
3. GRUMPY
NO.
4. NONRESPONSIVE

THE LOOMING DECISION

TOTE BAGS

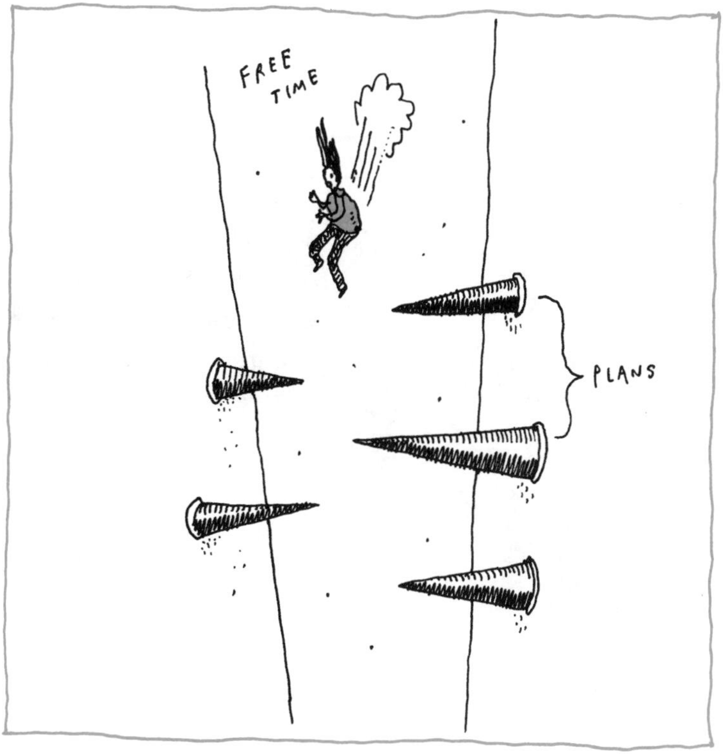
FREE TIME
PLANS

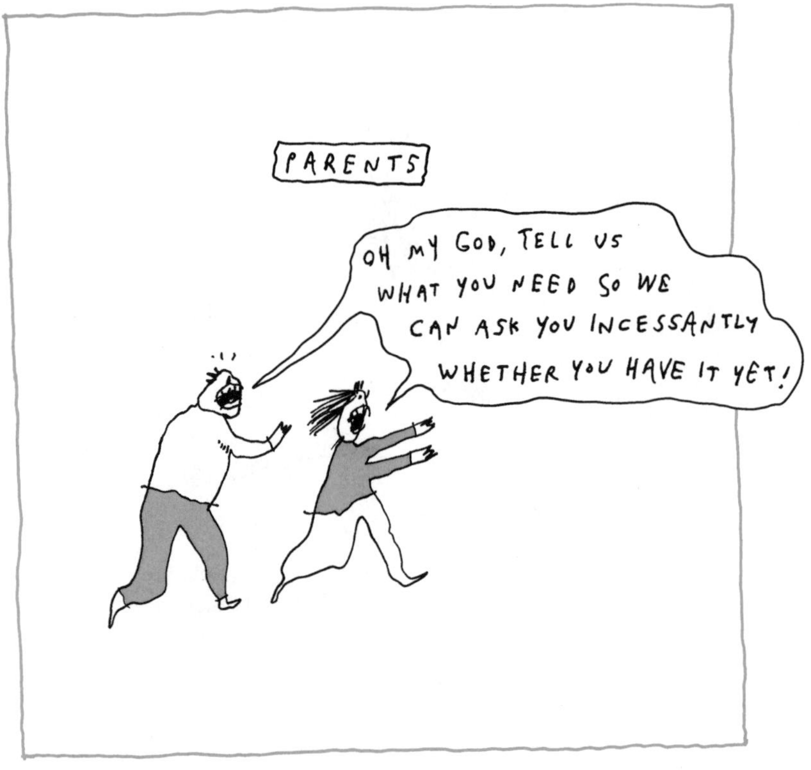
PARENTS
OH MY GOD, TELL US WHAT YOU NEED SO WE CAN ASK YOU INCESSANTLY WHETHER YOU HAVE IT YET!

GUILT TRIP
FROM PARENTS

SURPRISE
GUILT TRIPS
FROM AUNTS
AND UNCLES

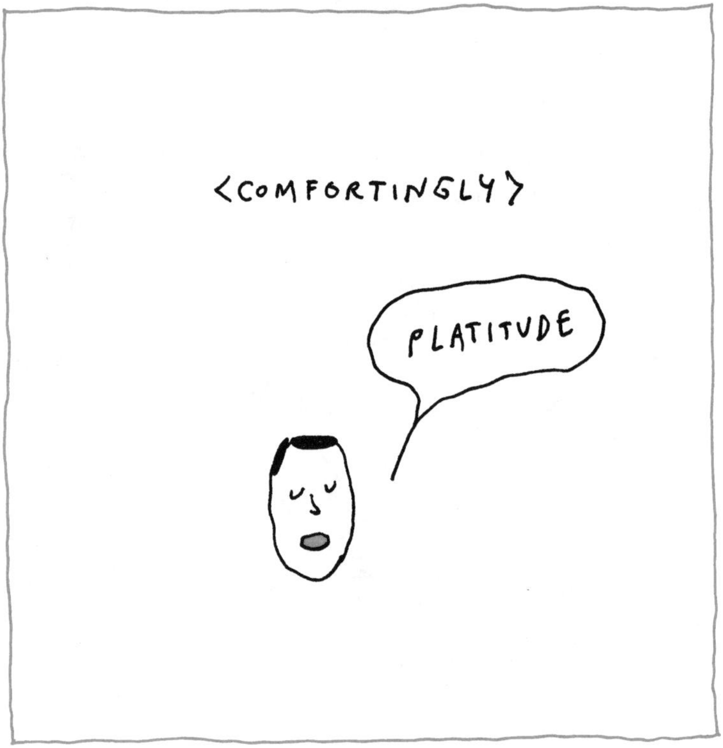
<COMFORTINGLY>
PLATITUDE

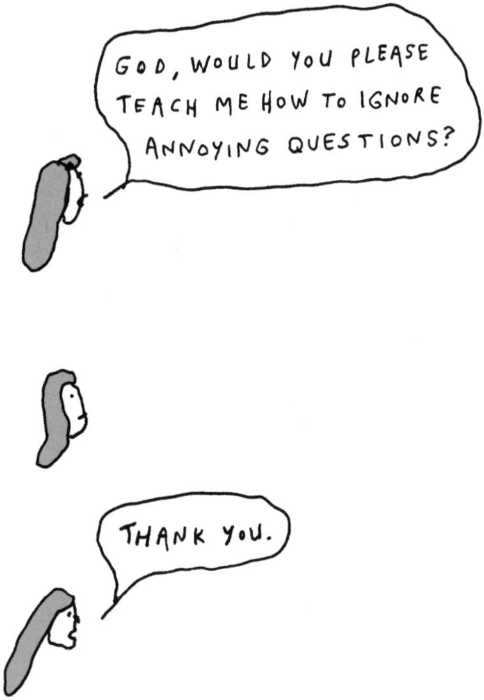
GOD, WOULD YOU PLEASE TEACH ME HOW TO IGNORE ANNOYING QUESTIONS?
THANK YOU.

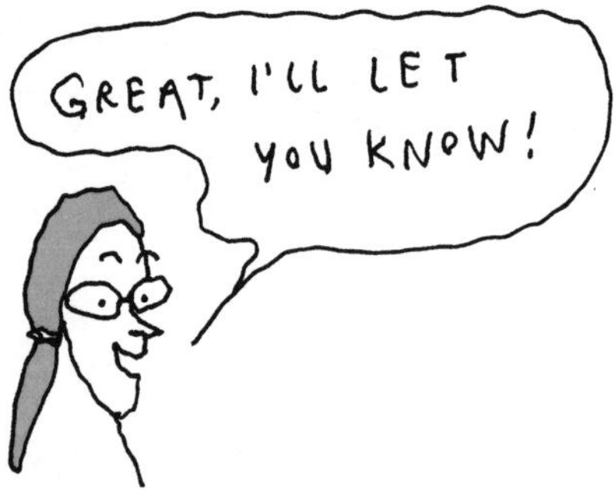
GREAT, I'LL LET YOU KNOW!

THE END

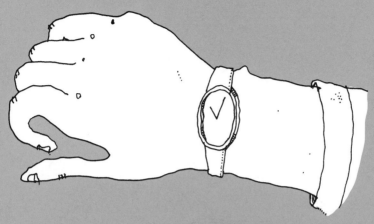

TIME,

SPACE,

AND

HOW TO NAVIGATE THEM

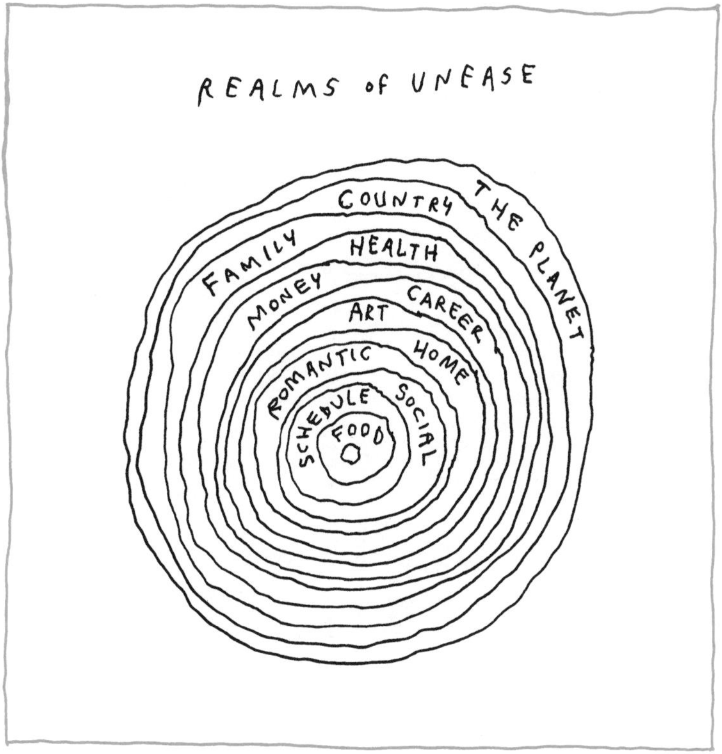
REALMS of UNEASE
THE PLANET
COUNTRY
FAMILY
HEALTH
MONEY
CAREER
ART
HOME
ROMANTIC
SOCIAL
SCHEDULE
FOOD

THE WORLD AT LARGE, WAITING TO BE OBSERVED

FORCES OF EVIL

BUBBLE OF PRIVELEGE

TYPES OF TIME

· NORMAL	OK
· TIME WON BY SAYING NO TO SOCIAL EVENT	SO, SO, SO MUCH PRESSURE TO MAKE IT WORTH THE SACRIFICE
· TIME GIFTED BY FRIEND'S CANCELLATION	WONDERFUL NO MATTER WHAT YOU DO WITH IT

286

DIAGRAM OF THE WORLD

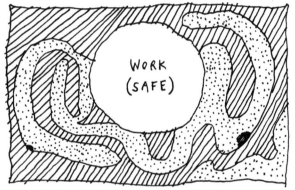

KEY ▨ = CONFUSING, DEPRESSING, AIMLESS HAZE

▦ = SURPRISING & DELIGHTFUL ADVENTURES

◼ = MIDDLE GROUND (VERY RARE)

THE DAY
EAT CROISSANT
RUN ON TREADMILL
READ BOOK IN BED

DEATH

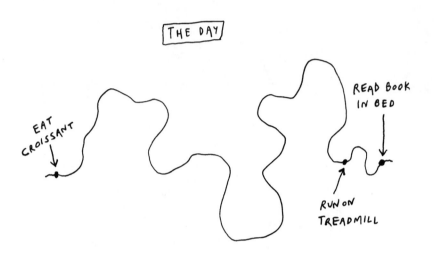

UP
LEFT OR RIGHT
LEFT OR RIGHT
DOWN

A SECOND PASSED... ANOTHER SECOND PASSED... ANOTHER SECOND PASSED... ANOTHER SECOND PASSED... ANOTHER SECOND PASSED... ANOTHER SECOND PASSED... ANOTHER SECOND PASSED... ANOTHER SECOND PASSED...

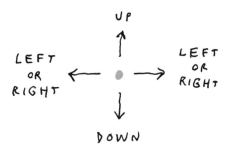

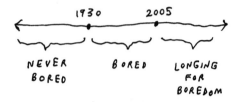

1930   2005

NEVER   BORED   LONGING
BORED   FOR
                               BOREDOM

TIMELINE

ABOUT TO COME INTO YOUR OWN

ABOUT TO COME INTO YOUR OWN

ABOUT TO COME INTO YOUR OWN

ABOUT TO COME INTO YOUR OWN

ABOUT TO COME INTO YOUR OWN

ABOUT TO COME INTO YOUR OWN

ABOUT TO COME INTO YOUR OWN

ABOUT TO COME INTO YOUR OWN

4   8   12   16   20   24   28   32

SCHEDULE

7 A.M. WAKE UP
   CHECK PHONE
   BRUSH TEETH
   CHECK PHONE WHILE PEEING

7:15 MAKE BREAKFAST
   CHECK PHONE
   EAT BREAKFAST
   CHECK PHONE
   PUT ON COAT
   CHECK PHONE

7:45 LEAVE HOUSE
   CHECK PHONE
   WALK TO SUBWAY
   CHECK PHONE
   GET ON SUBWAY
   CHECK PHONE
   WALK TO WORKPLACE WHILE CHECKING PHONE AND SENDING EMAIL

8:30 GET IN ELEVATOR
   SEND ANOTHER EMAIL
   CHECK PHONE
   CHECK PHONE WHILE POOPING

8:40-12 P.M. CHECK PHONE WHILE WORKING
   GET IN ELEVATOR WHILE CHECKING PHONE

12:15 CHECK PHONE WHILE WAITING FOR SALAD
   EAT WHILE CHECKING PHONE

1:00 CHECK PHONE IN ELEVATOR

1:05-6:00 WORK WHILE CHECKING PHONE

6:05 LEAVE WORK WHILE CHECKING PHONE

7:00-10:00 SEE FRIENDS, OCCASIONALLY SHOWING THEM
                          THINGS ON PHONE
10:05 LEAVE
10:06 CHECK PHONE
10:10 SUBWAY/PHONE
11-1 A.M. TEXT
1:05 GET READY FOR BED
1:20 CHECK PHONE

SCHEDULE IN HELL

- WAKE UP
- MAKE BREAKFAST
- LOITER
- EAT BREAKFAST
- LOITER OVER BREAKFAST
- CLEAN UP
- CLEAN UP MORE
- DECIDE, IN A LEISURELY
  MANNER, WHAT TO WEAR
- SHOWER
- BRUSH TEETH
- BUMBLE AROUND
- DRY HAIR
- PUT ON CLOTHES
- THINK ABOUT LUNCH
- BEGIN TO MAKE LUNCH

- MAKE LUNCH IN EARNEST
- SET TABLE
- SET OUT LUNCH
- EAT LUNCH
- SIT AROUND
- SIGH
- LOITER
- CLEAN UP LUNCH
- NAP
- FINISH CLEANING
- WHERE WERE WE? - OH YES.
- BEGIN TO THINK ABOUT DINNER
- TO BE CONTINUED...

THINGS THAT FELL INTO THE INTERNET

THE PAST
MYSTERY
VARIOUS STIGMAS
THE SELF
THE OTHER
PRIVACY
LONELINESS
CLOSENESS
SPECIFICITY
SHYNESS
CHILDHOOD

FREAKISHNESS

CULTURE
THE ARTIST
NATURE
FAMILY

HIYA HOW'S IT GOING WHAT'S UP?!
NEW YORK
NOT NEW YORK

CELLULAR MAKEUP OF PARK SLOPE*

VIOLENT RAGE
UNDEALT-WITH PAIN, AND FEAR OF BEING LEFT OUT
THIN MEMBRANE OF GOOD BREEDING HOLDING IT ALL TOGETHER

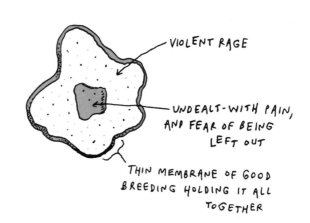

*AN UPSCALE NEIGHBORHOOD IN BROOKLYN

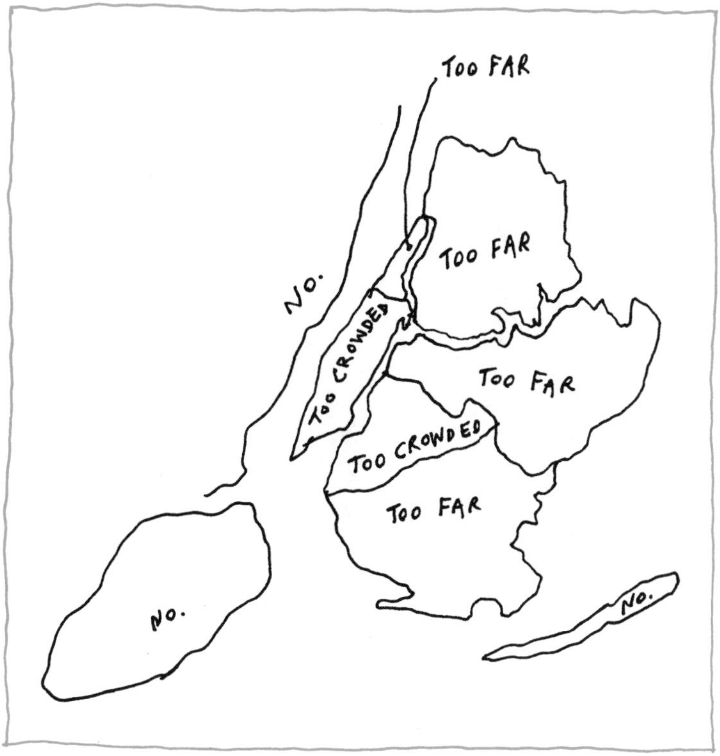
TOO FAR
NO.
TOO FAR
TOO CROWDED
TOO FAR
TOO CROWDED
TOO FAR
NO.
NO.

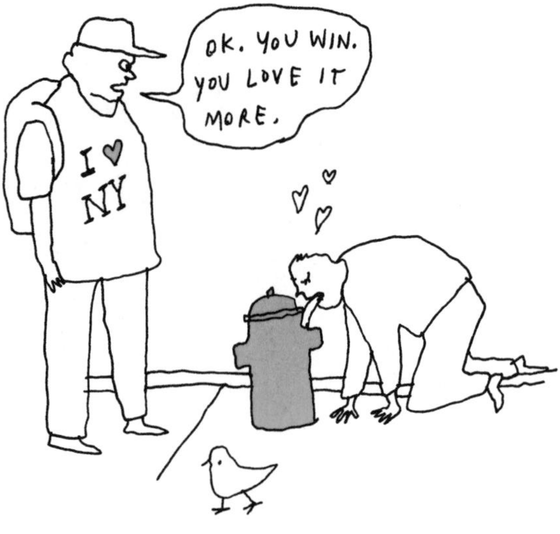
OK. YOU WIN.
YOU LOVE IT
MORE.
I ♥
NY

CITY LIFE

PROS	CONS
WONDERFUL, FASCINATING FRIENDS	UNENDING TERROR
WORK	
PEOPLE-WATCHING	
BUILDINGS	
FAMILY HISTORY	
MELTING POT	
PARKS	
ART	
HAPPENINGS	
GOOD TAKE-OUT	

OFFICES AVAILABLE (PART 1)

1. TABLE AT A HIPSTER CAFE IN THE EAST VILLAGE. (DOWNSIDES: IF YOU GET UP, SOMEONE WILL TAKE YOUR TABLE. IF YOU DON'T GET UP, SOMEONE WILL TAKE YOUR TABLE. A COLLEGE BOY WILL SIT TOO CLOSE TO YOU AND PLAY MIND GAMES WHEN YOU MOVE YOUR CHAIR AWAY, CREEPING CLOSER.)

2. TABLE IN A CAFE IN AN OLD-BOURGE PART OF BROOKLYN. (DOWNSIDE: YOU GET TO SPEND TWO SESSIONS THERE BEFORE THE BARISTAS START TO RECOGNIZE YOU AS A LOVABLE ECCENTRIC.)

3. TABLE AT A CAFE NEAR WHERE YOU LIVE. (DOWNSIDES: THE CAFES NEAR YOU ARE RUN BY STRANGE PEOPLE WHO DON'T SEEM TO UNDERSTAND WHAT A CAFE SHOULD BE. THERE ARE NO WINDOWS; THE SPACES ARE EITHER VERY HOT OR VERY COLD. ALTHOUGH YOU LIVE IN A BLACK NEIGHBORHOOD, THE CAFES ARE FULL OF WHITE KIDS WHO LOOK LIKE THEY'RE TRYING TO IMPERSONATE HIPSTERS.)

4. STUDIO SPACE, SHARED WITH FRIENDS. (DOWNSIDES: VERY, VERY FAR AWAY. BUILDING VERY EMPTY AND SOMETIMES INHABITED BY SCARY MEN. WHEN NO ONE COMES, YOU ARE HORRIBLY LONELY. WHEN SOMEONE COMES, SHE TAKES YOUR CHAIR.)

5. LIBRARY. (DOWNSIDES: SOME ARE VERY CROWDED; SOME ARE FULL OF SAD, DOWN-AND-OUT PEOPLE YOU RELATE TO TOO MUCH. THE GLAMOROUS MAIN BRANCH IS VERY CROWDED AND HAS NASTY, BUREAUCRATIC GUARDS.)

OFFICES AVAILABLE (PART 2)

6 AIRPLANE. (DOWNSIDE: YOU HAVE TO GO ON A TRIP.)

7. TRAIN. (DOWNSIDE: INEVITABLY YOU RUN INTO SOMEONE YOU KNOW, AND WHEN THEY ASK YOU WHO YOU'RE VISITING IN MONTAUK, YOU HATE YOURSELF.)

8. HOME. (DOWNSIDES: MESS. ROOMMATES. REMOTE NEIGHBORHOOD. JUST NO.)

9. RENTED APARTMENT IN FRANCE. (DOWNSIDE: SO EXTREME, YOU MUST REALLY BE IN CRISIS.)

10. PARENTS' HOUSE. (DOWNSIDE: THE CHILD INSIDE.)

11. FRIEND'S APARTMENT. (DOWNSIDE: LIKE YOU, YOUR FRIENDS ALL LIVE IN OUT-OF-THE-WAY PLACES. ONLY NOT THE SAME OUT-OF-THE-WAY PLACE AS YOU.)

12. THE CORPORATE OFFICE OF THE COMPANY YOU WORK FREELANCE FOR. (DOWNSIDES: FEAR OF BEING "FOUND OUT," QUESTIONED; NEED TO BE ON BEST BEHAVIOR AROUND THE HAND THAT FEEDS YOU, AND NOT TO BE SEEN WORKING ON UNRELATED THINGS.)

13. THE OUTDOORS NEAR YOU. (DOWNSIDES: WIND, NO DESK, UTTER INABILITY TO WORK.)

14. THE OUTDOORS FAR FROM YOU. (DOWNSIDES: WIND, NO DESK, UTTER INABILITY TO WORK, CRUSHING HOMESICKNESS.)

OFFICES AVAILABLE (PART 3)

15. UPSTAIRS PART OF DELIS. (DOWNSIDE:
THEY WERE NICER TEN YEARS AGO, WHEN
YOU CAME TO THE CITY, BEFORE THE CITY
GOT SO VERY RICH AND CROWDED. WHEN YOU
TRY TO CHASE THE CITY AS YOU FIRST FOUND
IT, YOU FEEL OUT OF TOUCH, LIKE A GHOST.)

16. BARNES AND NOBLE. (DOWNSIDES: TOO CROWDED,
FULL OF ANGRY TOURISTS. ALSO THE "15-MINUTE
TIME LIMIT.")

17. STARBUCKS. (CROWDED, DINGY, ANGRY.)

18. A NICER APARTMENT. (TOO EXPENSIVE.)

I LIVE HERE FOR THE MUSEUMS BUT I CAN'T BEAR THE MUSEUM CROWDS BUT

I NEED TO GET OUT OF THE CITY BUT I CAN'T BEAR PENN STATION BUT

1. "ALLOW" PEOPLE TO GO BEFORE YOU IN LINE. FEEL GENEROUS AND POWERFUL.

2. DO YOUR BEST TO HOLD ON TO YOUR PLACE IN LINE. FEEL LIKE THE ONE AWARE PERSON IN A SEA OF VIOLENT, GREEDY AUTOMATA.

OVERWHELMED BY CROWDS

LOOK AT PHONE

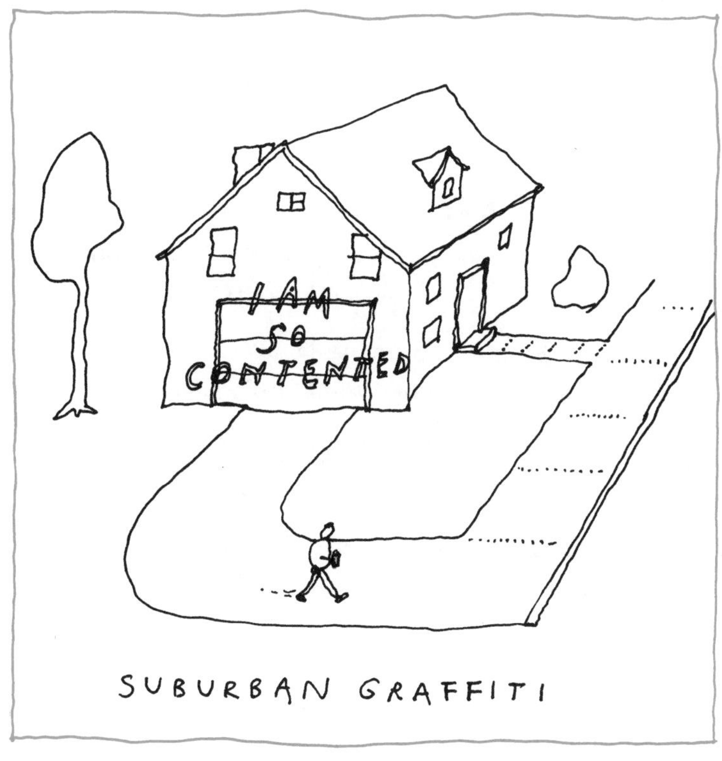
I AM SO CONTENTED

SUBURBAN GRAFFITI

THINGS PEOPLE SAY TO YOU WHEN YOU TELL THEM YOU ARE GOING TO VENICE

1. "YOU MUST GO TO GREECE."
2. "WHAT AIRPORT ARE YOU LEAVING FROM WHAT TERMINAL WHAT TIME?"
3. "I MET SOMEONE ONCE WHO LIVES IN FLORENCE. DO YOU WANT HIS NUMBER?"
4. "I BET YOU'LL HAVE A GREAT ROMANCE."
5. "RIDE A GONDOLA AND TAKE PICTURES!"
6. "LET'S SPEND A DAY TOGETHER THIS WEEK."
7. "CAN I VISIT YOU?"
8. "MAMMA MIA!"

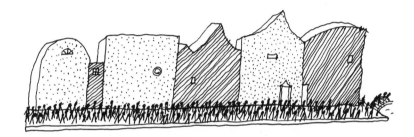

KEY

▨ = TOURIST TRAP

▣ = TOURIST-HATING ESTABLISHMENT

𝄐 = TOURIST

TRAVELOGUE

BEFORE BUYING SOMETHING:

WHAT AM I DOING HERE? WHERE SHOULD I HIDE?

VAGUE BLUR

AFTER BUYING SOMETHING:

(GREAT HARMONY OF BUILDINGS & TREES & YOU ARE PART OF IT; NEVER LEAVE THIS PLACE.)

1964

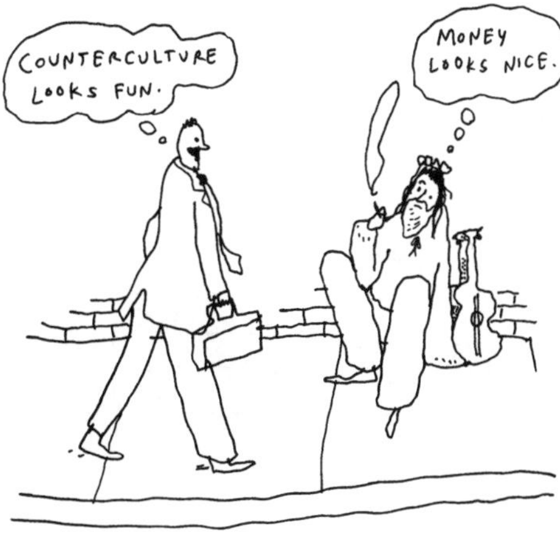
COUNTERCULTURE LOOKS FUN.
MONEY LOOKS NICE.

2016

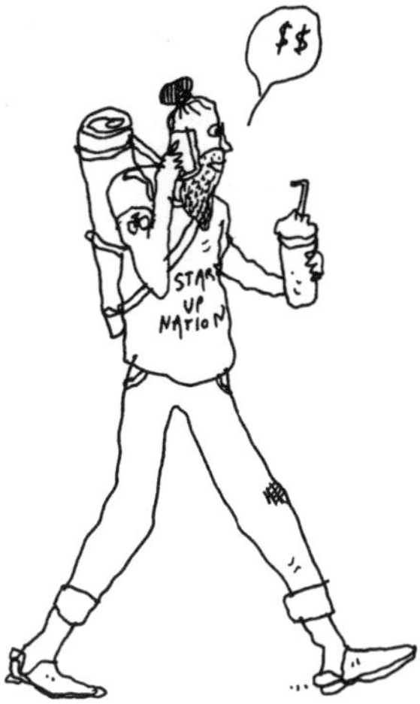
£$

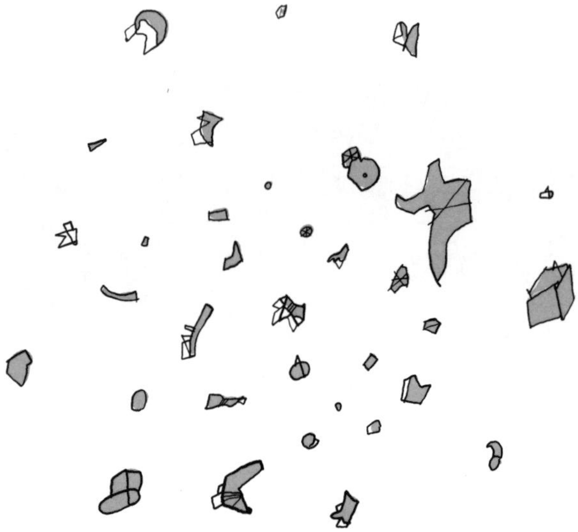

HISTORY: ASSEMBLE IT YOURSELF

FANTASIES

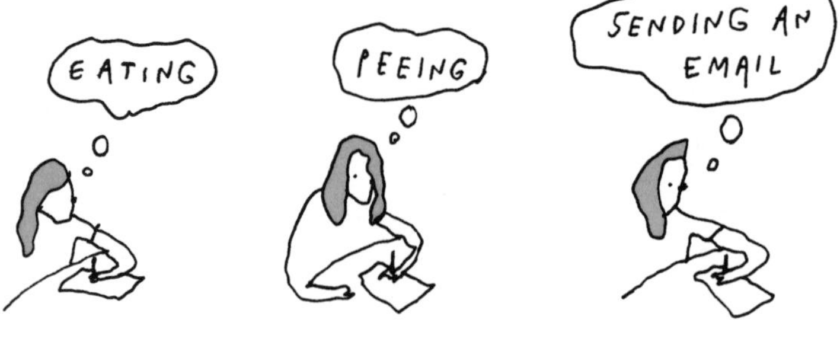
EATING
PEEING
SENDING AN EMAIL

THE PAST = WATER

THE MIND = SIEVE

———————————————————————————

THE PAST IS IN THE
      MEMORIES.
THE MEMORIES ARE IN
      THE EX-BOYFRIEND.
THE EX-BOYFRIEND IS IN
NEW JERSEY WITH HIS
      NEW GIRLFRIEND.

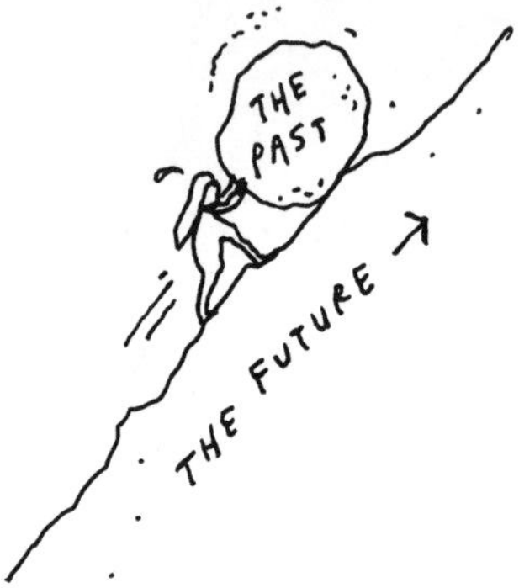
THE PAST
THE FUTURE →

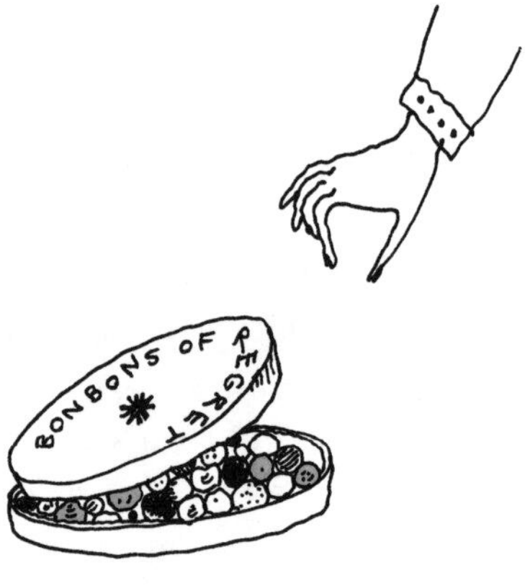
BONBONS OF REGRET

THE BIG
THINGS

THE LITTLE
THINGS →

SCALE MODEL
MOUNTAIN
MOLEHILL

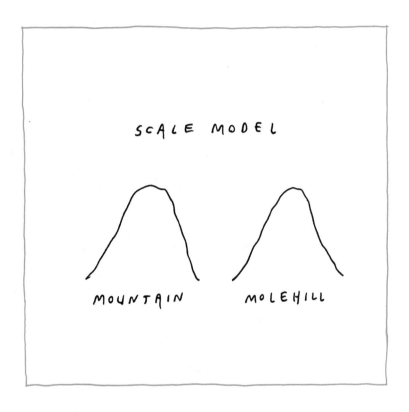

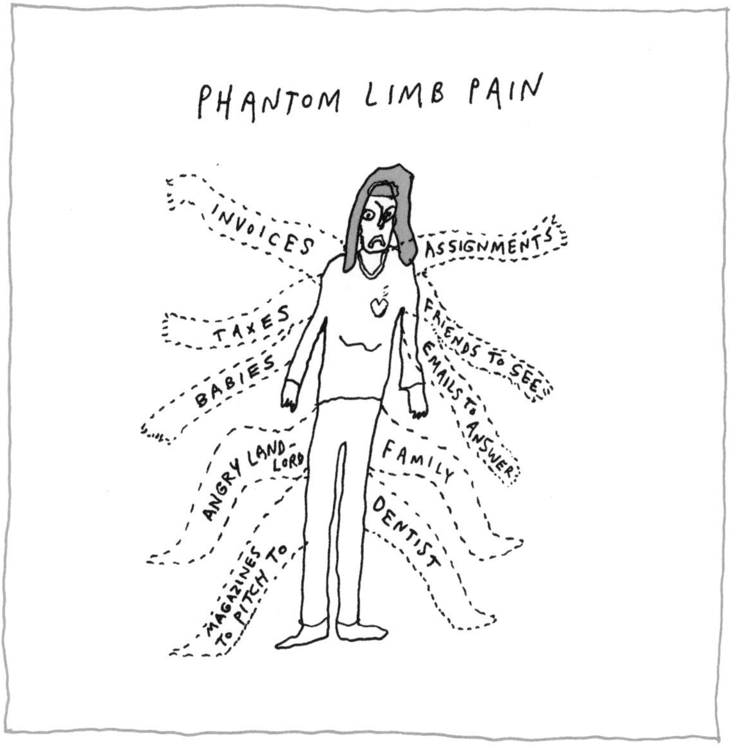
PHANTOM LIMB PAIN
INVOICES
ASSIGNMENTS
TAXES
FRIENDS TO SEE
BABIES
EMAILS TO ANSWER
ANGRY LANDLORD
FAMILY
DENTIST
MAGAZINES TO PITCH TO

THE STRENGTH TO
FILTER OUT SOME
PROJECTS IN ORDER
TO FOCUS ON OTHERS

THE FEAR OF
REFUSING TO TAKE ON
NEW CHALLENGES,
HIDING FROM SUCCESS

HOW HARD TO TRY

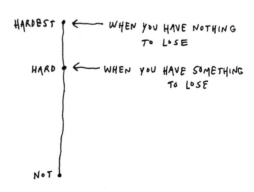

HARDEST ← WHEN YOU HAVE NOTHING
TO LOSE

HARD ← WHEN YOU HAVE SOMETHING
TO LOSE

NOT

WORK   FUN

CAT

YARN

WINDOW = POETRY

DOOR = PROSE

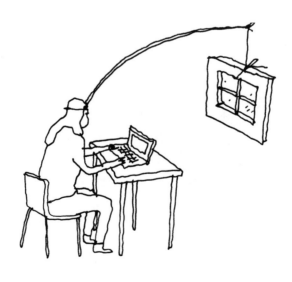

SCREENS
11 P.M.
7 A.M.
DREAMS

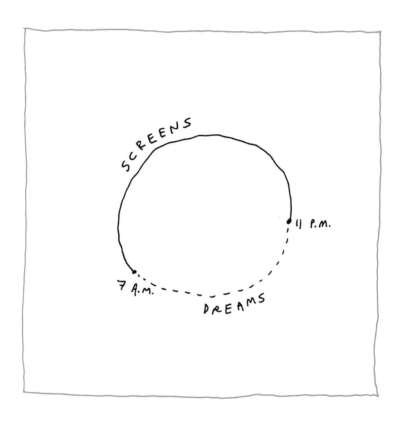

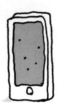

THE OFFENDING
OBJECT

STARING INTO THE VOID

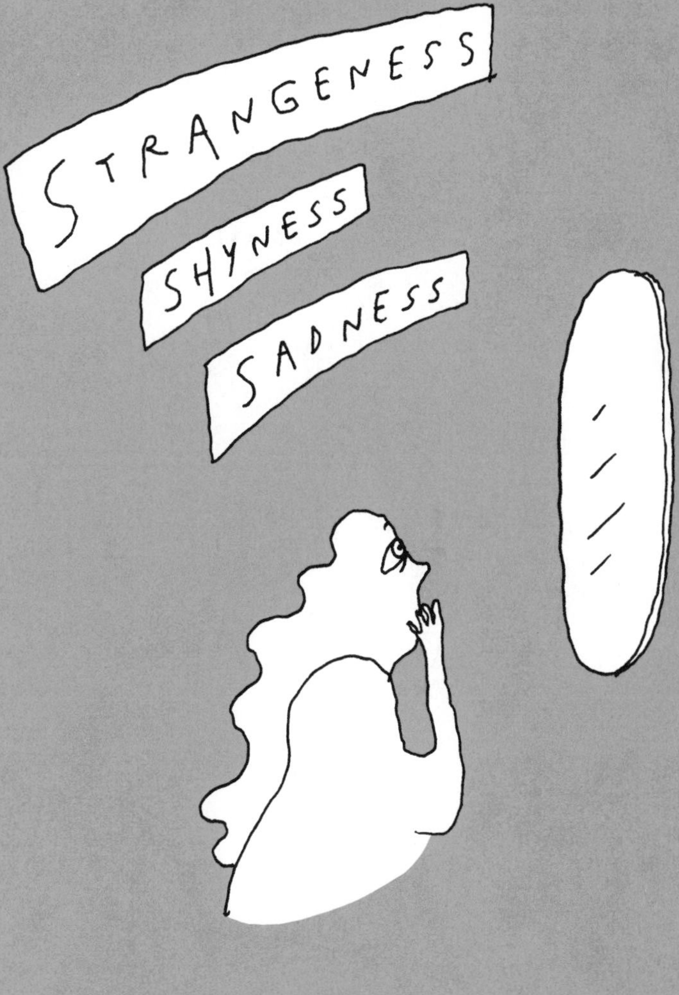
STRANGENESS
SHYNESS
SADNESS

AM I WEIRD
YES
NO
WHY
GENETIC ABNORMALITY
PARENTS
FORGOTTEN TRAUMA
HOW AM I WEIRD?

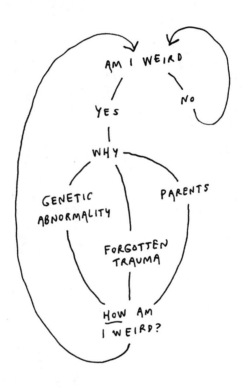

RINGS OF SELF-CONSCIOUSNESS

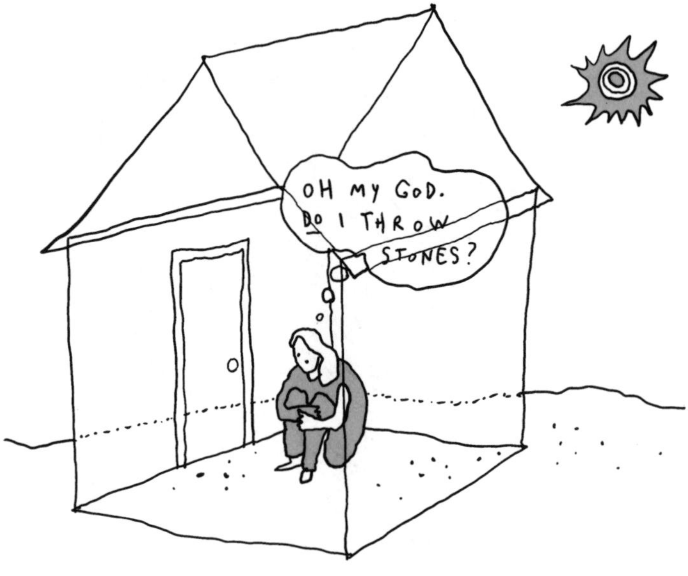
OH MY GOD.
DO I THROW STONES?

FEEL
OVERSENSITIVE

ACT
INSANE

MAKE PEOPLE
ANGRY

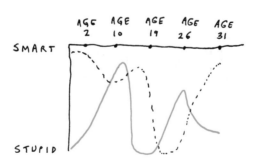

SMART

STUPID

AGE 2 AGE 10 AGE 19 AGE 26 AGE 31

KEY

☺ FEEL

☐ BE

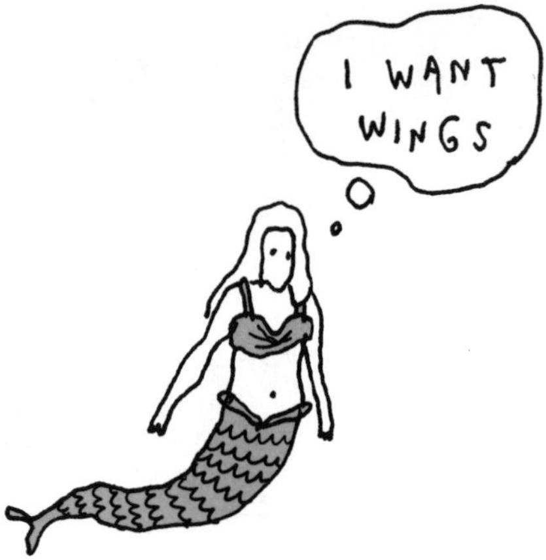
I WANT WINGS

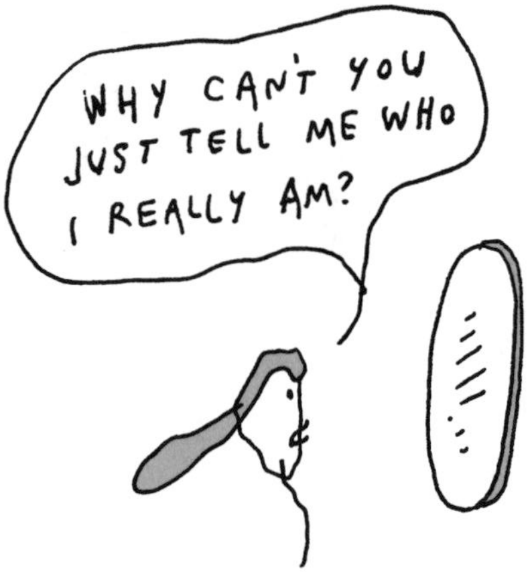
WHY CAN'T YOU JUST TELL ME WHO I REALLY AM?

THE PATHOLOGY OF THE MUMMY

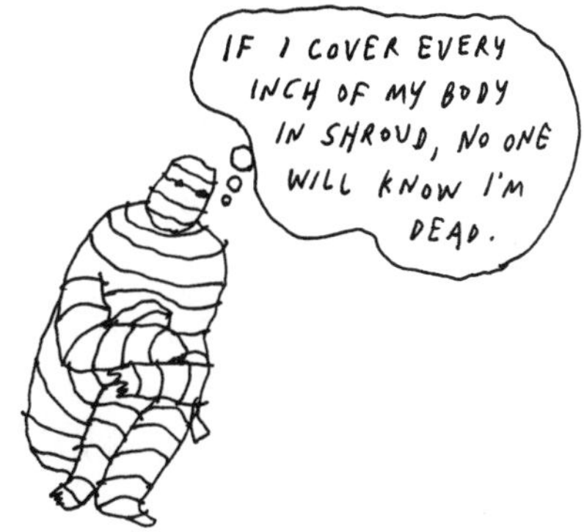
IF I COVER EVERY INCH OF MY BODY IN SHROUD, NO ONE WILL KNOW I'M DEAD.

INSIDE ME

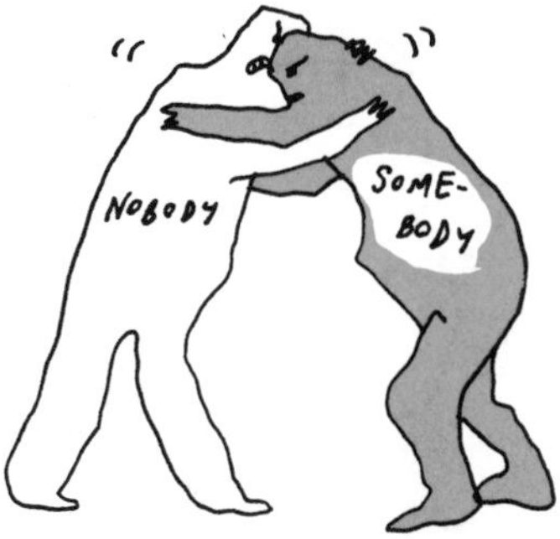
NOBODY
SOME-BODY

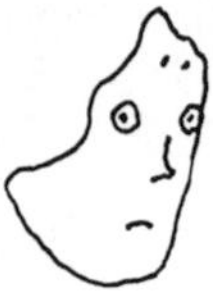

THE VERY BRIEF LOOK OF PANIC WHEN THEY REALIZE YOU DON'T FIT INTO ANY OF THE SOCIAL BOXES THEY KNOW OF

SELF-PORTRAIT

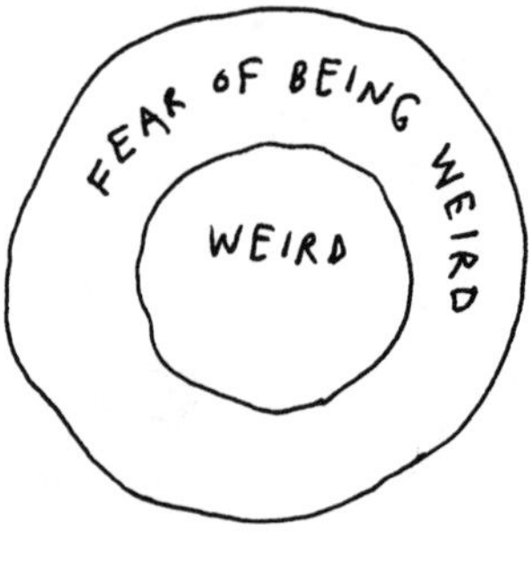
FEAR OF BEING WEIRD
WEIRD

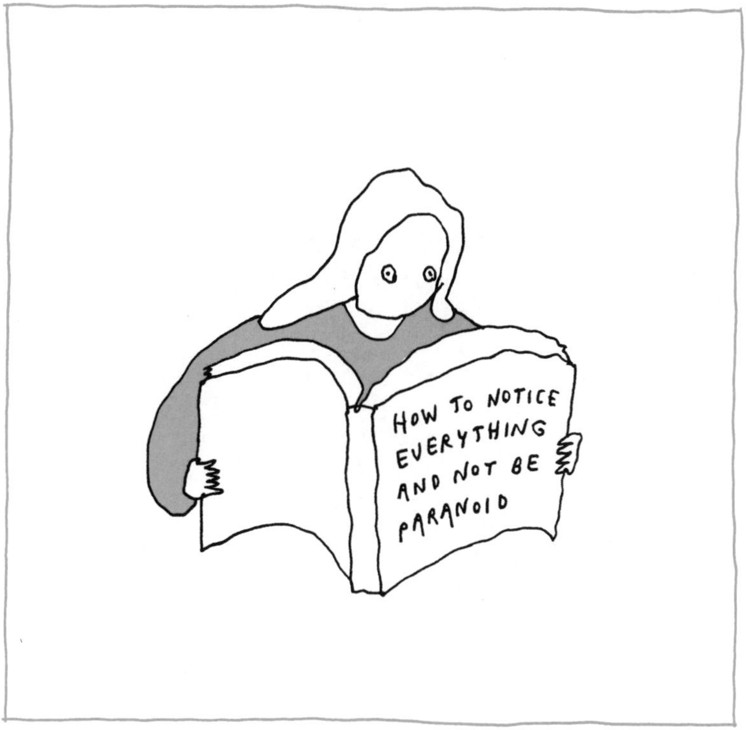
HOW TO NOTICE EVERYTHING AND NOT BE PARANOID

SELF-PORTRAIT,
WITH FEELINGS

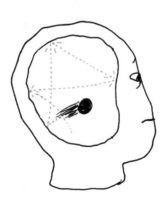

A THOUGHT

SHYNESS CHART

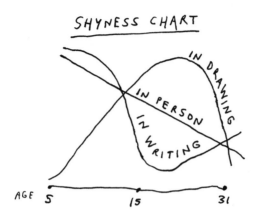

IN DRAWING

IN PERSON

IN WRITING

AGE 5 15 31

ON BEING STRANGE, AND FEMALE

DIFFICULTY OF NAVIGATING
LIFE WHEN YOUR NEEDS/
FEARS/ETC. ARE UNUSUAL
AND INTENSE

< ALWAYS TRYING HARD TO
MAKE SURE THE PEOPLE
AROUND YOU AREN'T HURT/
MAD/UNCOMFORTABLE
BECAUSE OF YOU

MY TWO DOMINANT PERSONALITY TRAITS

1. MUST MAKE EVERYONE COMFORTABLE AND HAPPY
2. CAN'T MAKE ANYONE COMFORTABLE OR HAPPY

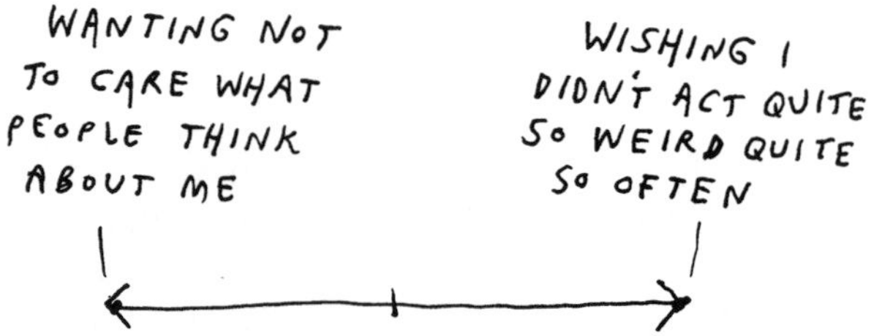
WANTING NOT TO CARE WHAT PEOPLE THINK ABOUT ME
WISHING I DIDN'T ACT QUITE SO WEIRD QUITE SO OFTEN

ONE MODEL

BORED   ANXIOUS

ANOTHER MODEL

BORED AND   NEITHER
ANXIOUS

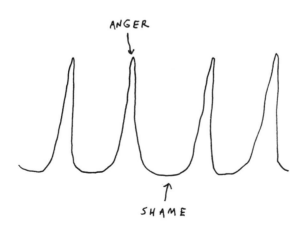

ANGER

SHAME

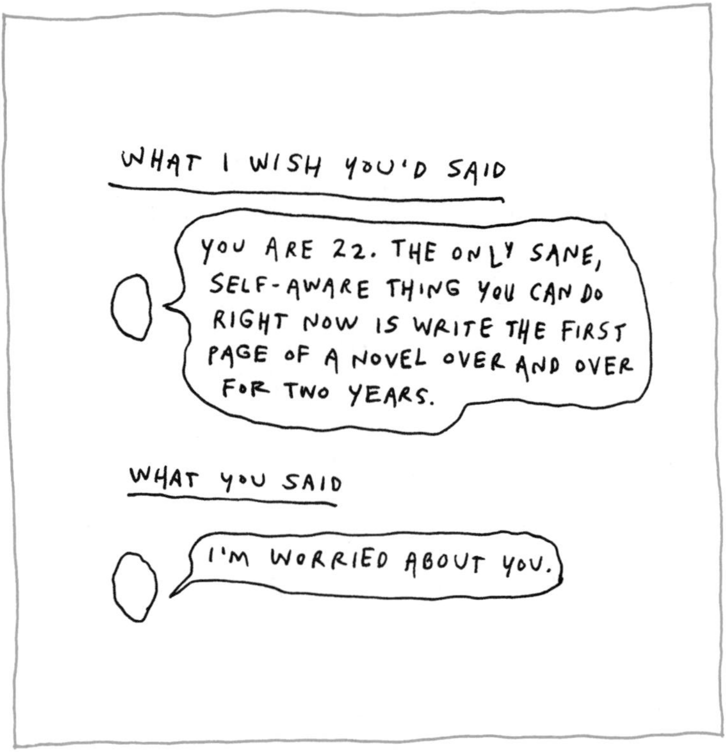
WHAT I WISH YOU'D SAID
YOU ARE 22. THE ONLY SANE, SELF-AWARE THING YOU CAN DO RIGHT NOW IS WRITE THE FIRST PAGE OF A NOVEL OVER AND OVER FOR TWO YEARS.
WHAT YOU SAID
I'M WORRIED ABOUT YOU.

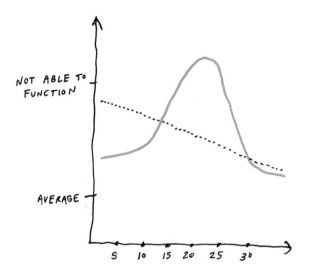

NOT ABLE TO FUNCTION

AVERAGE

5   10   15 20   25   30

KEY

[...] = WEIRDNESS

[ ] = SELF-CONSCIOUSNESS

I SAY	YOU SAY
"I AM NORMAL."	"SO WHY ARE YOU DOING THESE BIZARRE, NASTY, ANTISOCIAL THINGS?" ALSO: "STOP."
"IT IS A MENTAL ISSUE OF SOME SORT."	"WELL AREN'T YOU A SPECIAL LITTLE SNOWFLAKE."

☐ I AM SPECIAL

☑ I AM SPECIFIC

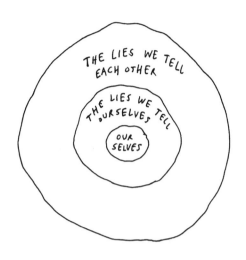

THE LIES WE TELL
EACH OTHER

THE LIES WE TELL
OURSELVES

OUR
SELVES

THE MARK OF
LOW SELF-ESTEEM

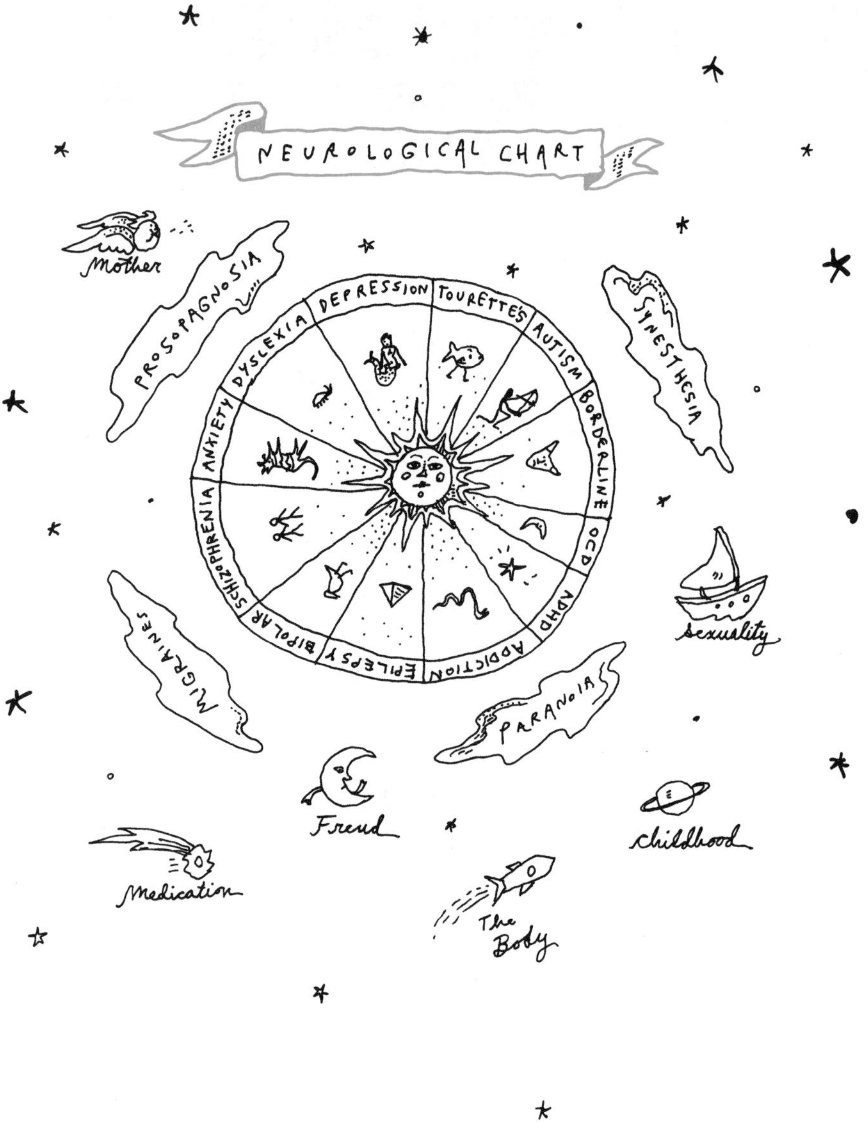
NEUROLOGICAL CHART
DEPRESSION
TOURETTE'S
AUTISM
BORDERLINE
OCD
ADHD
ADDICTION
EPILEPSY
BIPOLAR
SCHIZOPHRENIA
ANXIETY
DYSLEXIA
PROSOPAGNOSIA
SYNESTHESIA
MIGRAINES
PARANOIA
Mother
Sexuality
Freud
Childhood
Medication
The Body

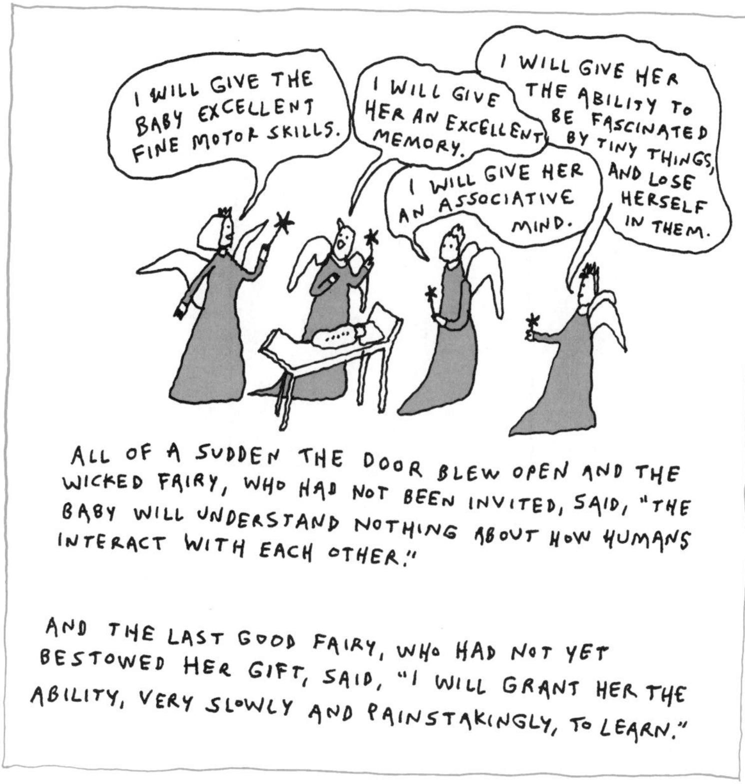
I WILL GIVE THE BABY EXCELLENT FINE MOTOR SKILLS.
I WILL GIVE HER AN EXCELLENT MEMORY.
I WILL GIVE HER AN ASSOCIATIVE MIND.
I WILL GIVE HER THE ABILITY TO BE FASCINATED BY TINY THINGS, AND LOSE HERSELF IN THEM.
ALL OF A SUDDEN THE DOOR BLEW OPEN AND THE WICKED FAIRY, WHO HAD NOT BEEN INVITED, SAID, "THE BABY WILL UNDERSTAND NOTHING ABOUT HOW HUMANS INTERACT WITH EACH OTHER."
AND THE LAST GOOD FAIRY, WHO HAD NOT YET BESTOWED HER GIFT, SAID, "I WILL GRANT HER THE ABILITY, VERY SLOWLY AND PAINSTAKINGLY, TO LEARN."

THE BOX

OUTSIDE THE BOX

TOO FAR OUTSIDE THE BOX

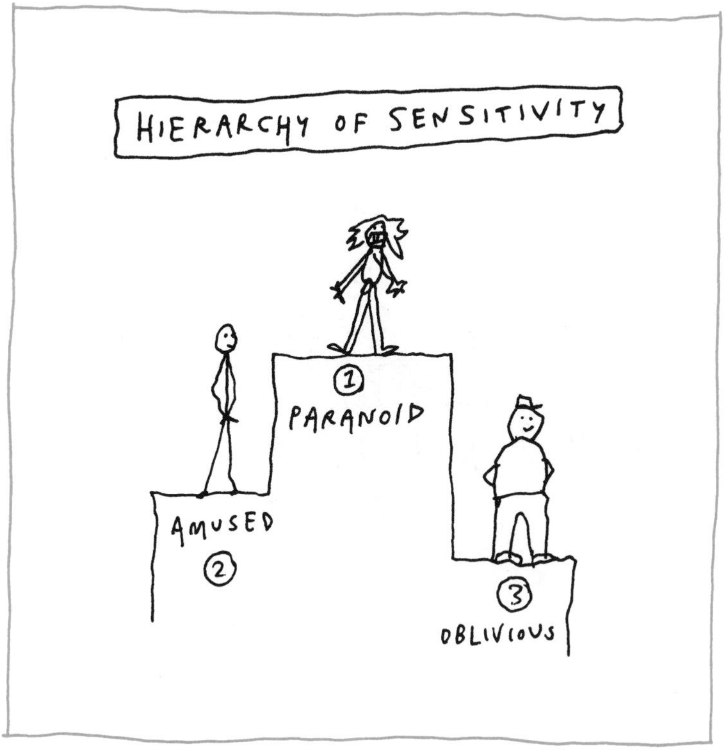
HIERARCHY OF SENSITIVITY
1
PARANOID
AMUSED
2
3
OBLIVIOUS

INPUT
OBSTACLE
OUTPUT

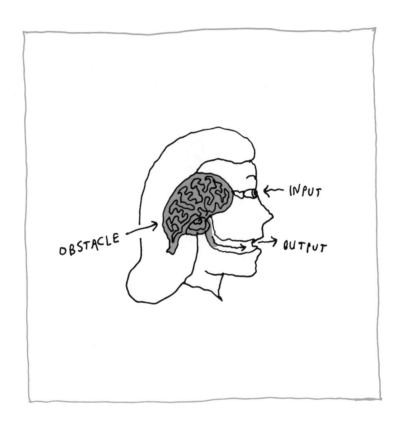

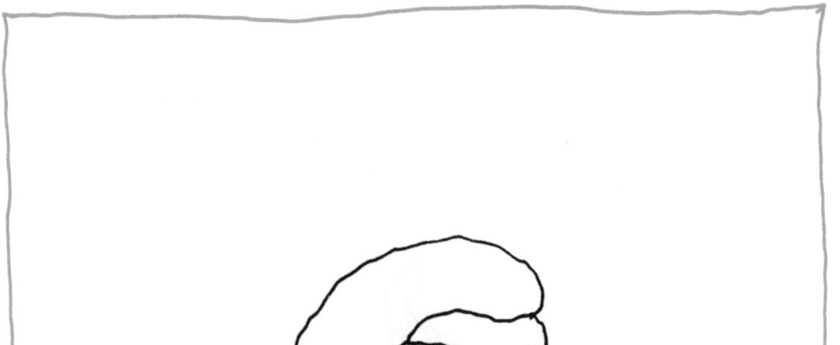

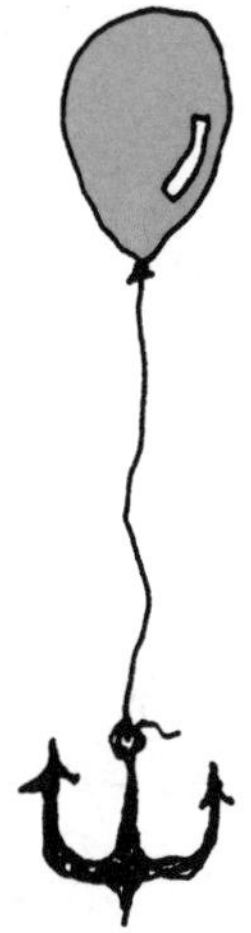

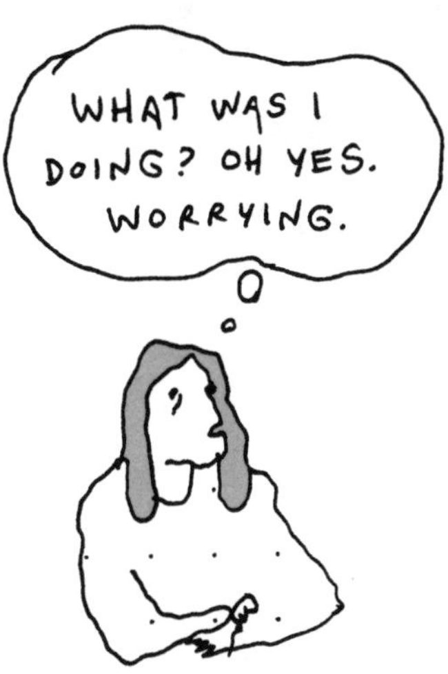
WHAT WAS I DOING? OH YES. WORRYING.

ADULT

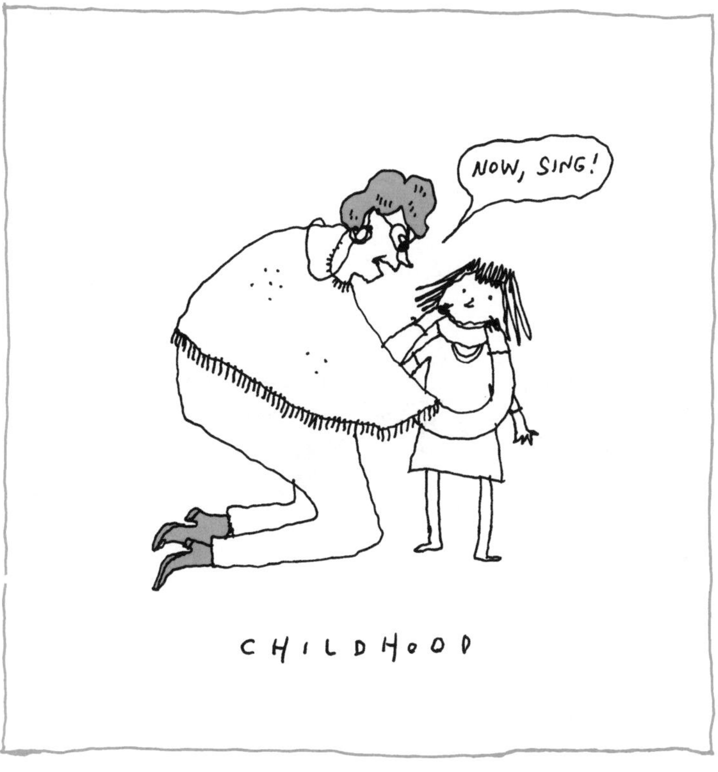
NOW, SING!

CHILDHOOD

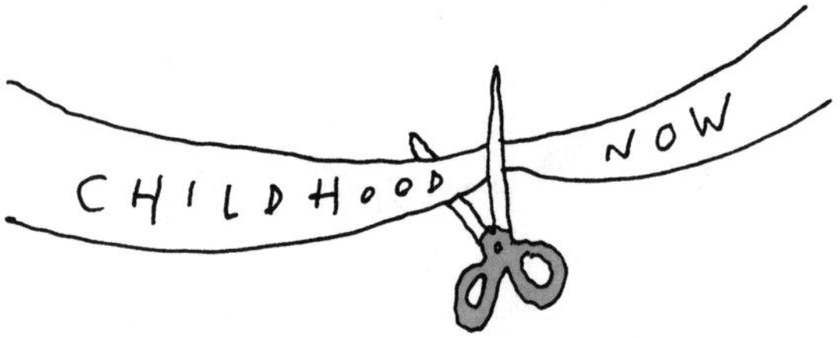
CHILDHOOD
NOW

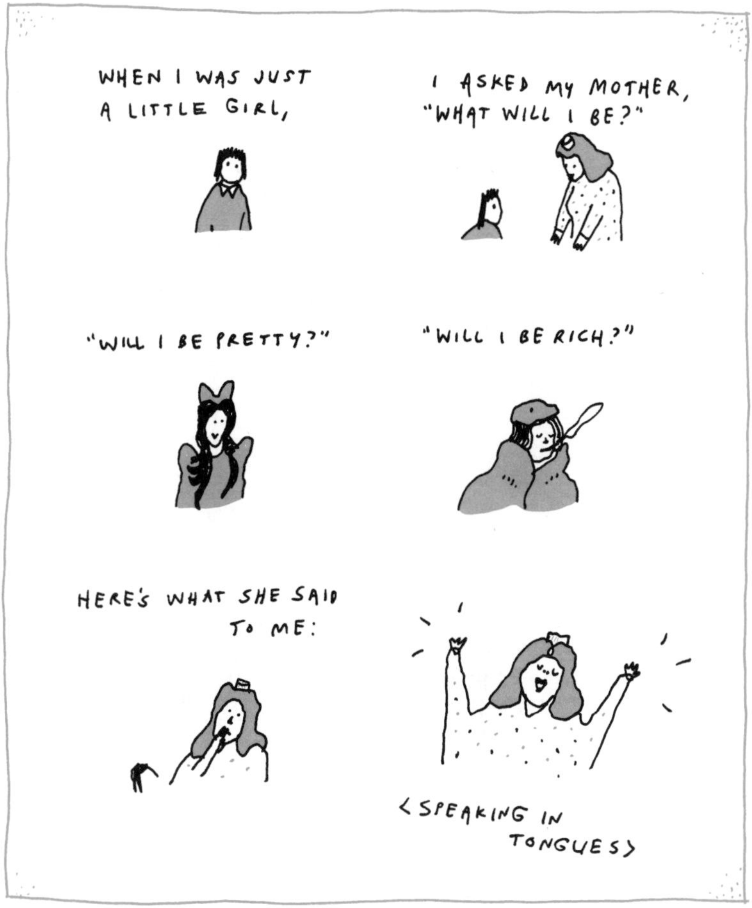
WHEN I WAS JUST A LITTLE GIRL,
I ASKED MY MOTHER, "WHAT WILL I BE?"
"WILL I BE PRETTY?"
"WILL I BE RICH?"
HERE'S WHAT SHE SAID TO ME:
<SPEAKING IN TONGUES>

CHILD
ADULT
ADULT
CHILD

CAN TIMMY COME OUT AND PLAY?

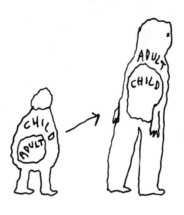

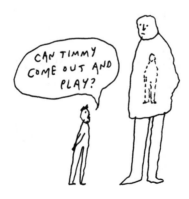

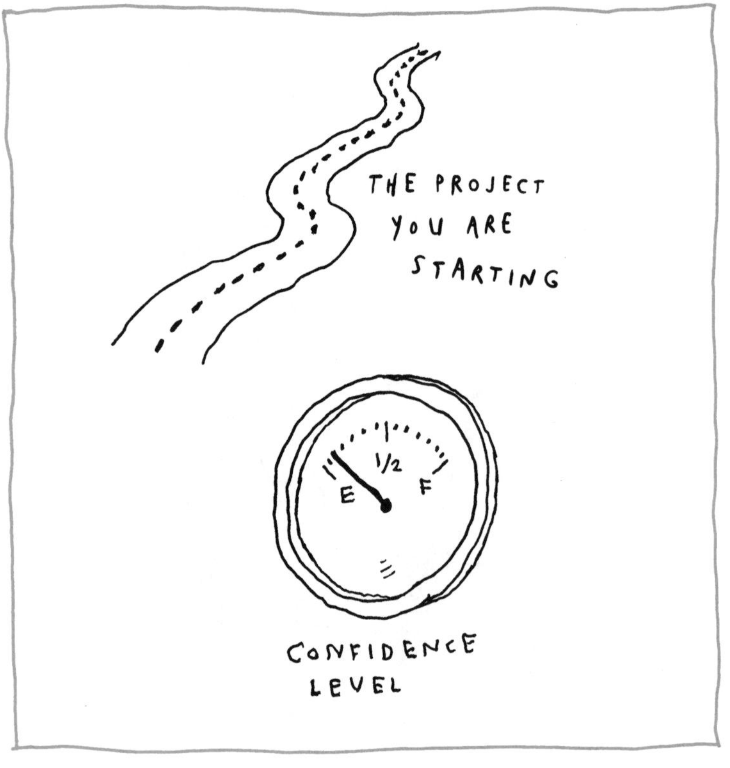
THE PROJECT
YOU ARE
STARTING
1/2
E
F
CONFIDENCE
LEVEL

THE FIRST STEP

351

A THEORY

HAPPY PERSON:
GETS ENOUGH
THINGS DONE
FOR TWO PEOPLE

SAD PERSON:
HUMANITY'S
COLLECTIVE
CONSCIENCE

A FUNDAMENTALLY LONELY
PERSON FIERCELY GUARDING
HER INDEPENDENCE

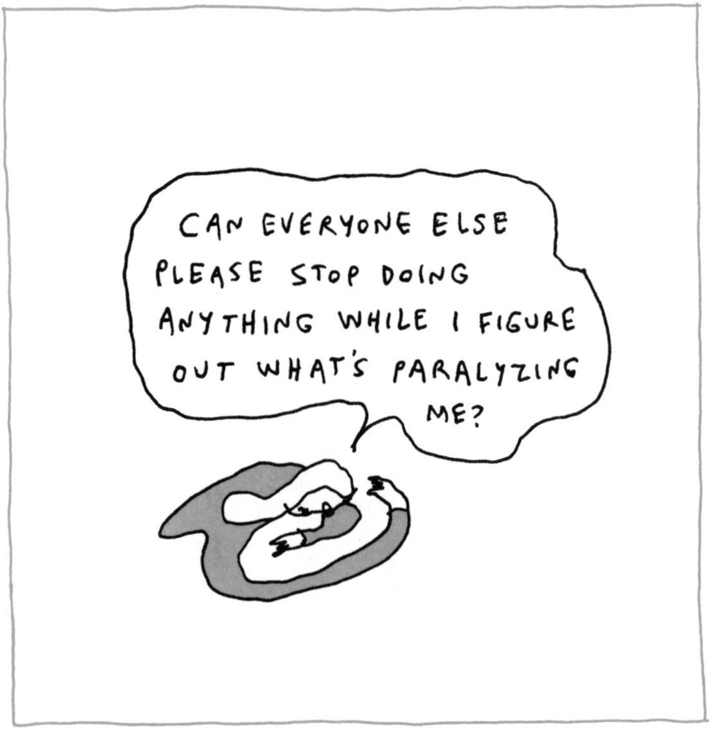
CAN EVERYONE ELSE PLEASE STOP DOING ANYTHING WHILE I FIGURE OUT WHAT'S PARALYZING ME?

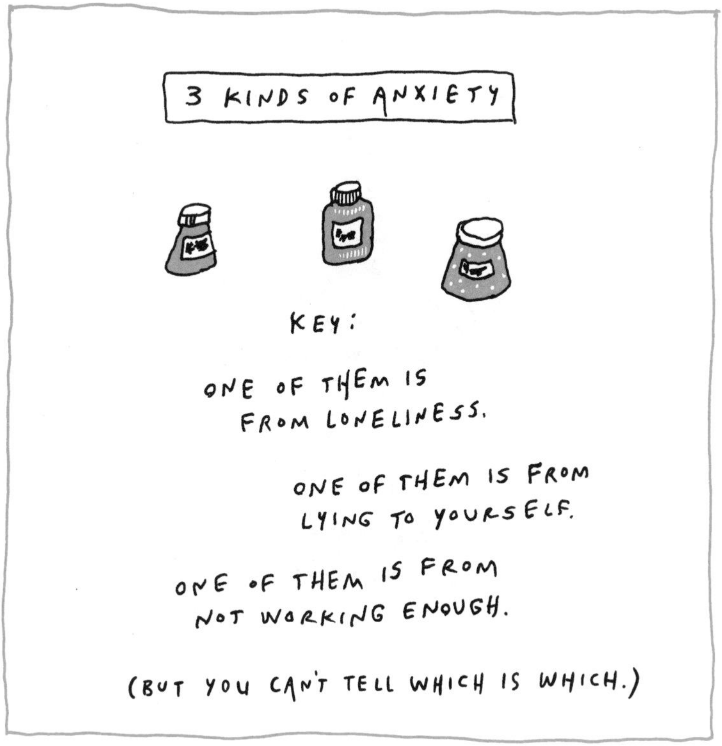
3 KINDS OF ANXIETY
KEY:
ONE OF THEM IS FROM LONELINESS.
ONE OF THEM IS FROM LYING TO YOURSELF.
ONE OF THEM IS FROM NOT WORKING ENOUGH.
(BUT YOU CAN'T TELL WHICH IS WHICH.)

EATING THE BRAIN OF
AN EASYGOING PERSON
(HELPS YOU RELAX)

HOW DO I GET OFF THIS HIGH HORSE?

CLEVERNESS
ANXIETY

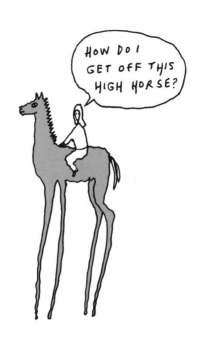

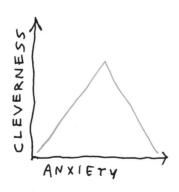

DEPRESSED   HAPPY

REALLY
CONFUSING
AND HORRIBLE

SHE
NEVER
BELONGED
HERE
ANYWAY

UPPERS	DOWNERS	DISTRACTORS
PARTIES	HUMIDITY	BUSYWORK
CAFES	UNCERTAINTY	PODCASTS
THE BEACH	DREAD	CLEANING
MUSIC		COFFEE DATES
SEX	OBLIGATIONS	SCHEMING
DRAWING	ABANDONMENT	ERRANDS
ART	WASTE	SLEEP

ANXIETIES

FOOD
MONEY
SCHEDULE
EXERCISE
WORK
TRAVEL
CAREER
SOCIAL LIFE
HEALTH
PEOPLE
BEING ALONE
NEATNESS
WEIGHT
MANNERS
CROWDS
PARENTS
DATING

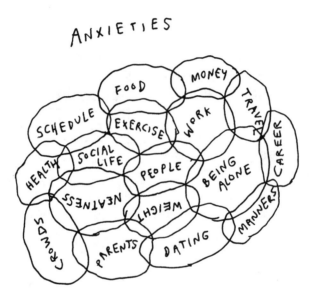

OH AND: DEATH.

MOOD: WORK

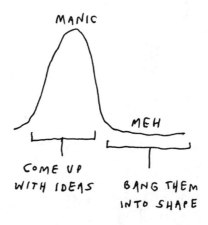

MANIC

MEH

COME UP
WITH IDEAS

BANG THEM
INTO SHAPE

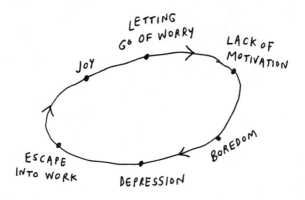

LETTING
GO OF WORRY

LACK OF
MOTIVATION

JOY

BOREDOM

ESCAPE
INTO WORK

DEPRESSION

362

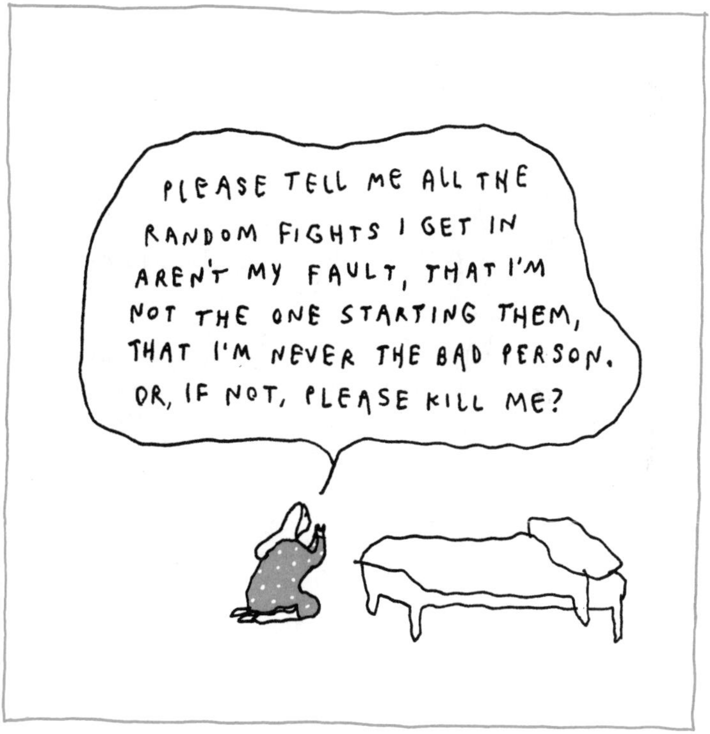
PLEASE TELL ME ALL THE RANDOM FIGHTS I GET IN AREN'T MY FAULT, THAT I'M NOT THE ONE STARTING THEM, THAT I'M NEVER THE BAD PERSON. OR, IF NOT, PLEASE KILL ME?

A GUIDE
MAJOR COWLICKS
INSOMNIA (NEW!)
SCALP PAIN (WHEN HAIR LONG)
OBSESSIVENESS
SPATIAL CONFUSION
TERROR
DEAD TOOTH (HURTS IN COLD WEATHER)
CANKER SORES
NEARSIGHTEDNESS
HEARTBURN (FROM PIZZA)
ASTIGMATISM
RINGWORM (GONE?)
PLASTIC
CRAMPS (LESS NOW)
NEED TO PICK AT THINGS, PULL OUT HAIR
CUTICLE STUFF
WRIST ISSUES (OCCUPATIONAL)
KNEE STUFF (FROM RUNNING)
VARICOSE ISSUES (FAMILY)
SHIN STUFF (SAME)
WEIRD NAILS (FROM WEIRD SHOES)
WART???
CRACKS
CALLUSES (RUNNING)

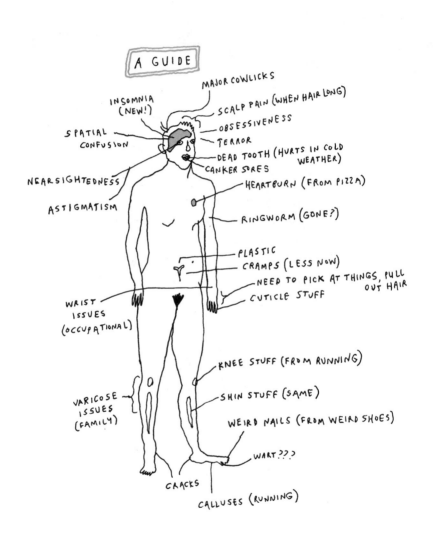

365

IF YOU'RE HAPPY AND
YOU KNOW IT, TURN THE
CORNERS OF YOUR MOUTH
UPWARD AND BARE YOUR
TEETH.

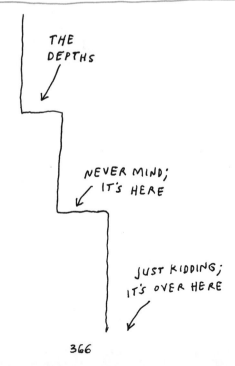

THE
DEPTHS

NEVER MIND;
IT'S HERE

JUST KIDDING;
IT'S OVER HERE

ALL-PURPOSE EMOTICON

DOGS BARK
CATS MEOW
PLANTS GROW
I REGRET

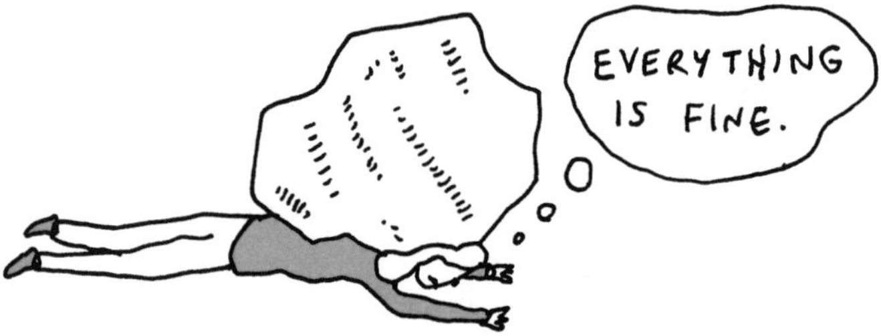
EVERYTHING IS FINE.

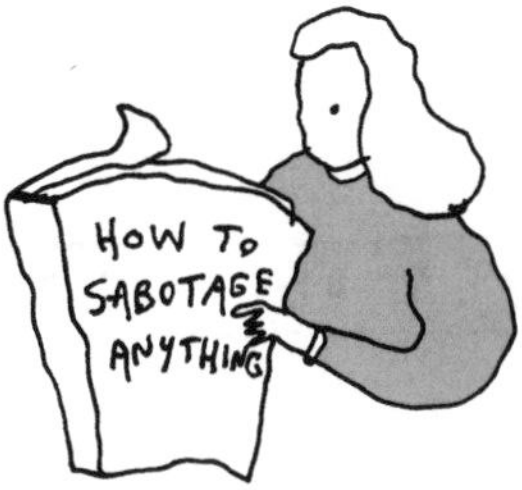
HOW TO
SABOTAGE
ANYTHING

THE OPTIMISTIC PESSIMIST

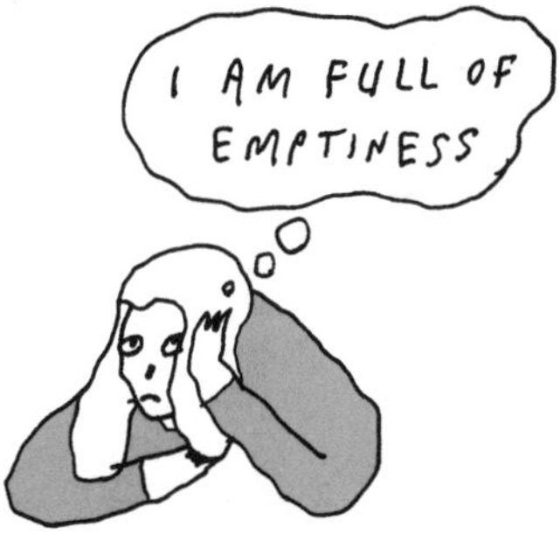
I AM FULL OF
EMPTINESS

TYPES OF SOLITUDE

BUBBLE

MIST

HOLE

VERY THICK
ONE-WAY MIRROR

PROUD SHIP

A THING

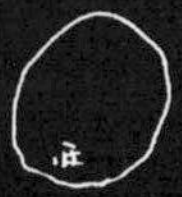

THE SAME THING, SEEN AT NIGHT

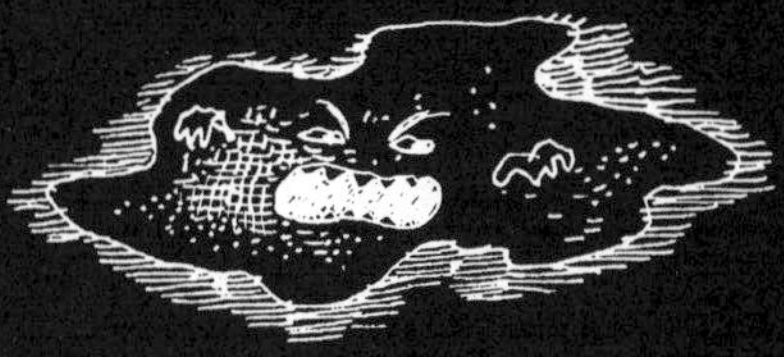

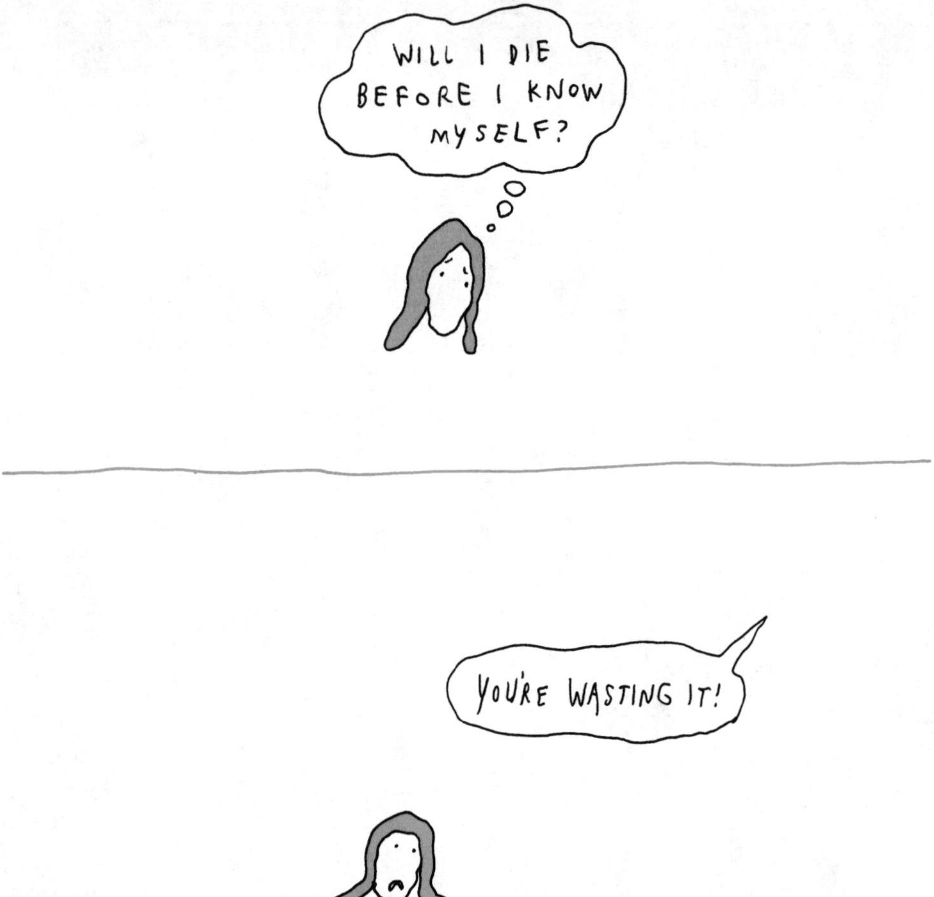
WILL I DIE BEFORE I KNOW MYSELF?
YOU'RE WASTING IT!

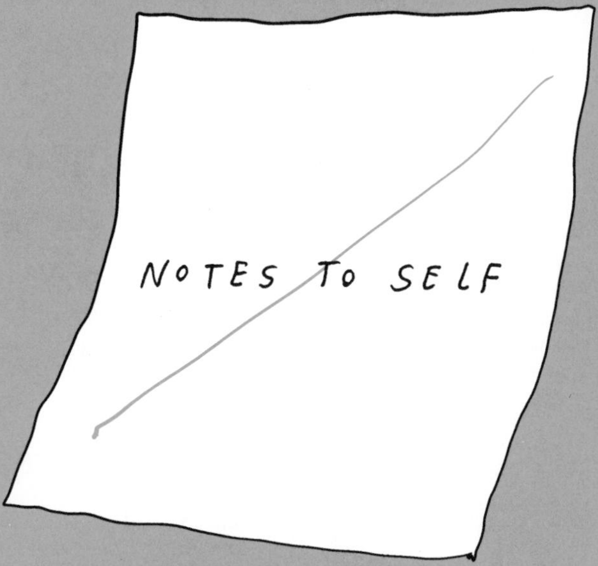
NOTES TO SELF

I AM A PUZZLE
I AM SOLVING.

THIS PUZZLE HAS NO PIECES.

CAN I EVER ATONE
FOR THE PAIN I HAVE
INFLICTED ON MYSELF?

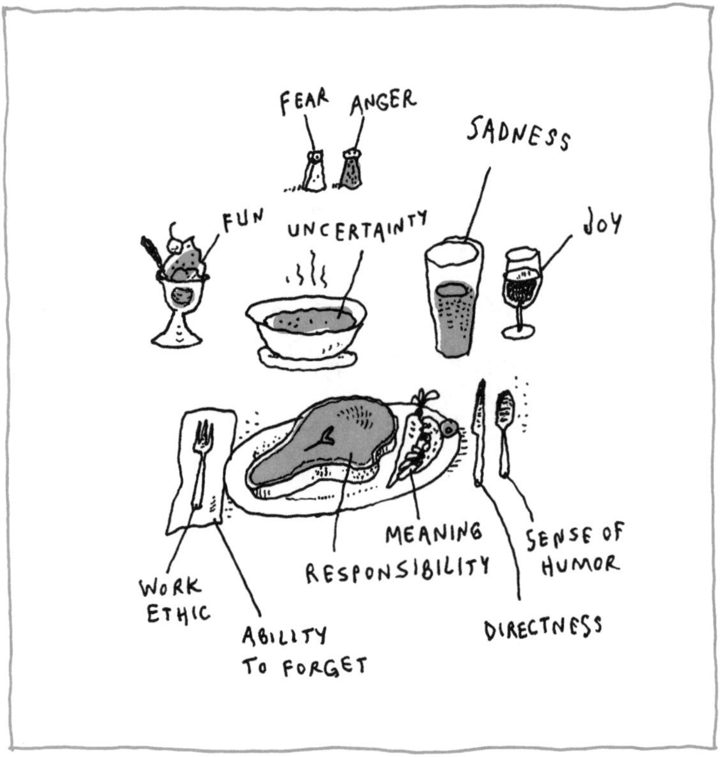

FEAR
ANGER
SADNESS
FUN
UNCERTAINTY
JOY
MEANING
SENSE OF HUMOR
RESPONSIBILITY
WORK ETHIC
ABILITY TO FORGET
DIRECTNESS

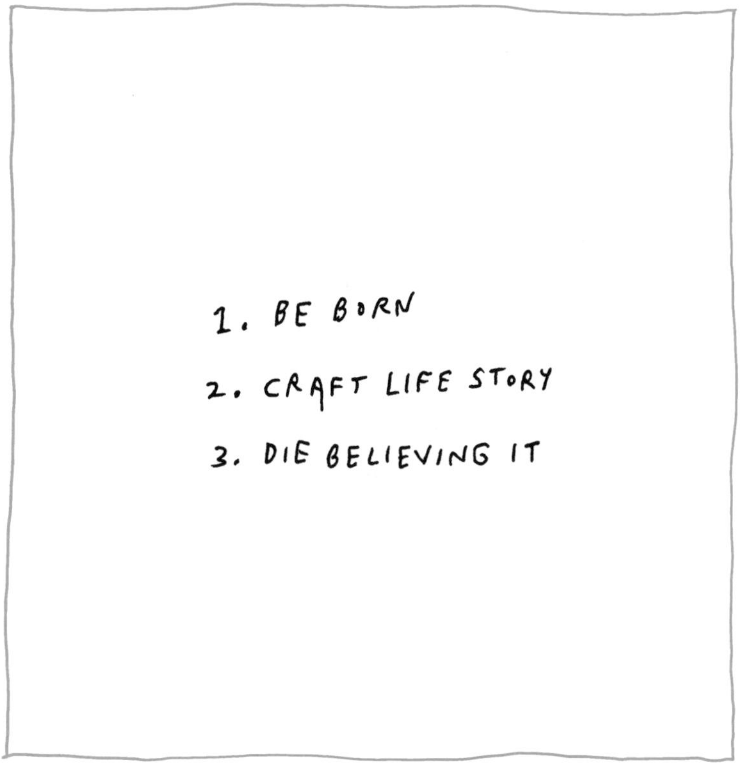
1. BE BORN
2. CRAFT LIFE STORY
3. DIE BELIEVING IT

NOT EVERYTHING
NEEDS TO BE
EVERYTHING.

HOW TO READ A BOOK

1. READ IT

2. CHANGE A LOT

3. REREAD IT

FEAR OF DROWNING. FEAR OF BEING MURDERED BY A MAN. FEAR OF ABANDONMENT. FEAR OF LOUD NOISES. FEAR OF BEING TOUCHED. FEAR OF BEING STARTLED. FEAR OF THE UNEXPECTED. FEAR OF BEING FOUND OUT. FEAR OF BEING IN THE WAY. FEAR OF REPERCUSSIONS. FEAR OF NOT BEING ABLE TO SAY NO. FEAR OF DYING. FEAR OF DYING BEFORE FINISHING BOOK. FEAR OF MAKING MEDIOCRE BOOK. FEAR OF NOT BEING HEARD. FEAR OF BEING A MONSTER. FEAR OF NOT BEING ABLE TO STOP. FEAR OF OWN OBLIVIOUSNESS. FEAR OF DRIVING AWAY FRIENDS AND EMPLOYERS. FEAR OF BEING ENSNARED BY FRIENDS AND EMPLOYERS. FEAR OF WILLFULLY BEING DELUDED. FEAR OF CHANGE. FEAR OF OWN STRENGTH. FEAR OF SNAKES.

THINGS THAT WILL FORSAKE YOU

1. YOUR JUDGMENT
2. YOUR ABILITY TO SAY NO AND OTHER THINGS YOU MEAN
3. YOUR ABILITY TO CONCENTRATE ON THINGS OUTSIDE YOURSELF
4. YOUR ABILITY TO CONCENTRATE ON THINGS INSIDE YOURSELF
5. EYE CONTACT
6. ABILITY TO SPEAK
7. ABILITY TO BREATHE
8. ABILITY TO STAY AWAKE
9. ABILITY TO SLEEP
10. YOUR FACADE
11. ALL SENSE OF PROPORTION

So IT WILL NOT BE EASY.
So THERE WILL BE PAIN.
So THERE WILL BE UNCERTAINTY.
So THERE WILL BE MISTAKES.
So THERE WILL BE REPERCUSSIONS.
So THERE WILL BE WORRY.
So THERE WILL BE REGRET.
So THERE WILL BE FAILURE.
So THERE WON'T BE A POINT.
So THERE WILL BE MISUNDERSTANDINGS
                ON EVERY SIDE.
So THIS WILL ALL BE FORGOTTEN.

THINGS I'VE LOST

3 GRANDPARENTS

2 DOGS

1 FAVORITE TEDDY BEAR (DOV)

1 FIRST FRIEND

1 SECOND FRIEND

MANY IRREPLACEABLE ROCKS

COUNTLESS OBSESSIONS (ALL REALLY ONE OBSESSION)

COUNTLESS MEN (ALL REALLY THE SAME MAN)

Too ANXIOUS TO BE NICE.
Too SENSITIVE TO BE EASYGOING.
Too DETAIL-ORIENTED TO SEE THE BIG PICTURE.
Too OBSESSIVE TO RELAX.
Too PRIVATE TO BE OPEN.
Too BRITTLE TO BE WARM.
Too PRINCIPLED TO LET SELF OFF HOOK.
Too SPECIFIC TO BE SUCCESSFUL.
Too HONEST TO BE KIND.
Too RIGOROUS TO LAUGH.
Too AMBITIOUS TO LET THINGS GROW.

WHEN I'M NOT
LAUGHING OR
CRYING OR
YELLING OR RUNNING
I'M DYING.

Q: WHO AM I?

☐ I AM WHAT IS INSIDE ME.

☐ I AM WHAT SURROUNDS ME.

☐ I AM WHAT COMES OUT OF ME.

TO YOU WHO SAID A SCATHING
"EXCUSE ME," AND THEN A
SARCASTIC "HAVE A NICE DAY":
MAY YOUR "POLITENESS"
BRING YOU "PLEASURE."

TWO WAYS TO MAKE A THING WORTHWHILE

1. STEP BACKWARD AND FIND THE HUMOR IN IT.

2. STEP FORWARD AND FIND THE MEANING IN IT.

	THINGS I DON'T BELIEVE IN	THINGS I DO BELIEVE IN
①	GHOSTS	NOTHING EVER DISAPPEARS
②	GOD	WE ARE SEEN
③	HEALING PROPERTIES OF CRYSTALS	INDIVIDUAL PERSONALITIES OF ROCKS
④	MIRACLES	SURPRISES
⑤	MAGIC	MEANING
⑥	PSYCHICS	INTUITION
⑦	RELIGIOUS DOCTRINE	HOLINESS OF STORY
⑧	MONETARY VALUE OF ART	HOLINESS OF OBJECTS, AND OF TIME
⑨	FAITH HEALING	POWER OF BELIEF
⑩	ASTROLOGY	ASTROLOGY AS STORY (SEE No. 7)
⑪	HAUNTINGS	THE LINGERING PAST
⑫	RELIGIOUS FIGURES	INVISIBLE THREADS BETWEEN PEOPLE
⑬	THE OCCULT	THE NEED FOR THE OCCULT

WAYS TO HAVE MEANING IN LIFE
(OTHER THAN LOVING SOMEONE)

1. BE SOME KIND OF GHOST THAT WANDERS AROUND SAYING, "THIS IS BEAUTIFUL, THAT IS BEAUTIFUL."
2. BE "GOOD" TO YOUR FRIENDS AND FAMILY AND THE WORLD.
3. BE ANGRY. SHINE.
4. HAVE WILD DREAMS OF "WHEN I WILL FINALLY COME INTO MY OWN." (IGNORE THE FACT THAT YOU ARE ALREADY 30).
5. PRETEND YOU'RE A CHARACTER IN A MOVIE (AGAIN, IGNORING THE FACT THAT YOU'RE 30).
6. USE SADNESS AS A FORM OF EXTREME FOCUS.
7. APPRECIATE WHAT YOU HAVE.

THINGS THAT MAKE ME PANIC #1 BEING AT A CROSSROADS WITH WORK. FINISHING IMMERSIVE AUDIOBOOK SERIES. HUMIDITY. LOOMING PLANS THAT INVOLVE UNUSUAL TYPES OF TRAVEL. INDEFINITE PLANS. HAVING TO SEE A PLAY. HAVING TO SEE A MOVIE. HAVING TO TELL A FRIEND I LIKED THEIR ART. BEING LOOKED AT. BEING STARTLED. SNAKES REAL OR IMAGINED. THE TIME BETWEEN AGREEING TO SEE SOMEONE AND FIXING ON A TIME AND PLACE. SITTING ON A BENCH IN THE MIDDLE OF A WALKING PATH. UNCERTAINTY. NARROW SIDEWALKS. A MESS I DID NOT MAKE BUT MAY HAVE TO CLEAN. LOSS OF CONTROL. NUTELLA. BEING REPRIMANDED. BEING SINGLED OUT. ASKING SOMEONE TO DO SOMETHING. WAITING IN LINE. WAITING FOR AN ANSWER. WAITING FOR A PHONE CALL. RESPONSIBILITY. LACK OF RESPONSIBILITY. LONELINESS. FIXED PLANS. NO PLANS. DAYTIME, NOT INCLUDING MORNING. ADMITTING TO MY FRIENDS HOW MUCH ALONE TIME I NEED. FOOD WITHOUT PORTIONS. KNOWING THERE WILL BE FOOD BUT NOT KNOWING WHAT IT WILL BE. NOT KNOWING HOW I'LL GET HOME. LONG STRETCHES OF TIME BETWEEN PLACES. NOT AGREEING WITH SOMEONE I RESPECT. SUBWAY TRANSFERS. SUBWAYS AT NIGHT. TAXIS. RUNNING OUT OF TOOTHPASTE (WHILE ON THE GO) AND FLOSS (AT HOME). BUREAUCRACY. TO-DO LISTS. BEING SUCKED INTO A CHORE SPIRAL. SURPRISES. RELATIONSHIPS THAT MAY OR MAY NOT BE. LATE-NIGHT GET-TOGETHERS. PICNICS. POTLUCKS. BEING ASKED A FAVOR. ASKING A FAVOR. RACCOONS. RANDOM COMMENTS FROM STRANGERS. INVASIVE INTIMACY FROM STRANGERS. MY OWN RUDENESS. BEING ASKED TO REPEAT MYSELF. BEING ASKED TO WRITE A CLEAR, FACTUAL PARAGRAPH. BEING ASKED TO TRY OUT FOR SOMETHING. EXPECTATIONS. BULLSHIT. FAKE SMILES. PHONY TONES OF VOICE. GUNSHOTS. ROADS WITHOUT SIDE-WALKS. FLASHING LIGHTS. NOT BEING ABLE TO BREATHE. MEETING UP FOR DINNER FIRST. UNNECESSARY PHYSICAL PROXIMITY. MOVEMENT IN MY PERIPHERAL VISION. CAR TRIPS. MATH. THE BILL (SPLITTING, PAYING, OR NOT PAYING). MARIJUANA. SINGING IN A GROUP. DANCING IN PUBLIC. DANCING IN PRIVATE. WEIGHT GAIN. JUDGMENT CALLS.

THINGS THAT MAKE ME PANIC #2   THE NEEDS OF LOVED ONES.
BEING SCOLDED. UNFORESEEN MOODS. MIDTOWN. BEING ACCOSTED WHILE
NOT WEARING A BRA AND/OR CONTACTS. RUNNING OUT OF DEODORANT.
ENDLESS REVISIONS. DISTRUSTING MYSELF. PUBIC HAIR (YEA, NAY, OR
OTHER). HAIRCUTS. LOUD NOISES. BEING WRENCHED OUT OF CONCENTRATION.
RIDING A BIKE ON A ROAD. PRETENDING TO BE EASYGOING. BEING
FORCED TO EAT. READING MAPS. WAITING FOR THE LIGHT TO CHANGE.
CHANGING INTO OR OUT OF RUNNING CLOTHES. GYM LOCKER ROOMS.
NOT BEING ABLE TO GET OUT OF THE HOUSE. HAVING TO ENDURE A
SO-SO PODCAST. BED BUGS. LUNCH MEETINGS. BEING INVITED TO
RIDGEWOOD, QUEENS. THANK-YOU CARDS (WRITING). GIFTS (GIVING).
NETWORKING. BEING CALLED UPON TO RECOGNIZE ACQUAINTANCES. TRAFFIC.
BOATS. RITUALS (HAVING TO KEEP THEM). RITUALS (FAILING TO KEEP THEM).
BADLY DEFINED LINES IN SUPERMARKETS. COURTSHIP. HAVING TO GET
A BARTENDER'S ATTENTION. TRYING TO BE CHARMING WHILE AVOIDING
ALL THE SUBJECTS THAT COULD POSSIBLY OFFEND. BEING ASKED TO
MOVE. CRAFTING A POLITE LIE. BEING PUT ON HOLD. FRATERNITIES.
SORORITIES. LARGE STROLLERS. SLOW GROUPS. DECIDING HOW LATE
TO BE. NAVIGATING FOR OTHERS. LYING IN BED. SOFT, MUSHY FURNITURE.
ILLNESS. TV. CLUTTER. FILTH. LETTING PEOPLE BORROW MY STUFF.
BOOMING VOICES. CUTE SNEEZES. CLICHÉS. AUTOTUNE. BEING IGNORED.
BEING TOUCHED. BEING CONDESCENDED TO. BEING INGRATIATED TO. WAITING
FOR SOMEONE TO "DROP IN." BEING ASKED TO "DROP IN." COOKING FOR
OTHERS. MOVING. WRITING CONDOLENCE LETTERS. TRAVEL PLANNING. BIG
DECISIONS. LITTLE DECISIONS. ARCHIVING OWN WORK. SENDING INVOICES.
THINKING OF A MEANINGFUL COMPLIMENT. EYE CONTACT. BEING APPROACHED
BY "FRIENDS OF FRIENDS." BATHING SUITS. HANGING OUT. REJECTION.
HIDING MY ANXIETY. CHRISTMAS MUSIC. BOY SCOUTS. GIRL SCOUTS.
GRAY AREAS. BEING FORCED TO CHOOSE A SIDE. A PACKED SCHEDULE.
MEAT. SPORTS FANS. WAITING FOR A PACKAGE. REMEMBERING OTHER
PEOPLE'S LIFE DETAILS. MESSING UP. OTHERS BREAKING INTO SONG.
BEING SPOKEN TO SARCASTICALLY. NAZISM. RACISM. CRUELTY. DECIPHERING
TERSE EMAILS. BEING ASKED IF THIS SEAT IS TAKEN. LONG TEXT
CONVERSATIONS. INVISIBLE OPPRESSION. PORN. PARADES. FACE PAINT.
MASKS. SLICKNESS. BEING LOOKED THROUGH. BEING HIT ON. LACK
OF IRONY. FAITH HEALING. MEANINGFUL CRYSTALS. NAPS.
SIGHTSEEING. HAVING MY TABLE SHAKEN.

THINGS THAT CALM ME DOWN

LOW LIGHT. EVENING. NIGHT. SITTING UNDER
FURNITURE. SINGING ALONE. DRIVING ON HIGHWAYS.
AIRPLANES. TRAINS. RUNNING. BIKING. BEING ALONE
IN A BEAUTIFUL NEW PLACE. A FREE EVENING.
HAVING MY OWN BATHROOM. GROUPS OF THREE.
FANCY PARTIES. AN UNEXPECTED FREE EVENING.
MUSEUMS AT NIGHT. WATER. FEELING LOST IN
A FAMILIAR PLACE. FEELING AT HOME IN AN
UNFAMILIAR PLACE. SEX. BEING COOKED FOR.
BEING TAKEN CARE OF. BEING SO SAD I STOP
BEING ANXIOUS. BEING AROUND HAPPY PEOPLE.
GOING TO A CAFE IN THE MORNING. GENUINE
SMILES. READING (NOT AS AN ASSIGNMENT).
DRAWING (AS AN ASSIGNMENT). GOSSIPING. HAVING
MY HEAD SQUEEZED. GRAND BUILDINGS (BUT NOT
SIGHTSEEING). OLD THINGS. ANIMALS. MEANINGFUL
STORIES. MUSIC. BEING MINIMAL. HAVING WHAT
I NEED. CLEANING. CITY PARKS. SILENT FILM.
EAVESDROPPING. KNOWING WHAT I WANT TO SAY.
FLOWERS. SNOW. EXOTIC FRUIT. SALAD BUFFETS.
HEIGHTS. SCHEDULES. HARD LIQUOR (IN MODERATION).
CAREFULLY CRAFTED SITUATIONS. MOVIES IN
THEATERS. PICKING FRUIT. BREAKING RULES,
MY OWN INCLUDED. CHECKING MY PHONE. PUTTING
MY PHONE DOWN. LONG TEXT CONVERSATIONS WITH
FRIENDS. BEING IN LOVE. NOT BEING IN LOVE. PEOPLE.
BREEZES. BEACHES. STRONG WIND. BEING ANGRY.
FANCY BARS. CLOUDY DAYS. REMINISCING. ESCAPE.
FORCING MYSELF TO LOOK AT PEOPLE. PERFORMING.
                    WIDE EMPTY SPACES.

THINGS I'M ASHAMED I CAN'T DO

DANCE · TRAVEL WITH PEOPLE · FOLLOW
DIRECTIONS · LIE · DAY TRIPS WITH PEOPLE ·
LONG HOLIDAYS · SIT THROUGH THINGS ·
SMALL TALK · RESPOND POLITELY WHEN
STARTLED · READ TO ESCAPE · GO TO
CROWDED MUSEUMS · TAKE COMPLICATED
SUBWAY RIDES · CHANGE MY ROUTINE ·
EAT GRATUITOUSLY CALORIC FOOD THAT ISN'T
VERY GOOD · DRINK BEER · WATCH LOUD
MOVIES · CASUAL SEX · HAVE HOUSE GUESTS ·
BE A HOUSE GUEST · BE POLITE TO A STRANGER
IN A CROWDED, NOISY PLACE · SHARE A SMALL
CAFE TABLE · EAT SOMETHING UNPLANNED FOR
BREAKFAST · WATCH MEN PLAY SPORTS · BE
SPONTANEOUS (OR RATHER, GO ALONG WITH
SOMEONE ELSE'S SPONTANEITY) · COLLABORATE ·
WORK FOR FREE · DO THE SAME THING OVER
AND OVER LIKE A GOOD ARTIST SHOULD.

CHORES

PILE OF PRESENTS TO BUY, WRAP, AND DELIVER TO FRIENDS
AND FRIENDS' KIDS.

PILE OF THANK-YOU NOTES TO WRITE AND MAIL.

PILE OF BOOKS TO BORROW OR BUY AND READ.

PILE OF BOOKS TO LEND OR RETURN.

PILE OF POSSESSIONS TO SORT AND KEEP OR DISCARD.

PILE OF GROCERIES TO BUY AND PUT AWAY.

PILE OF FOOD TO COOK AND SERVE, DISHES TO WASH AND PUT BACK.

PILE OF THINGS TO ORDER, PAY FOR, UNPACK, AND PUT AWAY.

PILE OF BOXES TO DISMANTLE AND TAKE OUTSIDE.

PILE OF THINGS TO WIPE.

PILE OF THINGS TO SCRUB.

PILE OF QUESTIONS TO LOOK UP, AND ANSWERS TO REMEMBER.

PILE OF PEOPLE TO APPEASE OR CHARM, VARIOUSLY.

PILE OF HYGIENIC NECESSITIES TO FULFILL, DAY IN, DAY OUT.

PILE OF OUT-OF-LEFT-FIELD REQUESTS FROM STRANGERS TO SORT,
AGREE TO OR GRACIOUSLY REFUSE, AND SECOND-GUESS.

PILE OF FAVORS TO DO, AND FAVORS TO ASK, CRINGING.

PILE OF LITTLE JABS TO METABOLIZE.

PILE OF AWFUL ENDINGS TO FORGET, AND KEEP FORGETTING.

PILE OF EMOTIONS TO HAVE AND PERFORM.

PILE OF EMAILS TO CHECK AND ANSWER.

PILE OF DEADLINES TO KEEP.

PILE OF EVENTS TO GO TO, OR APOLOGIZE FOR MISSING.

PILE OF OBLIGATIONS TO KEEP.

THINGS I'D LIKE TO BE TOLD

WHAT TO EAT AND WHEN

WHAT TO WEAR

WHAT SONG TO LISTEN TO

WHAT TO WORK ON AT ANY GIVEN MOMENT

WHETHER TO WORK IN CONCENTRATED SILENCE OR
WHILE DOING OTHER THINGS

WHERE TO SHOP AND HOW OFTEN

WHEN TO BE POLITE AND HOW

WHETHER TO EMBRACE THE LONELINESS, OR FIGHT IT,
OR IGNORE IT

WAETHER TO BE SERIOUS OR LIGHT

WHETHER TO APPRECIATE OTHERS OR SCRUTINIZE THEM

WHEN TO FIGHT MY NATURE AND WHEN TO CELEBRATE IT

WHEN TO BE RESPONSIBLE AND WHEN NOT

WHEN TO MAKE SACRIFICES AND WHEN TO REFUSE

WHEN TO FIGHT FOR SPACE AND WHEN TO WALK AWAY

WHEN TO SEEK LIGHT AND WHEN TO CARVE A PATH
THROUGH DARKNESS

WHAT I MISS

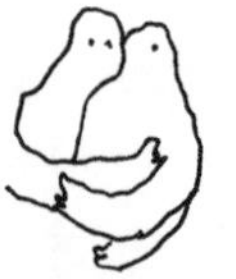

I MISS HAVING SOMEONE.
I MISS WALKING TO YOUR HOUSE.
I MISS TEXTING YOU.

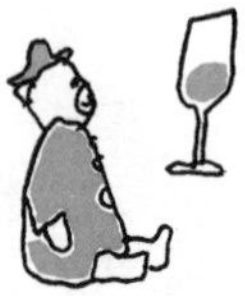

I MISS SITTING IN MY PLACE ON YOUR COUCH.
I MISS YOUR KIND SMILE.
I MISS YOUR BEAUTIFUL FACE.
I MISS YOUR SWEET APARTMENT, FULL OF KIND, INNOCENT THINGS.
I MISS HOW SMART YOU WERE.
I MISS YOUR SURPRISING SENSE OF HUMOR.
THE RANDOM, PERFECT NAMES YOU HAD FOR THINGS.

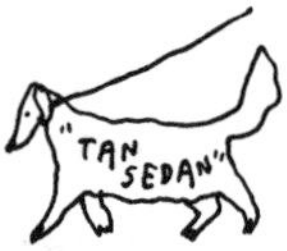
"TAN SEDAN"

I MISS THINKING I'D GET TO KEEP YOU,
EVEN IF THERE WAS TERROR IN YOUR EYES WHEN YOU SAID YOU LOVED ME.

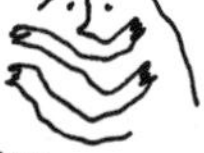

I MISS SLEEPING INTERTWINED, AND DREAMING THE SAME DREAM.
I MISS YOUR RECORD PLAYER,
AND THE SENSE OF HOME YOU CARRIED WITH YOU,
ALTHOUGH YOU'D NEVER REALLY BEEN AT HOME ANYWHERE.

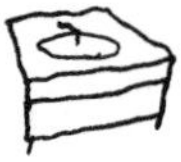

I MISS THE PAST YOU WOULDN'T TELL ME ABOUT,
AND MY TERROR WHEN YOU TOLD ME PARTS.
I MISS THE WAY YOU GRABBED MY PEN
AND COVERED A PAGE IN ANTEATERS.

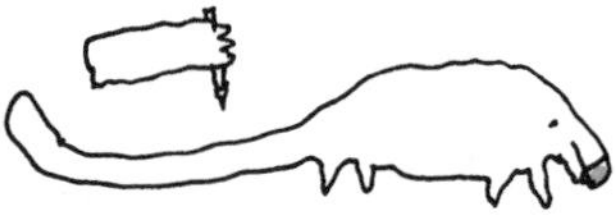

I MISS YOUR NERDINESS.
IS THAT WHAT IT WAS?
I MISS YOUR FRUGALITY.
YOUR MODERATENESS.
YOUR MORALS.
I MISS THE WORRY IN YOUR EYES
BACK WHEN YOU PAID FOR EVERYTHING,
AND THE WORRY WHEN YOU STOPPED PAYING.
I MISS THE PERSON YOU WERE AT DINNER PARTIES, WHO EXASPERATED ME
I MISS KNOWING WHO YOU WERE, UNDERNEATH.
I MISS THINKING THAT, IF WE COULDN'T BE PARTNERS, WE COULD STILL BE FRIENDS.
I MISS WHEN I STILL BELIEVED THAT.
I MISS PLANNING A FUTURE WITH YOU.
THE SMALL THINGS. THE BIG THINGS.

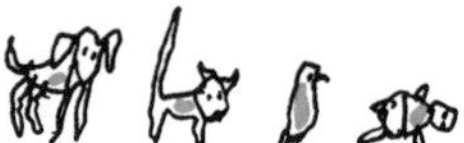

I MISS OUR LISTS OF NAMES: DOG, CAT, BIRD, BABY.

I MISS THINKING THAT, IF WE DIDN'T HAVE A FUTURE, WE AT LEAST HAD A PAST.
THAT WAS, FINALLY, THE LAST THING LEFT THAT YOU COULD TAKE FROM ME.
YOU TOOK IT.
I DIDN'T NOT DESERVE IT.
I MISS YOUR INSOMNIA, AND YOUR SLEEP, WHEN YOU DID. 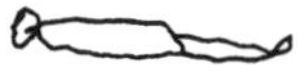
I MISS YOUR HUMANE MOUSETRAPS, 
AND YOUR HUMANE MICE. 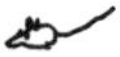
I MISS YOUR COZY MESS, AND YOUR EXCELLENT COOKING.
I MISS YOUR BEAUTY, AND YOUR SHREDDED OLD SWEATPANTS, AND YOUR FEAR
OF DISAPPEARING, FALLING BACK INTO THE DIRT.
I MISS COMPLAINING TO YOU.
I MISS WHEN YOU COMPLAINED TO ME.
I MISS FINDING INSECTS TOGETHER. 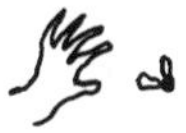
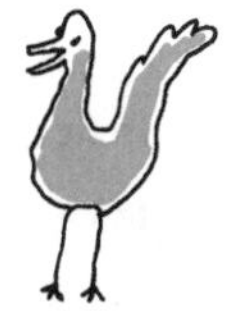
I MISS YOUR TURNS OF PHRASE ("IT'S NOT NOT"),
AND THAT YOU KNEW A LOT ABOUT A LOT (FOOD, WINE, BOOKS).
I MISS HOW LOW-KEY YOU WERE. HOW PLUMED AND HYPER I FELT
BY COMPARISON.
I MISS YOUR DEAD-ON SOCIAL DIAGNOSES, THE THINGS YOU LAUGHED AT.
I MISS YOUR INNOCENCE. FINDING PEANUTS IN YOUR BED. 
I MISS THE MARTINIS YOU MADE.
YOUR EXPERIMENTS ALWAYS WORKED.
I MISS WAKING UP AT NIGHT
TO FIND YOU EATING ICE CREAM IN THE OTHER ROOM. 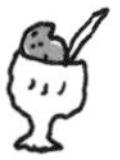
YOUR RAGTAG COLLECTION OF CUPS AND PLATES,
PICKED UP OUTSIDE YOUR HUGE, MUSTY BUILDING. 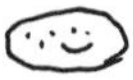
I MISS THE FOODS YOU LIVED ON, WHICH FEEL TOO PERSONAL TO LIST.
I MISS THE PARTS OF YOU I DIDN'T UNDERSTAND.
I MISS GETTING TO KNOW YOU.
I MISS HOW QUICKLY YOU DECIDED YOU LOVED ME. 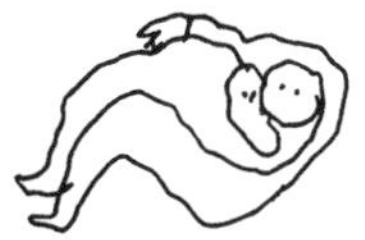
I MISS FOLDING YOU INTO MY LIFE, IN CERTAIN WAYS.
I MISS HOW QUICKLY YOU DECIDED. IT MADE ME FEEL SO SAFE,
AND SO UNSAFE.
I MISS WHEN I WENT ON A TRIP, AND WE EMAILED.
YOU ALWAYS WROTE BACK RIGHT AWAY. YOU WERE A SWEET MAN.
I MISS YOUR FORMALITY, AND HOW DISTRUSTFUL I WAS OF IT.
I MAY HAVE BEEN RIGHT.

I MISS HOW PASSIVE YOU GOT WHEN YOU WERE NERVOUS,
AND HOW MUCH IT SCARED ME.

I MISS HOW SWEET YOU WERE WHEN YOU EMERGED.
I PROMISED MYSELF I WOULDN'T BE SCARED ANYMORE.

I MISS YOUR POLITENESS, WHICH WAS KIND, IF OPAQUE.
I MISS YOUR EXCLAMATION POINTS.
I MISS HOW LITTLE SPACE YOU TOOK UP.
I MISS HOW EVERYONE ASSUMED WE WERE SIBLINGS.

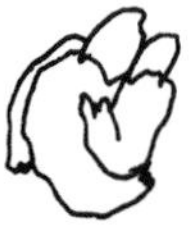

I MISS WEARING YOUR PANTS.
I MISS HOW, BEFORE IT GOT BAD, YOU USED TO HUG ME ALL NIGHT.
I MISS YOUR HEALTHINESS, AND YOUR HATRED OF CHEMICALS.
I MISS YOUR CLOTHES, WHICH SUITED YOU, AND YOUR BODY, WHICH
WAS ARMOR.
I MISS THE BOOKS ON YOUR SHELVES.
I MISS HOW FAMILIAR YOU WERE TO ME.
I MISS HOW YOU ADOPTED MY HABITS, AND IMPROVED THEM; MY
TASTES.

I LOVED RATS AND PIGEONS, AND SO DID YOU.
THE MUSEUMS WE LIKED. OUR PRIVATE JOKES, OUR DANCES.
WE HAD A FUTURE. I MISS IT.

I MISS YOU AS A LOVER, OR MAYBE AS A TWIN.
I MISS BEING ALONE BUT KNOWING YOU WERE THERE.
I MISS READING FROM THE SAME MAGAZINE ON A TRAIN.
I MISS WATCHING NATURE MOVIES WITH YOU.
I MISS HAVING FAITH IN YOU, AND YOUR FAITH IN ME.
YOU WERE MY HOME.

I MISS WAITING FOR YOU IN YOUR APARTMENT,
FOR YOU TO COME HOME.

☑ YES ☑ NO

- REMEMBER
- MISREMEMBER
- FORGET

ACKNOWLEDGMENTS

THANK YOU, FIRST OF ALL, TO MY INSTAGRAM FANS (MAY I CALL YOU THAT) FOR SEEING AND ENGAGING WITH MY ROUGH, PERSONAL DRAWINGS, AND FOR GIVING ME A REASON TO MAKE THEM. TO MY EDITOR AT RANDOM HOUSE, ANDY WARD, THANK YOU FOR HAVING THE ORIGINAL VISION FOR THIS BOOK, AND FOR WISELY AND PATIENTLY GUIDING ME AT EVERY STEP: SHAPE/SIZE/COLOR, CHOOSING DRAWINGS, ORGANIZING THEM INTO CHAPTERS. THANK YOU, MEREDITH KAFFEL SIMONOFF, MY LITERARY AGENT, FOR SAVING THIS BOOK WITH YOUR INTUITIVE AND ON-POINT VISUAL HELP, FOR ALWAYS POINTING OUT THE FOREST AMIDST THE TREES, AND FOR BEING SUCH A STRONG, SMART, SANE ADVOCATE. THANK YOU TO EVERYONE AT RANDOM HOUSE WHO HAS MADE THIS BOOK EXIST: SARAH FEIGHTNER AND CAROLE LOWENSTEIN FOR YOUR PATIENCE AND HAND-HOLDING WITH THE BOOK DESIGN; ROBBIN SCHIFF, FOR ALL THE WORK YOU PUT IN WITH THE COVER—I'M TRULY OVERWHELMED WITH GRATITUDE; EDWIN TSE, FOR ALL THE PHOTOGRAPHY AND THOUGHTFUL DESIGN HELP; CHAYENNE SKEETE, FOR BEING THE HUB IN THE WHEEL OF EMAILS AND LOGISTICS, AND PULLING EVERYTHING TOGETHER; ERIN RICHARDS, MARIA BRAECKEL, AND CARRIE NEILL, FOR BEING SO GOOD AT WHAT YOU DO; BETH PEARSON FOR THE PERCEPTIVE AND RIGOROUS COPYEDITS; JESS BONET AND LEIGH MERCHANT FOR THE GOOD IDEAS; ALSO TOM PERRY, NICOLE RAMIREZ, REBECCA BERLANT, AND HANNAH NEFF. THANK YOU SUSAN KAMIL, FOR YOUR KINDNESS. THANK YOU TO EVERYONE AT THE NEW YORKER—SPECIFICALLY, EMMA ALLEN, DAVID REMNICK, AND COLIN STOKES—FOR THE BEST JOB IN THE WORLD. BOB MANKOFF, THANK YOU FOR YOUR EDITORSHIP AND MENTORSHIP. I SHOULD HAVE SAID THIS LONG AGO, BUT THANK YOU LEAH WALCHOK, DAVINA PARDO, JOANNA SOKOLOWSKI, KRISTEN JOHNSON, JUDY KARP, AND DEBORAH SHAFFER, FOR PUTTING ME IN VERY SEMI SERIOUS. THANK YOU JORGE COLOMBO FOR YOUR GENEROUS DESIGN AND ILLUSTRATION ADVICE, RODRIGO CORRAL FOR YOUR EXCELLENT BOOK COVER CRITIQUE, RAFIL KROLL-ZAIDI FOR THE CAFE ARTICLE I TOOK THE QUOTE FROM, AND ROB RUSSELL, FOR THE PIECE OF WOOD ON THE COVER. HARRIET FINCK, THANK YOU FOR BEING MY ETERNAL SOUNDING BOARD, GURU, AND MY ROLE MODEL IN ART-MAKING. SCOTT GOODMAN, THANK YOU FOR YOUR WHIRLWIND OF HELP ON THE COVER, AND YOUR FUNNY, BRILLIANT AND HANDSOME PRESENCE. MICHAEL FINCK, THANK YOU FOR BEING MY MORAL BENCHMARK, FRIEND IN DISSECTING SOCIAL AND NATURAL MINUTIAE, AND FOR BEING A KIND AND GOOD DAD. GIDEON FINCK, THANK YOU FOR SHARING MY MEMORIES, AND FOR TEMPERING MY RETIRING PUNCTILLIOUSNESS WITH YOUR WARMTH AND (SORRY) SPARKLE. TO MY EXTENDED FAMILY AND PAST DOGS: THANK YOU. ROZ CHAST, STACY SCHIFF, AND ADRIAN TOMINE: A BELATED THANK-YOU FOR THE BLURBS ON MY LAST BOOK. MELINDA WANG, THANK YOU FOR THE SHOW AT EQUITY GALLERY, AND ALLI KATZ FOR THE SHOW AT KELLY WRITERS HOUSE. FOR DRAWING WITH ME: GABRIELLE BELL, KAREN SNYDER, LUCAS ADAMS, ED STEED, KEREN KATZ, LAUREN WEINSTEIN, ARIEL SCHRAG, TANIA SCHRAG, JULIA GFRÖER, JULIA WERTZ, AND SARAH GLIDDEN. TO OTHER FRIENDS— AND I HOPE YOU KNOW WHO YOU ARE—I AM SO LUCKY TO HAVE YOU IN MY LIFE. THANK YOU VARIOUS CAFES—KONDITORI, CLEVER BLEND, MCNALLY JACKSON, HUNGRY GHOST, THINK COFFEE—FOR HOSTING ME WHILE I DRAW. THANK YOU ANYONE OVER 40 FOR BEARING WITH THIS SMALL PRINT. LASTLY, THANK YOU, THE ALGORITHM.

Liana Finck IS A REGULAR CONTRIBUTOR TO THE NEW YORKER. SHE IS A RECIPIENT OF A FULBRIGHT FELLOWSHIP, A NEW YORK FOUNDATION FOR THE ARTS FELLOWSHIP, AND A SIX POINTS FELLOWSHIP FOR EMERGING JEWISH ARTISTS. SHE HAS HAD ARTIST RESIDENCIES WITH MACDOWELL, YADDO, AND THE LOWER MANHATTAN CULTURAL COUNCIL. HER LAST BOOK, PASSING FOR HUMAN, WAS PUBLISHED IN 2018.

@ LIANAFINCK
  └→ INSTAGRAM
    └→ TWITTER

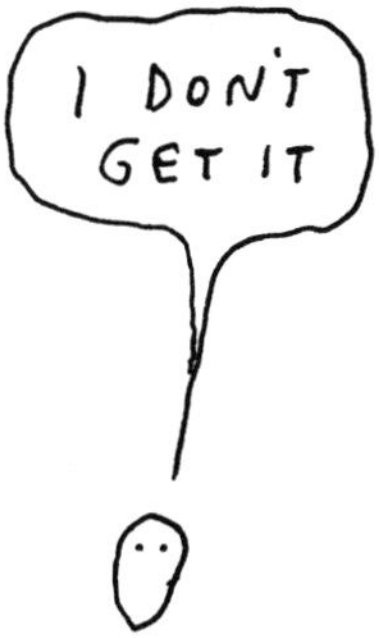
I DON'T GET IT

GRAPHIC NOVEL